ALSO BY DAVE MARSH

Born to Run:
The Bruce Springsteen Story

The Rolling Stone Record Guide: Reviews and Ratings
of Almost 10,000 Currently Available Rock, Pop, Soul,
Country, Blues, Jazz, and Gospel Albums

The Book of Rock Lists

Elvis

Rocktopicon: Unlikely Questions
and Their Surprising Answers

Before I Get Old: The Story of the Who

Fortunate Son

The First Rock and Roll
Confidential Report: Inside the
Real World of Rock and Roll

Sun City: The Making of the Record

Trapped: Michael Jackson and the Crossover Dream

Glory Days: Bruce Springsteen in the 1980s

The Heart of Rock & Soul:
The 1001 Greatest Singles Ever Made

Heaven Is Under Our Feet: A Book for
Walden Woods, coedited with Don Henley

50 Ways to Fight Censorship:
And Important Facts to Know About the Censors

Louie Louie: The History and Mythology of the
World's Most Famous Rock 'n' Roll Song; Including the Full
Details of Its Torture and Persecution at the Hands of the Kingsmen,
J. Edgar Hoover's F.B.I., and a Cast of Millions; and Introducing,
for the First Time Anywhere, the Actual Dirty Lyrics

Merry Christmas Baby:
Holiday Music from Bing to Sting

Pastures of Plenty: A Self-Portrait,
coedited with Harold Leventhal and featuring
the writings of Woody Guthrie

The New Book of Rock Lists

*Mid-Life Confidential: The Rock Bottom Remainders
Tour America with Three Chords and an Attitude*

The Great Rock & Roll Joke Book,
with Kathi Kamen Goldmark

Sam and Dave (for the Record series)

*Bruce Springsteen: Two Hearts:
The Definitive Biography, 1972–2003*

Forever Young: Photographs of Bob Dylan,
with Douglas R. Gilbert

Bruce Springsteen on Tour: 1968–2005

The Beatles' Second Album

360 Sound: The Columbia Records Story

OTHER BOOKS EDITED BY DAVE MARSH

George Strait, by David Cantwell (Liner Notes series)

Neil Young, by Brian Keizer (Liner Notes series)

Soul Asylum, by Danny Alexander (Liner Notes series)

Black Sabbath, by Mike Stark (for the Record series)

Sly and the Family Stone, by Joel Selvin
(for the Record series)

George Clinton and P-Funkadelic,
by David Mills (for the Record series)

*Up Around the Bend: The Oral History of
Creedence Clearwater Revival,* by Craig Werner
(for the Record series)

JIBES, BARBS,

TRIBUTES,

AND

RALLYING CRIES

FROM

35 YEARS

OF

MUSIC WRITING

KICK
OUT THE
JAMS

DAVE
MARSH

edited by
Daniel Wolff *and*
Danny Alexander

SIMON & SCHUSTER
New York   London   Toronto   Sydney   New Delhi

Simon & Schuster
1230 Avenue of the Americas
New York, NY 10020

First Simon & Schuster hardcover edition August 2023

SIMON & SCHUSTER and colophon are registered trademarks
of Simon & Schuster, Inc.

For information about special discounts for bulk purchases,
please contact Simon & Schuster Special Sales at 1-866-506-1949
or business@simonandschuster.com.

The Simon & Schuster Speakers Bureau can bring authors to your
live event. For more information or to book an event, contact the
Simon & Schuster Speakers Bureau at 1-866-248-3049 or visit our
website at www.simonspeakers.com.

Interior design by Lewelin Polanco

Jacket photographs from Alamy Stock Photo: Mary J. Blige and Elvis Presley by PA Images;
Bob Dylan by PictureLux/The Hollywood Archive; Nina Simone by Pictorial Press Ltd;
Paul McCartney by Abaca Press; Bono by Trinity Mirror/Mirrorpix

Jacket photographs from Getty Images: Kurt Cobain by Martyn Goodacre; Ice Cube by Al
Pereira; Patti Smith by Charles Steiner; photos of Madonna by Michel Linssen and Rob
Verhorst used as reference

With decades of thanks for Sandy Choron

Manufactured in the United States of America

10 9 8 7 6 5 4 3 2 1

Library of Congress Cataloging-in-Publication Data is available.

ISBN 978-1-9821-9716-2
ISBN 978-1-9821-9718-6 (ebook)

For Barbara

Contents

INTRODUCTION TO SECTION 3: 161
THE 2000S

BLOOD IN YOUR MOUTH:
The Writing of Dave Marsh

Since 1969, Dave Marsh has been writing about music like our lives depended on it. His friend, the critic Greil Marcus, has described Marsh's writing as "heartfelt, heart on your sleeve, blood in your mouth." In the 2020s, it may seem absurd that there was a time when rock and its audiences were not taken seriously, were mocked and even criminalized, when rock was a fighting matter. Dave Marsh came up in those times, and this collection, among its many virtues, argues for the value and possibility of rock, soul, and rap music, with blood in its mouth.

Marsh has always been clear about what he was fighting for. Maybe he captured it best in this collection's touching remembrance of the record producer and talent scout John Hammond that include some words from Hammond's memoir:

> I still would change the world if I could, convince a nonbeliever that my way is right, argue a cause and make friends out of enemies. I am still the reformer, the impatient protester, the sometimes-intolerant champion of tolerance. Best of all, I still expect to hear, if not today then tomorrow, a voice or a sound I have never heard before, with something to say which has never been said before. And when that happens I will know what to do.

Starting at Detroit's *Creem*, Marsh has spent years writing and editing record and concert reviews, profiles, columns, all while producing more than twenty books. In 1982, he started a newsletter, *Rock & Roll Confidential*—renamed *Rock & Rap Confidential* to reflect the rise and significance of rap and hip-hop—in part to more aggressively situate popular music within a political context. For Marsh, that means to ask and answer hard questions around the power dynamics of the music business, to recognize and fight music censorship, and to call out the racist assumptions that frame the critical categories and histories that we use to tell the story of popular music. The work collected here, from *RRC*, *Addicted to Noise*, and other outlets is the work of day-to-day journalism, of the writer in a daily conversation and argument. Selected by two of his collaborators and friends, the writers Daniel Wolff and Danny Alexander, *Kick Out the Jams* highlights the personal relationships and collaborations characteristic of Marsh.

This is the second collection of Marsh's music journalism. The first, *Fortunate Son* (1985), chronicled his work as a young writer for rock magazines like *Creem* and *Rolling Stone*. This collection begins around the time that Marsh left *Rolling Stone* after his first major commercial success with a biography of Bruce Springsteen, *Born to Run* (1979). Marsh was thirty-three when *Fortunate Son* came out, at a point in the history of rock when the baby boom generation of rock writers were wondering how and whether this music could age, how and whether it could be of value as its audience aged.

While many of his peers who grappled with those same questions—Greil Marcus, Robert Christgau, Ellen Willis, even Lester Bangs—have been embraced or even lionized by popular music studies, Marsh's work has faded from the critical conversation. This may be, in part, because Marsh can be so heart-on-his-sleeve emotional about rock and roll—an attitude some pigeonholed as rockist. But this collection shows that Marsh never championed rock and roll as the only avenue to freedom and justice—in fact, he's quick to point out when it's been used for the opposite purpose, as he does here in his pieces on Neil Young and Axl Rose. Anti-bohemian, uninterested, or often flat-out hostile to critical/academic debates, Marsh has always written for the general public and with a particular fondness for what he calls "the vulgar." If you've missed or dismissed his work as a result, *Kick Out the Jams* is an opportunity for rediscovery. I look forward to the dialogue it should start between Marsh and a generation of critics that has blown up genre categories and champions music that takes on the fight of Black Lives Matter.

Marsh has described himself as a "rock-drunk" kid; *Kick Out the Jams* is the sequel to that beginning. There's a maturity in these pieces, a desire not to escape through the music but to use it to embrace life's pain and complexities. It's adult in the best sense of that word. What shines through is the belief that rock and soul and rap and pop and folk are an opportunity for possibility, for hope. Not because they offer a free ride, but because the music—and the communal experience of making and listening to the music—gives us a chance to change ourselves and our communities.

Sometimes it gets lost in the noise of Marsh's fighting spirit, or his famous friends, but the guy can flat out *write* in a way that draws you into his passions. A big part of that is the openheartedness, his commitment to getting his energy on the page and to being understood. Whether he digs in on a long profile—like the ones here on Patty Griffin or the MC5's Rob Tyner—or just works up a couple of paragraphs in memory of the blues great Bobby "Blue" Bland, he gets you to hear what he hears. He doesn't reach for the most complex take, with flashy rhetorical moves for the sake of it. His voice is heart-to-heart, person-to-person. There's very little "insider" writing. Sure, he spends time in some rarified places, and lets us know about it (a dinner at Harold Leventhal's, backstage at a Springsteen show). Like all critics, he can sometimes reference things you may not know. But I've never felt like I needed specialized knowledge to understand Dave Marsh—be it theoretical, music biz, or even music references. A lovely example included here is his piece on the Chinese rock artist Cui Jian. The essay opens with Marsh on the road, popping in a cassette marked "Van Halen" and discovering Jian instead. His confusion and wonder, how he felt when he heard it in the car, captures the power of Jian's music better than if he'd tried to describe a scene or style. His best writing is an invitation.

But make no mistake, writing is work, and in a number of these essays he reflects on how the job has changed. He made his bones at a time when people could make a living as a music journalist. At the start of this collection, there were still significant print outlets for music journalism, despite their flaws, and new ones on the rise, like *Vibe* (1993) and *XXL* (1997). Print outlets are mostly gone, and while there is music commentary everywhere on the internet, getting paid for music or arts journalism is a hard road to hoe. But his pre-internet 1993 reflection here on how to handle the glut of new music is a prescient lament about the critic's job:

> For a musical omnivore like myself, the job is truly impossible. The time I spend trying to figure out dancehall is insufficient, my take on grunge too affected by my age and history, there were probably six or eight fine country voices that got by me while that fascinating but as yet undeciphered cumbia anthology was playing, and I've never heard Springsteen's *Unplugged* EP . . . Confronted by all this, I can only tell you that listening to everything is still the right way to go. You may not get there first with the new Mariah Carey review, but in the end, what you do tell people will add some perspective to what they're hearing and maybe even help keep the historical record straight. That's my version of the job, and I'm sticking to it for as long as I can make it last.

He sticks to it—to the music and what it means—because it's crucial to him, almost a question of survival. In a core essay here—a long reflection on Kurt Cobain's suicide in 1994 (the essay constituted a full issue of *RRC*)—Marsh describes the vision of rock and roll he believes in:

> If Kurt Cobain had grown up in the '50s or '60s or even the early '70s—if he was anybody from Lou Reed to Melissa Etheridge—his early encounters with rock & roll almost certainly would have represented a glorious possibility, a chance to communicate across all the gaps in our society—gaps of class, race, region, gender, generation, education, you name it. Used this way, rock & roll became not just a "way out" of impoverished working-class or straight-jacketed middle-class existence, but a method of absolutely transforming yourself, a means of becoming who you'd always dreamed of being, confronting your fears with the power to transmute them into assets, a chance to

be a hero not only to others but in your own life; to articulate out loud a vision of the world you'd previously have
been terrified to whisper into the mirror. Of such things is
freedom constructed.

Rock and roll doesn't provide easy answers here; it doesn't have magical
powers. But it's a means to an end, and that end is freedom. As Marsh says
in his remembrance of Pete Seeger: "Freedom meant everybody or it didn't
mean anything." For Marsh, freedom means calling out racism, fighting
the death penalty and helping others see how they can fight it, standing
up to corporate censorship, pushing back hard against Reaganism and the
rise of the right, yes, but also calling out Democrats like Bill Clinton and Al
Gore for not being much different (his takedown of Gore included here is
classic Dave).

When the music and the culture he loves is attacked—by politicians trying to make hay from the so-called evils of pop music, by censors condemning heavy metal or hip-hop, by the police harassing, arresting, and killing
people of color—Dave as a champion of the music feels the obligation to
resist. His first instinct is to fight back, even though (or maybe because) it's
an endless battle. He does so most effectively here by sharing information,
using his own voice to amplify others. In a 2002 piece from *CounterPunch*
after the murder of Jam Master Jay, Marsh quotes Davey D's (www.daveyd
.com) description of the war on the music: "Police departments all over the
country have been collecting and now have very detailed dossiers of rap
artists and who they're affiliated with. From New York City, which actually
has a 'rap task force,' to Oakland to Mountainview, California, where the
police chief sits down and determines what RAP acts are allowed and not
allowed to perform." This war is still on.

But the politics of the music doesn't only mean how music intersects
with activism or comments on social issues. One of the most important
through lines of this collection is Marsh working to better understand the
history of the music he loves—in essays on Elvis, James Brown, and Dorothy Love Coates, as well as lovely short obituaries along the way, Marsh highlights the founders of rock and soul, and reflects what they can and should
mean. Freedom requires that we know our history, and thinking hard and

long about what you know, why you know it, what's been kept from you and how it can shape your present. For example, in the pieces here reflecting on folk and blues anthologies, you can see Marsh working through the legacy of those genres in how rock was defined. His remembrance of the Birmingham DJ Shelley Stewart's coded on-air advice to young civil rights marchers stands out, with Marsh reveling in radio's ability to link and protect a community. It may be surprising to see how much time he spends writing about folk music, given his rock and roll roots, but these essays show how invested Marsh was in research and reflection on the past. That work becomes even more relevant and necessary as active forces continue to try to suppress the nation's history of Black culture and of White supremacy.

Marsh is quick to the draw, so when he loves something or someone, the writing is deeply emotional. The same is true for when he doesn't. These essays can be funny: "Madonna has entered the rarified ranks of those pop stars who function as lightning rods for assholes"; "if the most worthy new hero it can find is a bonehead shill like Jon Bon Jovi, whose synthesis of heavy metal and Bruce Springsteen sucks both into the vacuum of pure cliché, then maybe it really is time for rock to leave center stage." When he goes on the attack, he doesn't let go. The best example of that approach here is his ridicule of Bono's political work with the (RED) campaign, which hits the spot, but also feels over the top, with Marsh taking some cheap shots about Bono's hair and cosmetic work. Maybe it's good that Marsh never warmed to Twitter. He puts his dukes up fast.

This collection includes an essay that puts a different spin on Marsh's infamous lacerating tongue. "The Hero and the Blues" (1998) is a review of the CD *Safe House: A Collection of the Blues* compiled by the author Andrew Vachss, to accompany his book of the same name. In the essay, Marsh recounts, in careful detail, a story about how his father beat him for not getting a haircut when he was a teenager. He reveals that those beatings were a regular part of his life and describes the resulting shame and despair he carried. His willingness and ability to share that with his audience seems to have opened a pathway to a more compassionate voice from him in subsequent decades.

Perhaps the path to that compassion truly begins with the tragic death of Marsh's daughter Kristen Ann Carr in January 1993 from a rare sarcoma cancer. She was only twenty-one, and it was, of course, devastating to him and his family. He writes about it in many of the essays included here. It's clear that Marsh doubled down on using writing to work through pain and suffering, and he is remarkably open about the weight of her loss. He turns his writing, intellect, wealth, and connections to learning about cancer research, communicating it to others, and sustaining a foundation to support research. This is felt most powerfully here in the remarkable closing essay about the Texas singer-songwriter Jimmy LaFave, whose work Marsh has long admired. The essay follows LaFave's cancer diagnosis and his decision to refuse treatment. It's a heartbreaking moment when Marsh hits up against his abilities to help. Along the way, though, not only does he help you to understand how good a performer LaFave was, but also in clear, useful language he describes how sarcoma cancer works. Marsh writes, "I've seen *RRC* as an espousal of life against death. After watching my own child wage that struggle in literal terms, I know there's a way to live that message to your final breath. You do it by choosing the spirit of hope and affirmation that Kristen held so completely that she awed even her doctors."

I've been a fan of Dave Marsh's work since I first read his "American Grandstand" column in *Rolling Stone* in 1976. His voice captured the excitement and passion I was feeling for rock and roll as a young teenager, but it was a voice that welcomed me—it didn't exclude me. And as a female reader of rock magazines clearly aimed at young men, I also never felt verbally assaulted. His reviews could feel like a refuge from the sexism in the surrounding pages. He's helped me at many stages of my career, sometimes by making a phone call, but mostly by cheerleading, asking hard questions, and refusing to let me settle for an easy answer or wallow in disappointment. He always moved the conversation to figuring out what I was going to *do* about an obstacle, and how he could help. In addition to turning you on to a lot of great music, I hope this collection pushes you to act. Our lives depend on it.

—*Lauren Onkey*

Editor's Note

In selecting this work from three decades' worth of writing, we made some (perhaps arbitrary) distinctions.

We begin after the 1985 publication of *Fortunate Son*, subtitled: *The Best of Dave Marsh*. While *Kick Out the Jams* is in some ways a sequel to that book, be assured it is not "Second Best."

Dave Marsh was writing books during this period—some twenty-two in all—and we have not included excerpts from those, which are (or should be) still available. Ditto to liner notes.

Nor have we included the many unsigned pieces from *Rock & Rap Confidential*. Though many of these bear the distinct Marsh attitude and voice, they were written as collaborative, not individual, work, and we honor that.

So, what we have gathered here are some of the best of Dave Marsh's writing from the mid-1980s through the 2010s. Many of these pieces appeared in publications that are now hard to impossible to find. We scanned (thanks to Lee Ballinger) what may be the only complete set of *Rock & Rap Confidential*. Other work was only preserved through emails to friends.

While there's much we had to leave out, we hope this selection offers a portrait not just of an era—from Elvis to Trump, from Robert Johnson through Green Day—but of a writer wrestling with the American empire. What drives Dave Marsh remains, in his own words, "a raging passion to explain things in the hope that others would not be trapped and to keep the way clear so that others from the trashy outskirts of barbarous America still had a place to stand—if not in the culture at large, at least in rock and roll."

KICK

OUT THE

JAMS

Prologue

ELVIS: THE NEW DEAL ORIGINS OF ROCK 'N' ROLL

—*MUSICIAN*, DECEMBER 1982

E ach year, on August 16, the anniversary of Elvis Presley's death, Memphis State University hosts a memorial service and seminar in his honor.

The memorial service, which takes place in the early afternoon, includes testimonials and fervid witnessing from a great many of Presley's friends and colleagues, including the disc jockey George Klein, who acts as host, and even Sam Phillips, the somewhat reclusive producer of Elvis's great Sun recordings. The seminar, which immediately follows, is a rare occasion (in America) for serious public discussion of popular music issues, centering around a dialogue on the state of the Elvis image.

This year, coinciding with the publication of my book *Elvis* (Times Books), a critical biography, I was asked to deliver a speech on the state of the Presley image. The article which follows is a reworking of that speech; it sticks fairly closely to the original text, though I have added some detail and cleaned up some of my rather inelegant verbal grammar and syntax.

I thought the speech worth reprinting for a couple of reasons. First, because it places Elvis in a context in which he is rarely seen; and second, because it removes him—and in consequence, the music he founded—from the cultural isolation in which it is often trapped. Quite frankly, ever since a letter appeared in *Musician* several issues back questioning the appropriateness of references to Reaganism in a music magazine, I have been seeking a way to respond.

Like everything else, Presleymania has a political dimension. I hope this analysis suggests some of the richness of that dimension, not only for those who care about Elvis, but for anyone who cares about rock—or what is happening to the United States at the moment. At the very least, it reflects a perspective on the origins of rock which I do not believe anyone has suggested before.

Unfortunately, the only place to begin is with the rather ugly fact that Elvis is dead. We take this for granted, or avoid it with slogans such as "Always Elvis," but the fact of Elvis's death ought to astonish and outrage us. If he were alive, he would be only forty-seven years old, which is the very prime of life for a singer. Until we recover our sense of outrage about this loss, we will not begin to come to terms with Elvis's life and work.

Elvis didn't simply become sick; he did not have a terminal illness. Elvis Presley died of abuse, the majority of it self-inflicted, which had its source in his isolation, in his final years, from the rest of the world and in his absolute inability to connect sufficiently to share the details of his experiences with anyone else.

This is about the saddest thing one could say about anyone, much less someone who led the sort of public life that Elvis Presley did. So please forgive me if I refuse to look at Elvis and his life and image in isolation, as we usually do with stars. The only way I know to do homage to the singular nature of Elvis's fame is to place him *in* the world, not above it or beneath it.

Like any Elvis fan, I sometimes find it comforting to imagine him still alive. Despite all my mental pictures of how I might reach him and help him go on to make great music once again, this comfort never lasts long or even completely cheers me up. That's because the circumstances that caused Elvis to die young haven't been altered. We haven't learned the most fundamental lessons that the Elvis Presley story has to teach. So if Elvis did return, he would still wind up a lonesome wreck.

In any event, Elvis isn't coming back, or, if you believe otherwise, it will be too late when he does arrive to make any difference. But Elvis fans, from the very beginning, have had another related hope: we have always wanted to be like him. That doesn't necessarily mean that we wanted to look or dress or sing like him; we wanted to *be* like him, to tap into the same freedom, the wildness and dignity that Elvis combined so beautifully, allowing many of us to glimpse the concept of such a mixture for the very first time. In this sense, wanting to be like Elvis means creating a world that operates the same way that his music does: a world in which everyone would have the chance to be like Elvis. But this leaves some questions unanswered: Who was Elvis? What would be the terms of living in such a world? How close have we come to creating it?

Elvis Presley grew up in Tupelo, Mississippi. The Presleys were extraordinarily poor, the sort of people who, according to most of the cultural establishment of America, are not supposed to have creative voices in public life. Somehow, however, Elvis found a little more breathing space in which to think through his ambition than those who had come before him. His father, Vernon, was untrained and often ill (he had a bad back). Frequently, no one in the Presley household had a job; for a time, they actually lived on welfare, and for a while they lived in a government-sponsored housing project. Even so, Elvis didn't have to quit school and go to work when his father was laid up; he worked part-time, but he continued his education because the family's minimal income was supported by subsidized housing, and, when things were at their worst, by welfare money. As a result, Elvis Presley became the first person in his whole family to finish high school. As another result, Elvis Presley not only dreamed of being a singer, but also found time to look for ways to realize that dream.

The amount of talent that Elvis brought to this project was quite remarkable—unprecedented and, in my opinion, utterly unequaled. But the opportunities I have outlined weren't merely the product of Elvis's dreaming and scheming; they were the result of living in a society which, by design, offered people as poor as the Presleys a chance for that breathing space.

This design was the product of the realization that everyone was entitled to something more than just food and shelter; they also had the right to a certain amount of dignity. That is, society realized that it gained by relieving the poor of the social and economic humiliations, by giving them a chance to be productive and creative. And the proof that this system worked was named Elvis Presley.

The name for this design was the New Deal. It was absolutely instrumental in shaping the world that Elvis knew. Without it, I don't believe that he would have had the leisure in which to become a singer. For one thing, he would have been forced to go to work full-time much earlier, and for another, he might not have been able to maintain the idealism so crucial to his music.

Certainly it wasn't an accident that the great breakthrough for Indigenous American music, built on the music styles developed in this country over two centuries, occurred precisely twenty years after that New Deal began. Not only Elvis but Jerry Lee Lewis, Carl Perkins, Johnny Cash, and just about every singer at Sun Records grew up in an environment the New Deal shaped: a world in which TVA, WPA, and rural electrification played a central role, and a world of increasing personal dignity as a matter of policy. And what these singers had to say—about dreams and freedom, the way the world works and the way it ought to work—was also a product of that climate.

It should be obvious that the worst betrayal of the spirit of Elvis Presley and his music is occurring right now, with the deliberate dismantling of the New Deal's social programs and the simultaneous reneging on the social ideals those programs—and this music—represents. Those New Deal programs gave people more than food and shelter and some small income. They gave them the possibility of retaining some dignity even in the face of the worst poverty. And if that dignity is not the central kernel of what we loved and admired in Elvis Presley—well, then, you saw a different sort of hero than I did. It's the spirit of a waking dream of freedom, an easy conscience, self-respect, and most of all, equality among all people that calls to us from those records.

Thus, it isn't any surprise to me that the greatest effect Elvis had on American culture was to integrate it: to create an art so democratic that within it any kind of person would be treated on the same basis as any other, viewed with such compassion that it could finally be seen that what we had in common was far more important than those things that divided us.

For years, we have been told by those ignorant of the real history of

this country's popular music that Elvis Presley simply ripped off the innovations of Black musicians, that he was not a musical original, but simply
a thief, a usurper of rhythm and blues. That nothing could be further from
the truth may be demonstrated simply by listening to the original versions
of the songs that Elvis first recorded, and by comparing them with the Presley records. "That's Alright Mama," in Arthur Crudup's hands, is a simple
country blues; in Elvis Presley's style, it becomes something more complicated, more free-flowing, without losing its sense of the blues emotions,
but with an additional edge of freedom and grace. You can say something
similar about Wynonie Harris's "Good Rockin' Tonight," and about Junior
Parker's "Mystery Train," in relation to the Presley versions ("Mystery Train"
just might be the greatest single Presley recording). None of these comparisons will reveal Elvis as a thief. All of them will show that he radically altered Black blues and R&B styles, and not only by adding a component of
country & western accents.

What Elvis actually did was to *integrate* these styles, which is the reason that he is disparaged by people who do not find Johnny Ray or Benny
Goodman or Pat Boone—all of whom *did* rip off Black styles—at all offen-
sive. Elvis wasn't a threat because he stole from Black people—when has a
White American ever been condemned for that? He was a threat because, in
Greil Marcus's phrase, *he performed the union*, acted out our lip-service belief
in equality before our very eyes.

In this sense, the only comparable cultural blow in the movement for
racial equality of the post–World War II era was Jackie Robinson's. And for
a White Mississippian like Elvis to take the heat—well, it took an immense
amount of guts. And along with Sam Phillips and the other singers at Sun,
Elvis integrated American music and, equally against its will, American
broadcasting (at least radio broadcasting). And I know, as a person who was
brought up in Michigan amidst many of the same vicious racial lies that
people in Tennessee and Mississippi are taught, that Elvis Presley fundamentally altered many people's vision of how Blacks and Whites ought to
get along in this land.

That wasn't an accident. The New Deal, with its decision to reopen certain possibilities in America, set it up, not only by giving Elvis the space a
poor boy rarely has to find his artistic soul and by spurring his family in

their move from the country to the city, but by proposing that, if this nation were to succeed, then it would have to be one in which all the wires crossed. Elvis was the junction.

Elvis represented integration on a host of levels. For many Northerners, including myself, Elvis symbolized the idea that this was one nation, and that people with Mississippi accents could be as great as those who spoke like the folks on TV. Certainly, he represented a kind of sexual integration, between the frenzy of lust and the absolute modesty of personal love, between secular passion and religious ecstasy. And he incarnated the new ideal that our society should not be divided into one in which the rich spoke up and the poor shut up, but that it should become one in which all deserved a voice—even the rich, for those who think that only the poor are born funky. But especially the poor, because they have been unwelcome for so long in any area of the arts or media, except as foolish Amos 'n' Andy or Li'l Abner stereotypes.

All of this and some more is what Elvis meant, and you can boil it down to one word: integration. This is the ideal that propelled the New Deal imagination and if you listen to any Elvis record from "Mystery Train" to "Burning Love," you'll hear some fragment of it. People talk about the spirit in those records: in my view, this integration is the essence of that spirit.

This is a vision as old as America—older, in fact. But when Elvis was a boy, and all through his early days, it was a spirit abroad in the United States under the name New Deal.

We have now come to the point where the exact opposite of that vision is being preached: the so-called New Federalism. What this rise of the radical right really means is the repeal of the concepts of social and economic justice that made Elvis (and all of rock music) possible in the first place. Every day, a little more of that New Deal spirit is eroded and the message is driven home that this is not one big, integrated society, but two cultures, one high and one low; one privileged, the other restricted; one dignified, the other humbled; one respectable, one contemptible. In the midst of this political counterreformation, it's no wonder that Elvis Aaron Presley, who was the incarnation of the benefits of the New Deal and the integrationist movements, is presented as a fraud and a talentless know-nothing clown and that his audience is portrayed as a batch of ignorant suckers who fell for the biggest con job in national history.

This is the message of "neoconservatism," which means to redefine all of our social and cultural relationships. In this respect, Albert Goldman's version of Elvis is clearly a stalking horse for the new attitudes. If people will accept that Elvis was worthless *because* he was Southern, because his family background was not worthy of greatness and all the rest of it, then they will also accept the other lies the radical right sells. These lies can be heard from the lips of media commentators, educators, politicians, and other "respectable" persons, and they are amplified by the absolute contempt in which popular culture, and Indigenous American arts in particular, are held. All in all, what we now face is an attempt to deny that the entire cultural turmoil Elvis began and symbolized ever happened, or that what happened was meaningful. (This goes hand in hand with the neoconservative denial of the New Deal–derived movements for Black and female liberation, and of the victory of the '60s anti-war movement.)

Because Elvis is a great mirror of our society, it's easy for a writer like Goldman to spread the neoconservative theory over his life. In this version, Presley becomes an example of what such people really think of the poor, Southerners, the uneducated, the unprivileged (even, most absurdly, the uncircumcised). What's delivered isn't just a message about Elvis; it's a vision of the way the world ought to work, a precise inversion of the vision expressed in Presley's music (and the rock that follows from it).

What's going on here is a constant retraction of human dignity. Under such conditions, a phenomenon like Elvis Presley would be inconceivable. Allowing this theory to prevail would thus be the greatest dishonor we could do to Elvis.

People always want to know why Elvis screwed up and died. When he acted out the high school civics lesson version of the American Dream, which ought to be true, and found out it wasn't, it was like hitting a brick wall. He gave up, and as a result he got lazy; he stopped believing, and he started abusing both his body and other people, and he died.

The condition of Elvis Presley's memory in the coming years depends upon re-creating the dreams that he embodied. It requires a refusal of a world that is unequal and a willingness to battle for the ideals inherent in those dreams.

In his songs—which, for me, means in his dreams—Elvis Presley shows us a different world. It's tempting to say that he gave us that world, but that isn't true. That world is always present, as a hope or a chance, but no one, not even the true visionary who sees it clearly as Elvis did, can give it to us. Such a world must be seized and created, then preserved with care and devotion by everyone who wishes to live in it. Get lazy and stop taking care, and you end up as unfortunately as Elvis did: the dream world crumbles at your feet.

When Bruce Springsteen played Europe last year, he decided to sing an Elvis song which might tell the audiences in the countries where Presley never played what this American mythology was all about. (Every American rock singer must feel like an Elvis stand-in overseas.) He picked "Follow That Dream," but felt that the words didn't speak as clearly as the music. So he wrote some new lyrics, which got to the essence of the matter. I like to imagine Elvis singing them:

[Every man has] a right to fight for the things he believes

For the things that come to him in dreams

And if we can follow that dream, wherever that dream may lead, then we will have honored Elvis Presley, and his image and music will be preserved.

But if we let our country be ripped in two, allow the spirit of fairness and equality that he represented to die, then Elvis will seem to history not a hero but only a noble fool—though even then, he'll never look as foolish as we will for letting it happen.

INTRODUCTION
TO SECTION 1

1984–1989

What was happening at *Rolling Stone* when I was there (1975–1980) was similar to what happened at *Creem* (1969–1973): they were going someplace I wasn't going. Because I had this very specific idea of what I was supposed to do to be a writer. One part of that was, I was trying to capture something that hadn't been captured. Almost like a film.

Nobody else—at *Creem* and *Rolling Stone*—even really understood what I was trying to do. I'd go further: Nobody else even knew I was trying to do something! I didn't take it personally. And I tried to take it as comedically as possible. But I had some specific ideas of what this music's about, what I'm about, what Detroit's about . . . A lot of that's in *Fortunate Son*. Or a whiff of it. It's almost literally true that I knew from when I left high school what I was going to try to do.

I knew what was not being written, and I wanted to write it. I guess I mean to say: none of this was accidental. Why did I give up on *Rolling Stone*? Jann Wenner was a great editor for me. But I thought they were moving it far too quickly toward just being an alternative piece of journalism. And I didn't think that would work. What was being left out? The idea that there was something new in the world and that nobody was saying it. Even as they were thinking they were talking about that very thing, they weren't. There was this whole separation—not of church and state—but of ridiculous and serious.

So, we started a monthly newsletter, *Rock & Roll Confidential*, later *Rock & Rap Confidential*. The first issue went out

in May 1983—two years into Ronald Reagan's presidency—
to only a few hundred committed rock fans. The idea came
from Lee Ballinger. And communism. I understood that (1) it
needed to be done by several people, not just one. And (2) it
needed a tone of voice. You weren't able to get those things
in standard journalism. Standard journalism is against you
having a voice. It isn't interested in mockery. Or in anything
that's fabulous. Basically, I had a sense of the underlying ridic-
ulousness of everything that was serious. Everything. And if
you could bring that forward . . . But you had to do it right. You
couldn't destroy the old; you want to build on the old.

—D.M.

CHRISSIE COMES HOME

—RRC #10, MARCH 1984

Raves for what's trendy or just fashionable tend to cheapen the dialogue about rock, especially when words like *classic* and *masterpiece* are applied to albums as fundamentally flawed as the likes of Big Country. The Pretenders' *Learning to Crawl* makes you realize how irrelevant such superlatives have become. With this album, Chrissie Hynde is more clearly in charge than ever before, and she succeeds on almost every level: even her angry humor has never been so sharp, especially in brilliant musical jokes like "Time the Avenger," an inversion of the Outsiders' "Time Won't Let Me."

Yet discussions of Hynde's album have centered around two issues that are only marginally relevant: the deaths of band members James Honeyman-Scott and Pete Farndon and the fact that four of *Learning to Crawl*'s tracks have previously been issued as singles. The latter is a genuinely dumb charge, ignoring the fact that this album attempts a complete statement, in which each song is a necessary element; Hynde isn't repeating herself, or saddling her listeners with filler, because in the context of *Learning to Crawl*, "Middle of the Road," "2000 Miles," "My City Was Gone," and "Back on the Chain Gang" take on new meaning and have their old ones refreshed and enriched.

Death itself saturates side one of *Learning to Crawl*, in which the most compassionate as well as the angriest songs—"Middle of the Road" and "Time the Avenger"—reflect what amounts to a one-way dialogue with

Honeyman-Scott and Farndon, as well as Hynde's absolute refusal to acqui-
esce in the face of so much mortality.

Learning to Crawl is also another dialogue between Hynde and people
who can't talk back—not just the dead band members, but also her own in-
fant daughter and ultimately, the necessarily anonymous mass of listeners.
Into this suspended conversation she pours everything she knows: a sense
of roots and a sense of rootlessness ("My City Was Gone"), a profoundly
fearful sense of the future, and a jaundiced yet completely empathetic gaze
at the present ("Thumbelina"). In the best songs on this album (the only
truly weak one is the messy "I Hurt You") Chrissie Hynde speaks as wife,
mother, rebel, lover. As far as I can tell, she isn't posing, just incarnating all
these roles. Stripped of Honeyman-Scott's flamboyance, her own vision is
sharper than ever, because it has to be.

Finally, what's most engrossing and heartening about *Learning to Crawl*
is the way it fits into a period stifled by silly concepts of renewed British
Invasion, revamped Beatlemania, and other fads. Hynde is the most important U.S. expatriate since Jimi Hendrix; songs such as "Thumbelina,"
"Middle of the Road," "My City Was Gone," and "2000 Miles" represent
her first attempt to grapple with America and what's happened in the decade since she left. The album also focuses on the loss of personal identity
that comes from sensing a loss of geographic or social place. In the process,
Learning to Crawl taps sources of current public despair and rage that only
Elvis Costello, Bruce Springsteen, and a few rap performers have begun to
fathom. That is, like all genuinely great albums, *Learning to Crawl* finally
doesn't fit into its period—it redefines the time in its own image, exposing
what's fraudulent and silly in present goings-on, suggesting a way forward.

Rather than the sop of Anglophile fashion, Chrissie Hynde offers
something braver and more enduring: herself at the end of a taut rope. At
the other end is her audience. From the degree of slack and tension, we
can begin to measure what 1984 will really be like—and not only on the
turntable.

DANCE WITH THE DEVIL

—*RRC* #17, OCTOBER 1984; DAVE MARSH AND GREIL MARCUS

It was inevitable that Ronald Reagan would make an imperial endorsement of Bruce Springsteen's music, as he did at Hammonton, New Jersey, on September 19. "America's future rests in a thousand dreams inside your hearts," Reagan proclaimed. "It rests in the message of hope in songs of a man so many young Americans admire: New Jersey's own Bruce Springsteen. And helping you make those dreams come true is what this job of mine is all about."

Both the speech and the endorsement were based on unsound premises. Reagan was in the process of proclaiming his administration a victory for prosperity and Pax Americana at a time when unemployment and destitution are rife and hundreds of soldiers have been killed in battle as a direct result of his policies. And the "message of hope" that he—or his speechwriters—found in the music is anything but undiluted, as anyone who has heard Springsteen's last four albums must be aware. But bizarre as it was, Reagan's fiat wasn't out of context. The rightist movement he represents means to appropriate everything and anything that uses any kind of American patriotic symbolism in its quest for a return to "social purity" and the worst values of the nineteenth century.

Not that one would know any of this, or have a proper impression of what Springsteen is really singing about from reading mainstream press accounts. Springsteen has now reached a peak of media celebrity. The context for Reagan's foray into Bossmania was established in a four-minute report by Bernard Goldberg on the September 12 *CBS Evening News* with Dan Rather. Goldberg's piece was well put together and generally kept the story straight until it reached its final line: "His shows are like old-time revival meetings, with the same old-time message: If they (i.e., his fans) work hard enough and long enough, like Springsteen himself, they also can make it to the Promised Land." Since Goldberg was talking about a performance that included "Johnny 99," "The River," "My Hometown," and "Born in the U.S.A.," he seemed to be engaging in a willful misreading of the show's content.

The next day, George Will, who also saw Springsteen at the Capitol Center, checked in with his nationally syndicated column. Will had attended the show at the invitation of Max Weinberg and his wife, Becky, who had mysteriously found him amusing on ABC TV's *This Week with David Brinkley*. (They also invited Sam Donaldson, who didn't show; so much for liberalism in broadcast journalism.) In the course of a clumsy encomium, Will managed to contort the experience beyond recognition, ending in a burst of free market bluster: "If all Americans—in labor and management, who make steel or cars or shoes or textiles—made their products with as much energy and confidence as Springsteen and his merry band make music, there would be no need for Congress to be thinking about protectionism." In other words, if you find slapping bumpers onto compact cars less fulfilling than singing rock & roll songs in front of adoring masses, fuck off. Will's column did not note that he had left the concert one song into the second set, though not before he finally unknotted his ugly yellow bow tie.

It was Will's column that led directly to the Reagan speech, no surprise since Will has been a Reagan stooge since the 1980 campaign. (He was up to his neck in Debategate, before his colleagues declared that a nonissue.) Within twenty-four hours, the White House had contacted Springsteen's agent, Barry Bell, to ask if the singer would appear with Reagan at the Hammonton rally! They were politely told that Springsteen was busy touring. Apparently, the Reagan campaign staff then decided that if they could not have an endorsement-in-fact, they'd simply swipe an endorsement-by-default, allowing Reagan to declare an affinity between his works and Springsteen's. Thus did Reagan move from being the Teflon President to the Fly Paper President, a man incredibly difficult to shake off.

Springsteen often closes his show by saying, "Let freedom ring—but remember, you gotta fight for it." But his battle is only beginning, for the display of patriotic symbols on his LP cover and at his shows (all those waving flags) offers Reagan and other Rightists an easy opportunity to practice the distortion in which they specialize. Reagan's speech put him on the spot, and it didn't take Springsteen long to make his move. Twenty minutes into his first show afterward, in Pittsburgh on September 21, he stopped to say, "The president was mentioning my name the other day and I kinda got to wondering what his favorite album musta been. I don't think it was the *Nebraska* album. I don't think he's been listening to this one." Then he went into "Johnny 99," his song about an autoworker whom unemployment drives to murder. Later, Springsteen spoke of walking the Capitol Mall from the Lincoln Memorial to the Vietnam Veterans Memorial, concluding, "It's a long walk from a government that's supposed to represent all of the people to where we are today. It seems like something's wrong out there when there's a lotta stuff being taken away from a lotta people that shouldn't have it taken away from [them]. And sometimes it's hard to remember that this place belongs to *us*—that this is our hometown."

Springsteen no more lives in a Promised Land than the rest of us; his words acknowledge this. It's sad, in a way, that he had to make what was already obvious completely explicit, but that's part of the price we pay for having a government that twists and distorts facts so badly and "news" media that accepts these distortions at face value. The only other public statement of recent weeks that has depicted the full derangement of our situation—the only other that dared to challenge the unspoken presumption that everything in America is not only all right but improving—came from another rocker, Elvis Costello. Costello appeared on *The Tonight Show* on September 17 and, before the biggest audience of his career, on a program that has been a virtual nonstop Reaganite party both on the stage and in the audience for the past two years, sang his anti-Reagan song, "Peace in Our Time." But he did it with an amended line: "There's already one spaceman in the White House," he spat, giving the lyric the full ferocity of which he is capable. "What you want the same one there again for?" The venom of Costello's singing blasted apart the illusion of the perfect harmony; needless to say, it was met with dead silence. It's hard to imagine a greater tribute.

This is the day of the Big Lie, not just about the meaning of music but about the situation in Latin America, the Middle East, and in the heart of America itself. The ability to speak not just loudly but clearly (which Elvis Costello has done ever since "Less Than Zero") is utterly essential. And Bruce Springsteen didn't leave his ugly incident behind in Pittsburgh, because he can't. Reagan is truly the Fly Paper President in his ability to ignore all refutations of his mendacity, and the next time he visits New Jersey, he's likely to try the same campaign gimmick. Or will it be John Cougar in Indiana, Bob Seger in Detroit, or someone in your hometown?

What's up for grabs right now isn't just an election, much less the meaning of rock & roll songs. It's the meaning of America itself that's at stake. What we can't repeat is the awful error of the sixties, ceding all images of patriotism to the opposition. And rock stars can't fight this war alone, not if there's any chance of winning. It's up to the rest of us to also find ways of thinking and speaking clearly and of acting effectively *together* in order to reclaim our country and our future.

FREIGHT TRAIN BLUES

—RRC #29, OCTOBER 1985

S itting in the bar of a Detroit hotel, I bumped into photographer Joel Bernstein, who mentioned that he'd shown Neil Young the comments in *RRC* 19 about Young's enthusiasm for Ronald Reagan. Bernstein said that Young felt his quotes were misleading, since they were condensed from a much longer interview. But when I asked if that meant that Young had been quoted inaccurately, Bernstein said no. "He supports Reagan," he said. "He thinks he's good for the country."

Young's new album, *Old Ways*, has been hailed as a departure, his first LP of country music and his best since *Rust Never Sleeps*. *Old Ways* may very well be all of those things, though it must be said that the comparison to *Rust* is about as meaningful as claiming that any given Bob Dylan album is his best since *Blood on the Tracks*. "Best since" is not a criterion of greatness; more often, it's an excuse for mediocrity. As it happens, "Misfits" might be Young's first really great song since those on *Rust*, but it's no departure, and it has a lot more in common with *Everybody Knows This Is Nowhere* than anything that ever came out of Nashville. *Old Ways* is Young's most successful album in some time—but that's because it abandons his forays into futurism and concentrates on nostalgia, which has been his major preoccupation since "Sugar Mountain" and "Helpless."

What's Neil Young nostalgic for? The wayward wind, the open highway, cowboys, doping and drinking, but more than anything, the way the world used to be, when America was young, strong, prosperous, undefeated. One source of Reagan's appeal to Young (and those who think like him) is that RR promises that he can restore that world. Listen to Young, speaking in the September 7 *Melody Maker*: "In the Carter years, everybody was walking around with their tails between their legs. . . . Militarily, we had a lot of disasters and a lot of things that never should have happened and that maybe were mistakes in the first place, although it's hard to say.

"People were being killed everywhere before we went over to try to help, and we went over and tried to help them and we fucked up. But y'know you can't always feel sorry for everything that you did. Obviously, I wish no one had to die in any war but war is, ah, a dirty game . . ." Hard to believe that this is the man who wrote, "Four dead and Nixon's coming." Today Young implies that America should not regret the invasion of Cambodia, which is what those kids at Kent State were protesting when they were murdered by the National Guard.

So Neil Young is a meathead about politics. Does that make him a musical monster? Obviously not. Some of our greatest musicians—Elvis Presley, Ray Charles, and James Brown come readily to mind—are equally reactionary. But there's a difference. Young is celebrated as a pop writer of great intellect and vision, which rock's other right-wingers have not been. (The exception is Bob Dylan, and given Young's very visible Dylan fixation throughout his career, Dylan's shift rightward might even have been an impetus for Neil to make his move.) Young doesn't just endorse what has been happening to the U.S. and the world in the past five years; he justifies and rationalizes it.

This has been going on in Neil Young's music for a long time. But the real question is whether it makes any difference what Neil Young says. Obviously, *RRC* believes it does. Take *re-ac-tor*'s best song, "Southern Pacific," in which Young mourns the passing of the railroads and specifically complains of the plight of railroad workers: "I ain't no brakeman, ain't no conductor / But I would be though, if I was younger."

My father spent more than thirty years working for a railroad, mostly as a brakeman and conductor. I wonder if Young has any idea of what has happened to men like my dad in the past decade. In 1983, my father—only fifty-six years old—was forced to retire from the railroad because of disabilities caused by heart disease and two forms of cancer. It took almost a year for the insurance company to rule that his disability was legitimate. A few weeks before he died last summer, it did. Yet my father was still waiting—impatiently, angrily, and with a great deal of fear that added to his pain—for the government to decide the same. Had he managed to continue drawing breath for a few more months, he might have been confronted with the spectacle of having to return to a job that had literally sucked his life out of him, even though he could often barely walk across a room. For most of the time, he *could* walk, and under the current rules, if you can walk, you can work, and if you don't, you're a welfare cheat.

Neil Young's support of Ronald Reagan is an endorsement of that policy and dozens more exactly like it. They are policies that he has never had to reckon with for one day in his privileged life. And, perhaps most importantly, they are policies that he makes as chic as his often gorgeous and frightening imagery, as palatable as his cracked, lonesome voice. And that's why, no matter how many fascinating songs Neil Young may write and sing for the rest of his career, it would bother me not at all if he never did another. He may be good, but that doesn't mean he's not my enemy.

FIFTEEN LITTLE GIRLS
HIDING IN THE BACKSEAT

—*RRC #30*, NOVEMBER 1985

B y rights, the forces that want to censor rock ought to be on the run. The Parents Music Resource Center (PMRC) has now been exposed as a classic example of concealed conflict of interest and double-dealing. Although the PMRC denied for the first five months of its existence that it had any "membership" beyond its officers, a letter written by the group to the Recording Industry Association of America was signed by the wives of sixteen senators and congressmen, including the wives of five members of the Senate Commerce Committee, which held the September 19 hearings on "porn rock"; the wife of Senator Strom Thurmond, who presides over the Senate Judiciary Committee, which will determine the fate of record industry tape tax legislation; and the wife of Thomas Downey, co-chairman of the Congressional Arts Caucus and recipient of the RIAA's 1984 Cultural Award.

Nor were the signatures the only dirty little secret involved in the rock debate. For instance, Tipper Gore finally revealed in *Rolling Stone* that Kandie Stroud, the "journalist" whose *Newsweek* article helped stir national debate about song lyrics, is in fact a PMRC consultant. And internal documents prove beyond a doubt that RIAA president Stanley Gortikov, at least, was not only willing to give PMRC a ratings code but was willing to at least consider a blacklist of artists who didn't conform to the censors' standards. (Full details are in my article "Sympathy for the Devil," *Village Voice*, October 8.)

The idea of a warning label appeasement of the PMRC was explicitly rejected by eight record companies, including two, A&M and MCA, which had previously accepted it. During late September and the first week of October, serious opposition to censorship appeared to be mounting within the record industry, spearheaded by Frank Zappa and Danny Goldberg, of Gold Mountain Records. Goldberg formed the Musical Majority and enlisted support from the American Civil Liberties Union and Los Angeles mayor Tom Bradley, the only elected official who has opposed rock censorship.

The censors have now regrouped. President Reagan attacked rock lyrics in a mid-October speech; the *New York Times* has run two op-ed pieces attacking rock records and exactly zero supporting the music or the Constitution, while the highly ideological *U.S. News & World Report* devoted its October 28 cover to the topic. David Zucchino's story in the November 7 *Rolling Stone* made it crystal clear that while the PMRC has diluted its original ratings proposal, it plans to push ahead with the rest of its program, blacklist and all.

Record industry response ranges from sluggish to nonexistent. Goldberg got around to an official rerelease of Keel's album, featuring "The Right to Rock," but didn't get back to the fans who called offering to support the Musical Majority. The American Civil Liberties Union, Goldberg's partner in founding the Musical Majority, has also been inactive since the hearing. Debbie Kresh signed on as the Musical Majority's publicist but has been given nothing to publicize. An advertising campaign that was supposed to be at least partly funded by Island Records has never materialized. Word on the street has MTV basing its new broadcast TV ad campaign around the censors' attacks, but in the most self-destructive way: replacing "I want my MTV" with "I got corrupted by MTV" or the like.

Because the industry has done nothing, the issue now is not whether rock should be censored but how; not whether rock stars are corrupting the morals of American kids, but what should be done about it. In part, the lack of action can be explained by the fact that many in the rock business feel ashamed of the music and its audience—like the RIAA's Stanley Gortikov,

who, at the New Music Seminar, had the audacity to echo the PMRC by
reading the same excerpts from the Mentors' "Golden Showers," with its
elaborate references to sniffing anal vapors.

If the record industry chooses to fight, it has all the ammunition it
needs to win. For example, the least effort at doing some research would
have turned up for Gortikov what *RRC* reader Greg Reibman of Dallas
learned by calling Enigma Records: despite all the publicity given it by the
PMRC, the Mentors' *You Axed for It!*, which contains "Golden Showers,"
has sold all of three thousand copies—a fraction of the sales of the label's
album by Stryper, the Christian heavy metal act.

Even more heartening has been the public response. I have spent hours
on the radio from Boston to Los Angeles, and everywhere, even on shows
where the host is rabidly right wing, both rock fans and those who loathe
the music understand that what's going on here is a fundamental attack
on the First Amendment. Winning the battle against rock censorship on a
national basis would not only be simple—it might even be easy.

But without organization and national education of the audience about
the real issues, the results are likely to be dismal. Look at what just happened in San Antonio. Promoter Jack Orbin agreed to help Lynn Gladhill,
president of Parents Against Subliminal Seduction, set up a screening panel
for rock shows he presents. Gladhill interviewed Nikki Sixx of Mötley Crüe,
and she approved of the group's October 6 appearance at San Antonio Convention Center. Gladhill's role as de facto censor is a major *defeat*, no matter
that it temporarily lets Orbin conduct his business. The San Antonio deal
establishes a precedent that can allow any well-connected group of censorship fanatics to control musical expression through a region and perhaps,
eventually, the whole country.

THE LONESOME DEATH OF FOLK MUSIC

—RRC #33, FEBRUARY 1986

I n the booklet that accompanies *Biograph*, his boxed set retrospective, Bob Dylan forces a theme to emerge. For the first time in many years, he credits his sources among bluesmen and traditional Appalachian folk singers, even acknowledging a few deceased contemporaries. Yet, he tells Cameron Crowe, he was never a folk singer. "Folk music was a strict and rigid establishment. If you sang folk songs from the thirties, you didn't do bluegrass tunes or Appalachian ballads." Dylan should know—he was castigated as a heretic and traitor for his genre-mingling even before he electrified his music.

Biograph itself doesn't contain any of Dylan's performances, so it can't really make sense of the extent to which he'd mastered a stunning variety of traditional material. To learn about that, you have to dig up the ten-record bootleg box *Ten of Swords* (Tarantula).

"If it was worth my while, I could put together a ten-record set of unreleased songs, songs that have never gotten out and songs that have been bootlegged," Dylan recently told *Time. Ten of Swords*, over eight hours long and containing material only from 1961 to 1966, is filled with a lot of the music he must have been thinking about.

The readily digestible highlights of *Ten of Swords* are the rock & roll tracks from '65 and '66, especially the live ones. But what's most extraordinary about the set is the way it builds a comprehensive picture of Dylan as a master of traditional folk and blues material. There's a beautiful seven-minute version of "Barbara Allen," the litmus test of folk singing; Dylan crooning "No More Auction Block," from which he got the melody to "Blowin' in the Wind," and a Robert Johnson medley kicked off by "Kind Hearted Woman Blues." Heard alongside their sources, Dylan's own "Hollis Brown," "Don't Think Twice," "Mr. Tambourine Man," and little-known originals like "Man on the Street" and "Percy's Song" seem natural extensions. They have the same groove, the same lyricism, the same awareness of what Ralph Ellison called "that quality which makes for the mystery of the blues: their ability to imply far more than they state outright and their capacity to make the details of sex convey meanings which touch upon the metaphysical."

In this context, Dylan's breakthrough to rock seems inevitable, a one-man encapsulation of the development of American folk and popular music. It's the natural outcome of two streams finally converging and overflowing, like the great confluence of waters that takes the Mississippi from a tiny stream near Dylan's hometown in Hibbing, Minnesota, to the broad expanses of the Delta a thousand miles south. You can read about this process and observe its many transitional moments, but nothing quite compares to the vivid roar with which Dylan picks up his guitar and crashes through the dams and levees.

In the years when Dylan made the earthshaking music on *Ten of Swords* and *Biograph*, those isolated strands of American music still qualified as types of folk music: uniquely regional expressions with integral roots in specific communities. But Dylan's creative convergence (or for that matter, Elvis Presley's) was only possible because such communities were in the final stages of disintegration. The process started in the twenties as the South industrialized and the first great migration out of the region's rural areas began. World War II and the postwar boom completed the job of transferring the Black and White farmers of the South to the cities: Chicago, Detroit, New York, but also Memphis and Atlanta.

The results for folk music were inescapable, beginning with the first recordings of country songs in the twenties, which led to both the country music industry and the folklorist revival. But the real transformation began with Muddy Waters's electrification of the blues in the late forties, then continued with the innovations of the great rock and soul singers of the fifties and sixties. Elvis and Jerry Lee Lewis, Wilson Pickett and Tina Turner are all obvious products of this great shift from rural to urban, agricultural to industrial, regional to national.

This is a story that can't really be told through the music of one performer, even one as omnivorous as Bob Dylan. You can get a better handle on it by also listening to the season's other great boxed set, the seven-volume *Atlantic Rhythm and Blues, 1947–1974*. But if you're too young to have experienced that transition, I doubt that you can really grasp what it was like to have Aretha Franklin, Mahalia Jackson, Mother Maybelle Carter, and Skip James all bouncing off one another, their music publicly exposed to mass media security, yet always reflecting the quite separate communities from which they came. It fell to Bob Dylan to create the greatest synthesis of these remnants, which makes him both the truest heir of folk music and its ultimate executioner.

Today, there is no folk music, even though the music industry is built around and shaped by the descendants of folk forms. You can't create music that speaks to any significant number of people except by mingling not only those folk remnants but also forms of technology that those communities never imagined: TV, the movies, synthesizers, modern recording studios. What's presented as folk music today—the likes of Phranc and the Washington Squares—does have a connection to the urban wing of the "folk movement" that was inspired by Dylan and Joan Baez, the Kingston Trio, and Peter, Paul and Mary. But that connection doesn't lead toward the future; it simply evokes a past that has vanished. There won't be a folk revival of any scale for the best possible reason: we aren't those people any longer.

If a Dylan revival were possible, now would seem to be the moment. In addition to his charity appearances, *Biograph*, and his upcoming tour with Tom Petty and the Heartbreakers, this spring will see the publication of Robert Shelton's *No Direction Home*, a massive biography twenty years in the making. But such a revival isn't likely. The revamping of American culture is now so complete that the majestic and beautiful music Bob Dylan created seems to emerge from a time warp. Though Dylan is recognized today as a great lyricist, his brilliance as a performer is all but unknown. But even if *Biograph* and *Ten of Swords* are no longer seeds to be sown, they still offer a harvest to be reaped.

JOHN HAMMOND: REMEMBERING THE CONSCIENCE OF AMERICAN MUSIC

—MUSICIAN, OCTOBER 1987

John Hammond was much more than the greatest talent scout in the history of American music. He discovered Billie Holiday, Aretha Franklin, Bob Dylan, Bruce Springsteen, Charlie Christian, Benny Goodman, Count Basie, and a host of others, and nurtured talents from Bessie Smith to Stevie Ray Vaughan. But Hammond was also impresario of the legendary "From Spirituals to Swing" concerts, a record producer, a music critic, and a lifelong fighter against racism. His death in July at age seventy-six removes from the music scene one of its indisputably great figures. As James Lincoln Collier wrote in *The Making of Jazz*, "The importance of John Hammond to jazz history cannot be overestimated. No other nonmusician, and indeed only the major instrumentalists, has had as broad an effect on the music as he did." With little exaggeration, that judgment could be extended to all Black-based American popular music.

In a sense, then, everyone who works with and cares about that spectrum of American music—whether jazz or rock or gospel or R&B or any of their offshoots—is an heir of John Hammond. And that's why it's worth telling a little bit about what it was like to spend some time with him.

I had the opportunity and used it often during the last few months of his life, because Hammond and I were neighbors on the East Side of New York. We'd known each other reasonably well for several years, initially because I'd written an enthusiastic review of his 1977 autobiography, *John Hammond on Record*, and then from Friday morning dalliances at the corner candy store, which at one point had a couple of worthwhile pinball machines. Venerable as Hammond may have been, patrician as his upbringing as an heir of the Vanderbilt and Sloane fortunes left him, he was never happier than when "bangin' on them pleasure machines," as one of his discoveries put it. His assistant, Mikey Harris, carried the number of the pinball arcade in Times Square because it was the best place to find John when he couldn't be located anywhere else.

Hammond never wanted it known, but he'd been seriously ill for a couple of years as a result of a series of strokes and heart attacks. Late in 1986, his wife, Esme, died of AIDS and he was thereafter not only sick but heartbroken. Still, he carried on, and if he couldn't leave the house much anymore, his dozens of friends could come to him, and they did in droves. Between the visitors and the telephone, Hammond was never out of touch with a stream of relatives, friends, musicians, writers—the whole gamut of associates developed in half a century of enthusiasms and battles.

Visiting an invalid is nothing pleasant, but Hammond's apartment remained heavily trafficked because, even at his sickest, he was never less than an ardent conversationalist, and when you hit on one of his enthusiasms or stumbled across a *bête noire*, he sprang to life, eyes afire, voice firm and strong, ready as ever to articulate and defend his ideas. What I'm trying to say, I guess, is that even at a fraction of his former authority John Hammond remained a great man. And since the illness had quelled at least a fragment of his mercurial irascibility, a sweeter one than ever before.

There was one afternoon that I will never forget, not only because it taught me something about John's personality, but because it was one of the musical experiences of a lifetime. His nephew, David Oliphant, brought over some old blue-label Columbia 78s. John asked to hear one in particular,

"Old Fashioned Love"/"I Surrender, Dear" by a Red Norvo septet that he'd recorded in 1934. "Old Fashioned Love" turned out to be nothing special, but "I Surrender, Dear" was a revelation. The tune was nothing but a corny Tin Pan Alley pop ballad, but out of the syrup arose, in the first few bars, an unbelievably beautiful ("Marvelous!" John would say, in his upper-class tones) trombone solo by Jack Jenney. By the time that ended, everybody in the room was on the verge of tears; by the time the needle was lifted off the disc, a couple of us had gone over the edge.

Hammond wiped his eyes with the sleeve of his robe. "I don't get sentimental often," he said (and it was true), "but that record always gets to me." I was sufficiently stunned to spend a lot of time over the next few months lurking in the Red Norvo section of America's best-stocked record stores. (No luck so far.)

Later that same day I showed John a copy of *Yankee Blues: Musical Culture and American Identity* by MacDonald Smith Moore. It's a study of New England classical composers and their opposite numbers, the promoters and composers of jazz and modernist music. Hammond figures prominently in the book, and I wanted to ask him if he agreed with a passage: "Hammond yearned for an 'Ur-jazz,' elemental and earthy as Bessie Smith's blues. Yet Hammond was a moving force in the racial integration of jazz bands. He wanted to integrate people, but not music."

Where I got the nerve to read those sentences, I'll never know. John listened with composure, something that might not have been true when he was feeling better. When I finished, he made a sour face, not quite a sneer. He pointed at the turntable where lay the Red Norvo 78. "That's the answer," he said.

Which it was. The band Norvo led that day was integrated, at a time when almost no one else in the world—let alone Jim Crow America—was recording Black and White musicians together. (It would be a year or two yet before anyone had the guts to bring together Black and White players on a public bandstand—John Hammond, again.) But the song they were playing was smooth as Guy Lombardo; there was nothing self-consciously bluesy about the performance, its tempo was sedate. It was a perfect synthesis of the musical styles our culture encourages us to think of as "Black" and

"White." Indeed, a great deal of its beauty derived from the perfect balance the group achieved with those two modes of music-making.

Hammond was so little bothered by Moore's assessment, I think, because he knew just what he was not: a snob. That doesn't mean his tastes were anarchic, just that he determined what he loved and what he loathed on a more substantial basis than race or personal style. He was wide open, because he was rarely, if ever, concerned with defending turf. Instead, he listened and, because he wasn't a snob, he heard what others could not (or at least recognized it well before they understood what it was they were hearing). This accounts for Hammond's distaste for what he considered the excessive self-consciousness of Duke Ellington and the giants of bop, and for the seeming incongruity of discovering Springsteen *and* Holiday, Basie *and* Dylan. Such false distinctions never interested Hammond, any more than did the stricture against mingling art and politics. Nobody who went as a privileged White teenager to Harlem in the late '20s and later helped save the Scottsboro Boys, nobody who joined the board of directors of the NAACP, founded Cafe Society and initiated "From Spirituals to Swing," all as the means of expressing his outrage at the way his beloved artists were treated, could suffer under any such delusion.

We have lived through times when almost everyone has contended that the range of American music was narrow. John Hammond built his whole life on the belief that it was broad. With his passing, the myth of John Hammond will be built, and it should not be that he was unique, some sort of freak. Instead, we should remember those open ears. There is nobody reading this magazine who doesn't love at least some of the music he helped create. And there's nobody who won't benefit from following his example, expressed in the final words of his autobiography:

> *I still would change the world if I could, convince a nonbeliever that my way is right, argue a cause and make friends out of enemies. I am still the reformer, the impatient protester, the sometimes-intolerant champion of tolerance. Best of all, I still expect to hear, if not today then tomorrow, a voice or a sound I have never heard before, with something to say which has never been said before. And when that happens I will know what to do.*

PIECE OF
MY HEART

—RRC #59, JULY 1988

I got a call the other day," Aretha Franklin began at the top of her 1973 hit, "Angel." "It was my sister Carolyn saying, 'Aretha, come by when you can, I've got something that I wanna say.' And when I got there, she said, 'You know, rather than go through a long drawn-out thing, I think the melody on the box will help me explain.'"

The song Carolyn wrote for her sister was as intimate as anything Aretha has ever allowed herself, which I suppose means that it spoke for both of them. "Too long have I loved, so unattached within," she sang. "So much that I know, that I need somebody so." Aretha sang those words out of the deepest longing and loneliness, so ravaged by the end of the third verse, you can hardly believe she's gotten that far.

But then backing voices come in, telling her, "He'll be there, now don't you worry / Just keep lookin' and just keep cookin.'" They carry her out of the spirit of hope triumphant. And for fifteen years, they've often carried me that way, too.

Carolyn Franklin was always there for her sister. She must have been among those backing voices on "Angel," and maybe that's why they have that buoyant spirit. Certainly, it was she who gave the song its tragic spirit, because the other hit Carolyn wrote was "Ain't No Way," the most achingly lovely of heartbreak ballads. Carolyn arranged the original "Piece of My

Heart" for their sister Erma. She and Aretha came up with the idea to do "Respect" by singing it together during a break in a session.

Carolyn Franklin was only forty-three when she died of cancer in late April. But her music continues to keep a lot of us going, day-to-day; and as far as I can tell, that makes it eternal.

CRYING

—RRC #69, JANUARY 1989

R oy Orbison is so magnificently present in his best records that, even though his death was national news, he just doesn't feel gone. And why should he? With his sensational work with the Traveling Wilburys, Orbison's present on the charts for the first time in nearly two decades, and later this month Virgin will release his new album, *Mystery Girl*.

Orbison's career spanned the whole history of rock & roll, from rockabilly ("Ooby Dooby") to big-beat ballads ("Only the Lonely") to plain old big beat ("Pretty Woman") to the Beatlesque folk-rock of the Wilburys and the mystical adult balladry that makes parts of *Mystery Girl* feel like a Van Morrison LP with a Tex-Mex accent. His music can be tough to describe because it fits no genre or regional style. In the end, the best way to put it is to say that he was a rocker, meaning that he made music for the recording studios more than the stage, using every resource that came to hand, from country and classical to the wailing norteño-influenced high notes that rang through so many of his hits. And he was damn proud of it. In 1981, I congratulated him on winning his only Grammy (so far), for a country duet with Emmylou Harris, and his response, while polite, was almost derisive: "Yeah, and it's the last damn *country* Grammy I'll ever win. I'm a rock & roll singer."

Roy claimed that title, even while many other singers of his generation stayed wary of it, because he was a lifelong outsider. Partly because he looked so strange (geeky even without the Ray-Bans), but mainly because his story was so much like his own songs. Ironically, Roy Orbison the outsider struck a universal chord. The greatest of his records says it all in the very first line: "Only the lonely know the way I feel tonight."

Mystery Girl picks up and extends the overarching themes of Orbison's career and Roy sings like a god across the whole record, even on songs as weird as "Windsurfer" or as draggy as Elvis Costello's "The Comedians." While the Bono-produced title track has a special eloquent power, *Mystery Girl* achieves its real greatness with "In the Real World" and "The Only One," the songs in which Roy looks his legendary past in the eye and dares to disagree.

"The Only One" is a Stax/Volt review of the self-pity that lurks at the center of rock & roll and makes a bitter mockery of the "Only the Lonely" story by making it obvious how common even the most profound sense of alienation must be. "You're the only one with a broken heart / The only one who's afraid of the dark," Roy sings, his voice as tearful as ever. "The only one in a crowded room / The only one who sees the gloom." But as the details accumulate, the absurdity of the premise is unmistakable. Wallowing, Orbison discovers the truth and, because his voice is an instrument that cannot lie, he's redeemed. The story really might not be that far from "Only the Lonely," which, after all, ends with the singer going out to love again— but now he knows why.

If Orbison isn't best known as the voice of the lonely, then it must be as the king of all dreamers. The most heartbreaking lines in all his songs come at the end of "In Dreams": "Too bad that all these things / Can only happen in my dreams," he sings, and his voice picks up that norteño quaver, "Only in dreams, in beautiful dreams." "In the Real World" takes that idea by the throat: "In dreams we do so many things, we set aside the rules we know," Roy begins. "If only we could always live in dreams / If only we could make of life what in dreams it seems," and you figure you're in for another lonely ride. But then he changes pace and the music picks up, guitars strumming with a different Mexican flavor: "But in the real world, we must say real goodbyes / No matter if the love we leave will live or die." He sings the song not with regret that he's renouncing his dreams, but proudly, because he's learned to accept that there are parts of dreams that just can't be lived out. If he sounds weary, it's the weariness of a soldier victorious after a long battle—with himself. Roy Orbison could have no greater epitaph.

ACTS OF CONTRITION

—*RRC #67, MAY 1989*

The worst thing about the furor over Madonna's *Like a Prayer* may be that it obscures such an excellent album. But that just proves that Madonna has entered the rarified ranks of those pop stars who function as lightning rods for assholes.

The best thing about that furor is the opportunity it offers to examine the forces behind corporate sponsorship and music censorship. Pepsi claims it didn't know Madonna's video would debut on March 3, the day after Madonna's fairly tame Pepsi commercial first aired worldwide, and that it hadn't received permission to view it beforehand. (The company refused to tell *Variety* whether it had asked for such permission.) The video features Madonna saving a Black man from being lynched and then making love to him. The video's metaphors are entirely and clearly Christian; the man is obviously a Jesus stand-in. The subtext is equally plain: Madonna advocates integration (she even prays to a Black saint) and, in the most forceful way, violates one of the most powerful taboos of a racist society.

Almost immediately, a conservative Italian Catholic group began protesting the video's "blasphemy." Soon thereafter, Rev. Donald Wildmon, the Tupelo, Mississippi, preacher who runs the American Family Association (AFA), a pro-censorship pressure group, began to kick up a similar fuss in America. Wildmon threatened a boycott of all Pepsi products, and within days, he—not Pepsi—announced that the ad had been pulled after only the single showing. Pepsi didn't admit to canceling the commercial until early April.

It's strange Pepsi prefers Donald Wildmon to Madonna as a spokesman. Wildmon's made a name for himself by counting the acts of alleged violence and sexuality on various television programs. But his many notable religious allies are beginning to back away from him now, after *Freedom Writer*, an anti-fundamentalist newsletter, exposed the persistent anti-Semitism of his statements. Archbishop John L. May of St. Louis; Robert M. Overgaard, president of the Church of the Lutheran Brethren; and James M. Lapp, executive secretary of the Mennonite Church, have all condemned Wildmon's anti-Semitism. Yet every mainstream news account of Wildmon's boycott call portrayed AFA as a legitimate watchdog group, Wildmon as its honorable spokesman. And the only reporters to discuss the controversy's racial aspects were syndicated gossip columnist Liz Smith and *USA Today*'s Edna Gundersen. Pepsi meekly said only that it had "had discussions with Wildmon."

But to ignore Madonna's race-mingling is to misunderstand not only her controversies but her art. She is the first White female superstar to reach the top using Black contemporary music. (By comparison, Janis Joplin would have had to emulate Aretha or Martha Reeves rather than Bessie Smith.) Like the current video, her best records acknowledge, revel in, play with the ironies inherent in the fact that Donna Summer's true successor as the queen of dance music is a sometimes-blond Italian American. On *Like a Prayer*'s "Love Song," she works with Prince as nimbly as any collaborator he's ever had, and no wonder—she's as much a changeling.

If her ability to mix hedonism and liberation is somewhat at odds with reality, that doesn't mean it isn't exactly as uplifting as it means to be. The reality for Pepsi and Donald Wildmon is that the music makes you want to dive in, participate, get happy with the spirit. Not just the spirit of breaking down the barriers, but the spirit of finding yourself, which is Madonna's other great theme.

That's why Madonna's sponsorship deal felt more like a betrayal of her own best instincts than any since the Who's. But, perhaps through being continually reviled and trivialized, Madonna has learned to delight in trashing expectations. This time, she's done it to everyone: first her fans, by accepting the deal; then Pepsi and her business advisers, by destroying it; then her critics, by demolishing it with a great record and one of the most ambitious videos ever put together.

Madonna is Madonna. As millions of Wannabes must have learned by now, copying her is a ticket to oblivion. So the message to young bands is already clear: sponsors can and will withdraw their dough at the slightest sign of controversy. Certainly, if Pepsi will do it to Madonna, any random brewery will do it to a more anonymous up-and-coming act. And the sponsors clearly will *not* stand up for controversial music, no matter how popular. If anything, as all the industry's sponsorship pimps have been quick to tell the trade papers, sponsors will demand more and more control over the music that they subsidize.

Thank God they didn't get the chance with *Like a Prayer.*

CHINA GROOVE

—RRC #71, SEPTEMBER 1989

E veryone has a list of unforgettable first encounters with great records. Mine includes hearing the Animals' "House of the Rising Sun" during one of my first shaves and nearly amputating a lip; being awakened at 4 a.m. for a job I hated by Len Barry's dreadful "1-2-3" and being snapped into full consciousness when Dylan's "Positively 4th Street" followed; "Papa's Got a Brand New Bag" while stuck at a railroad crossing with my R&B-hating father; "Every Breath You Take" on a Black-oriented dance music station at four o'clock on an August Sunday afternoon.

Such surprises don't happen so often anymore. When I'm alone in the car, which was the place the radio used to be a brother, there is now a cassette machine. Sometimes, I pile a stack of tapes in the passenger seat and just take off aimlessly. That's what I was doing one night last winter when I reached over and picked up a box labeled "Van Halen." Lee Ballinger had sent it to me, but I couldn't remember why. Van Halen didn't have a new album on the way and we rarely trade bootlegs. But I was just on a rainy night cruise, so I snapped it in and braced myself.

What emerged was an acoustic guitar and an accordion and then the singer came in, chanting in a language of which I didn't know a word. The music was pretty, kind of the way Peter Gabriel's can be, and the singing undercut it totally. I let the tape run, not understanding a syllable of what the guy was going on about, but transfixed anyway. By the time the first verse was over I'd figured out the artist and the record: Cui Jian ("Sway Jen") and Ado's *The New Long March for Rock and Roll*.

A few weeks before, our friend Pam Yates had written from China, where she was working somewhere west of Shanghai on the first Chinese-American feature film coproduction. She'd heard Cui Jian's music and got excited enough to arrange to make a music video of a song from his new album. When Yates next had some time in Beijing, she shot "No More Disguises" in Tiananmen Square [*RRC* 66].

That was in January and Yates's letter described working with Cui Jian and Ado, his multinational group (the drummer is from Madagascar, the bassist is Hungarian, the others Chinese). She compared them to Bob Dylan, but I heard it as something that took place at the intersection of Gabriel, Bowie, and Springsteen. The heartbeat rhythms, the sax sonorities, the major key melodies (with surprisingly little of the minor key modalities our ears consider "Asian") made the music closer to American radio rock than any other foreign-language stuff I'd ever heard. Chinese, with its guttural intonations and short words, is perfectly suited to rock and roll. But these guys also have the nerve to end the fourth track on side B with Roy Bittan–like piano flourishes and count off the next one in a voice that sounds like John Lennon's.

Entranced as I was by Cui Jian's music, I didn't talk about it much because I had heard only rough mixes and the circumstances were so odd I didn't completely trust my perceptions. Then the demonstration came, and Pam was back in town and she sent over a copy of the finished album and it sounded even better—hard, sweet, bleak, angry, slashing, celebratory, tricking up reggae beats, AOR fetishes, art-rock allusions into a sound that connected directly at the heart.

She also brought home the unedited footage of the "No More Disguises" video, although she had no money to finish it with. The record had been officially released in Taiwan and Hong Kong, but not in the People's Republic, and the lyrics to "Disguises" make it easy to see why: "In the future my eyes will not look at you, and my longing will always remember," Cui Jian sang, weeks before a Chinese insurrection had even glimmered in Western media eyes. "My freedom also belongs to heaven and earth, and my courage belongs to me alone." He sang those lines in a tone of bleak rage. "My ability to endure is no longer exhausted, my sincerity is no longer in tears," he said. "My strength is no longer false, my anger is no longer repentant." He sang as a Chinese patriot, as the voice of May's demonstrations.

The completed "No More Disguises" video begins in the square before dawn, with the streetlights on and no people around. As titles float across the top of the screen, people begin drifting across the square like ghosts; only when the music picks up intensity do they become fully substantial. Suddenly, as Cui Jian declares, "Your freedom belongs to heaven and earth / Your courage to you alone," the camera zooms across the vast empty space of the square to the giant image of Mao, and then dissolves to shots of individuals up against a wall: soldiers, children, peasants, businessmen, a Tibetan, a trendy girl with the greatest green-striped gloves you've ever seen. The music explodes and recovers, Cui Jian bearing down on every sound, the drums banging a backbeat supported by synth and rumbling guitar. Then begins solarized black-and-white footage of the demonstrations, as dreamlike as the video's beginning, interspersed with shots of the band, of everyday life in the square in full color, of the saxman on a back street. At the end, a trio of images spells out the complexity of Cui Jian's vision: that amazing guy who faced down the tank in the square; Cui Jian himself, again declaring, "My courage belongs to me alone"; people filing away from the square at the end of a day's work, isolated, crowded, heads down.

Cui Jian already has a Chinese-American audience and I was able to purchase *The New Long March* in New York. But some U.S. label ought to release this wondrous music and its accompanying video (so far shown only at the New Music Seminar), and help it find an American audience. Not to prove any points about world pop or freedom of expression but because, in the end, if our courage really does belong to us alone, our freedom to heaven and earth, it is the job of artists to bring those ideas together. And Cui Jian does the job.

INTRODUCTION TO SECTION 2

The 1990s

There was something in the music, and it was pretty clear by then that if I didn't write about it, nobody was. Nobody else was going to try to write about any of the class stuff. Nobody even understood that it was there to talk about, mostly. And anyway, what did it have to do with anything? You had to reinvent the wheel. And I wasn't even interested in wheels; I wanted to fly! That's arrogant, but it's true.

My daughter Kristen dying changed everything. My heroes had been rock stars, mostly. But the patients—the kids—became my heroes. And the doctors and everyone at Sloan Kettering. We started the Kristen Ann Carr Fund to try to support them.

The most important thing I did in that period of time—to me—was when I played Santa Claus for the kids at Sloan Kettering. 'Cause here are kids confronting the most profound despair. And kids are smart; kids know that they're dying when they're dying. Kristen was twenty-one; still pretty damn young. No, everybody doesn't lose eventually. And no, everybody doesn't die at thirteen. And yes, you have every right you care to have to be and act furious.

My wife Barbara essentially had her entire raison d'être torn out of her body, and she got up the next morning and she did what she had to do. And the reason she did was, if she hadn't, she would have betrayed Kristen and violated her in some fundamental way. We kept trying. And that's a lesson about politics and about a lot of other things.

—*D.M.*

AFTER THE REVOLUTION: THE LEGACY OF THE MC5

¬MUSICIAN, NOVEMBER 1990

S omewhere there exists an alternate universe in which the MC5 became the biggest band in history—bigger than the Beatles (their ambition), bigger than Chairman Mao (their manager's). A universe in which thousands of their direct descendants express the White Panther Party's three-point program—rock 'n' roll, dope, and fucking in the streets—by accelerating social change through a musical fusion of Sun Ra, John Coltrane, the gutter-tongued rhythm and blues of Andre Williams, and pre-psychedelic, non-nonviolent Anglo-rock glommed from the Who and Them.

In this universe, everyone wears black leather trench coats and spangled stage costumes, guitarists wiggle through power chords, singers storm and stomp as they bash drum kits with out-of-control mike-cord lariats, skinny blond drummers bead sweat 'cross naked chests as they struggle to fit Keith Moon rolls into Elvin Jones–based patterns, while the crowd demands that anyone as wimpishly literary as the Velvet Underground "Kick out the jams, motherfuckers! Or get off the stage."

I know this universe because my active career as a rock 'n' roll fan began as one of the several thousand MC5 fans who followed the band's adventures around Michigan and the upper Midwest from 1967 through its disintegration in the early '70s. I know it because, with the band and its manager, John Sinclair (the self-styled "cigar-chomping psychedelic gangster" now best known as the subject of a John Lennon song), and those other fans, I dreamed it.

About the only resemblances between that universe and the one *Musician* inhabits are that the bassist remains stock-still at the back of the bandstand, and that those power chords and quasi-revolutionary concepts occasionally loom up as signposts to a better way of life.

By now, though, such offshoots are grown hydroponically, thrashers and punkers with their roots tangled and distorted because they're cut off from the twin sources of the Five's sonic fury: the frenzied frustrations of Motor City R&B's spiritual energy clashed with the intellectual anger of Midwestern bohemian dreams crashing to earth amid the multiple disasters of racial backlash, psychedelic crap-out, and Vietnam psychosis. Today's misunderstanding of high-energy Michigan rock is exemplified by the fact that most historians credit the Stooges, the Five's exquisitely comic doppelgänger, as one of the era's and the area's pre-punk prime movers. An error at least as significant as calling the Yardbirds more influential than the Stones, or ranking Joe Tex ahead of Otis Redding.

Make no mistake: Iggy and the Stooges were a great band, one of the most unsettling groups ever to seize a stage. But the MC5's shows were of a whole other order, as great in their own sizzlingly seismic way as the Who's or the Stones' or Springsteen's or Dylan's, and for exactly the same reason: they had every intention of changing the whole world, every time out, and on their best nights, the band and those paying attention realized some incredible fragment of that ambition and were transported to a state where that alternate universe wasn't just a possibility but the actual Truth, not only what was Going to Happen but what was actually Happening.

The Five presented themselves with such sudden, gaudy force that getting a fix on them, no matter how close to the site you happened to stand, proved virtually impossible. Originally, they were just a pack of rock rats from the downriver, downscale suburb of Lincoln Park. They weren't especially "progressive" the way that term is understood today: rather than Anglo-popsters, they were greaser soulsters, and the MC5 moniker evolved, I always suspected, partly because it had that biker/car club ring to it.

Sometime in the early mid-sixties, the Lincoln Park brigade did hook up with the local avant-garde, in the form of beatnik painter Michael Davis, who soon left his canvases for the bass guitar. A few blocks away, Trans-Love Energies' Artists' Workshop struggled to liberate poetry and jazz from the art ghetto. The Five were actually the first clear test of John Sinclair and company's thesis that ordinary rock 'n' roll street kids would thrive if thrown together with the avant-garde on equal terms. The Trans-Love credo, "There is no separation," seemed to mean "There is no condescension." In Sinclair's "Coat Puller" column in the old *Fifth Estate*, he once confessed to reading *Hit Parader* because they did good interviews and "besides I kinda like knowing what Ringo eats for breakfast."

To see the Five in those days—singer Rob Tyner playing harp on "Empty Heart" or "C.C. Rider" till his mouth was shredded and bleeding, or performing the ritualized atomic explosion of "Black to Comm" and thus holding its own on a bill with Joseph Jarman's ensemble or various other elements of the Art Ensemble of Chicago—was to experience not the *idea* of revolution but a form of the real thing. It was the Velvet Revolution as played out within the cultural matrix of Detroit, which is to say partaking of jazz, gospel, rock 'n' roll, psychedelic, and comic strip attitudes.

The Five were police targets, all of them. Sinclair made himself the Motor City's most notorious pot fiend, and managed to get sent up to the state pen for ten years for giving two joints to an undercover narc (the same guy who'd given him his *second* bust, so go figure). Meantime, the rest of the band's "management company," a hippie conglomerate earlier known as Trans-Love Energies, moved to collegiate Ann Arbor, absorbed various psychedelicized SDSers and the like, and became the ultramilitant White Panther Party, with its uniquely salacious political program (and a genuinely stupid name that has led to the widely mistaken belief that they—we—were some kind of White supremacists. The first point of the WPP's program was actually "Full support of the Black Panther Party's 10-point program," which ought to settle the issue).

Ludicrous as it may seem, the WPP attracted the direct interest of the FBI's Cointelpro (through which human agency I do not know or I would most certainly be tellin'); several of its members were arrested for (ineffectively) bombing an Ann Arbor CIA office and wound up on the Ten Most Wanted List. Meantime, the Five themselves managed to get busted for all sorts of things, ranging from illegally wrapping themselves in the flag to obscenity (the cry "Kick out the jams, motherfucker" probably remains illegal in most states, not only Florida) to shoplifting sunglasses.

The MC5 lived and worked at a killing pace and pressure. By the late seventies, three-fifths of the group were in governmental rehab in the federal penitentiary at Lexington, Kentucky, site of a Burroughs-ian nightmare—going cold turkey under armed guard while sequestered in the company of nothing but other dope fiends. They'd made three albums: a classic 1969 debut, cut live at their major haunt, Detroit's Grande Ballroom, and panned in *Rolling Stone* by none other than Lester Bangs in his major-league rock-crit debut (he later recanted); *Back in the USA*, a more conventionally tuneful 1970 set beloved of critics and garage-punkers for its breathtaking trebly sound (actually the result of excessively zealous EQing by novice producer Jon Landau—he later recanted); and the out-of-nowhere *High Time*, featuring marvelous late psychedelia, sexual/religious outrage (as in "Sister Anne"), quasi–science fiction and bizarre jazz workouts ("Skunk"), all held together by wizard producer/engineer Geoff Haslam (who recanted by, as far as I know, disappearing from the record-making machinery).

Thereafter, the Five basically dropped off the face of the earth. For a while, guitarist Fred Smith (not the one from Television) led a band of Detroit all-stars called Sonic's Rendezvous, but that didn't really go anywhere; since marrying Patti Smith (who I guess wrote the part of "Frederick" not directly lifted from "Because the Night" about him), he's become a recluse. Guitarist Wayne Kramer endured various minor-label adventures in both the U.S. and UK; he's most recently been found ensconced in Key West, working up a sci-fi rock concept with Mick Farren (whose Deviants were England's answer to the Five). Drummer Dennis Thompson and bassist Michael Davis played in Destroy All Monsters with Ron Asheton, the brilliant-if-Naziphile Stooges' guitarist/bassist, and then I lost track of 'em. Rob Tyner stayed home, raising his three kids and working with all manner of Motor City musicians from aspiring postpunkers (the Orange Roughies) to all-girl power poppers (the Vertical Pillows) to an assortment of country singers, Vietnam veterans, metalloids, and weirdos. John Sinclair now runs the Detroit Council on the Arts.

What survived was the band's guitar sound, expropriated by the Dolls' Johnny Thunders and handed down to Glen Matlock and Steve Jones of

the Sex Pistols. And, among musicians, a vestigial wariness of revolutionary politics as profound and well-embedded as the fear of snakes among
ordinary mortals.

Tyner's *Blood Brothers* (R&A), the first solo album by any of the Five,
appears a bit more than twenty years after *Kick Out the Jams*. It sounds a lot
like it leaked in through a tear in the fabric that separates our universe from
the one the Five dominate, opening with a slash 'n' burn cover of "It's Only
Rock and Roll" that for once sounds as if both singer and band really do like
it, no apologies, and winding up with "Grande Days," a bemused look back
at the site of Tyner's original crimes and misdemeanors, and "D.A.N.A.," a
grand sci-fi shaggy-dog story. It's straight-ahead postmetal grunge, two guitars, bass, and drums pounding out a panic. If not revolutionary, it remains
totally rebellious. If not cosmic, it's at least out there.

"It's Only Rock and Roll" kicks off with raw power chords and a choir-
like chorus chanting, "I know it's only rock and roll, but I like it." Tyner
leaps in with a decisive "Yes, I do" that razors away Mick Jagger's irony. The
song becomes not a sarcastic question but an answer. And with it, Tyner
becomes the Motor City shaman he's always longed to be—an Art Warrior.
In this guise, he's outfitted himself with an all-leather wardrobe, mainly
meat diet, and an affection for military cutlery that helped keep his video
of "It's Only Rock and Roll" off MTV. Tyner commonly tops off his togs with
bits of self-made armor, fashioned from the *RoboCop* detritus in which the
decaying Motor Megalopolis now abounds. This causes certain problems
for a family man, though not the ones you'd expect. "Whenever I go out in
public in armor, people treat me perfectly normally," Tyner says. "But when
I wear a suit jacket, they just don't take me seriously."

He means to be taken seriously, too. Tall, hefty, and Hendrix-haired,
Tyner operates in a wisely avuncular mode that has made him confidant of
stars like Ian Astbury of the Cult and creative co-conspirator of even such a
tempestuous individualist as Lester Bangs (to whom *Blood Brothers* is dedicated).

Tyner tells a story that explains what he's learned in almost twenty years
of woodshedding since his last album. His basic explanation of where he's
been for twenty years is that in 1972 he "fell through a hole in time," where
he fought with the Union Army in the Civil War, bagged a saber-toothed

tiger, and found a moment sixty years from now when the beer is so fine that other drugs are neither necessary nor desirable. But he also says that, on this plane, "I've been changing diapers and I'm ready to rock 'n' roll."

If this makes him sound like Detroit's answer to John Lennon, it should. He has the same sardonic wit, the same perpetually investigative curiosity, and a similar range of skills. An able cartoonist, he worked out the *Blood Brothers* cover using an Apple graphics program on his first try. He writes for the page as well as song lyrics. But when Lennon "fed the baby," he had somebody else to cook the food and clean up the dishes. Tyner and his wife, Becky (whose costumes were a key element of the MC5's act and whose catered cuisine has energized many a Detroit rock show's backstage), are on their own, in a small house in suburban Berkeley (boyhood home of Eagle Glenn Frey, perhaps the Michigan musician least influenced by the Five).

As the armor suggests, however, Tyner's not your ordinary Mister Mom. He also "spent a lot of time doing research in paleoanthropology, especially Native American studies. I became very interested in the study of mankind, where we came from, why we do what we do. I studied the question of violence. Why do people love violence? Being a person who has portrayed violence so much, I know they enjoy it. And I came to a startling conclusion. I don't think we're descended from monkeys. I think we're descended from lemurs—primitive forest creatures who live in fear. It's not our aggression that causes us to be violent. It's fear." He says that he finds this conclusion "endearing, in a kind of way."

It's "Renegade," *Blood Brothers'* first original song, that defines Tyner's renewed point of view. "You see, I once fought in a revolution," he sings, "I was searching for a more radical solution / But my comrades turned and started shootin' / I had to make my getaway."

Like all great music, the MC5's was about love, "love in spite of circumstances," as Tyner says of *Blood Brothers*. So the MC5 remain the rock concert experience against which I measure all others, because getting lost in that music, as you were meant to, became a vehicle for finding yourself. It was as scary, as exhilarating, and as worthwhile as it sounds. No wonder the men who made it happen were so depleted that, since then, they've done very little. Although he'd in many ways treated himself more considerately than any of the others, by mid-'88 Tyner found himself hospitalized, on the verge of full systemic failure. He survived, he says, through tapping his own shamanism after Becky brought him a copy of Joseph Campbell's *The Masks of God.*

Tyner always kept himself a little aloof from the core madness of the Five's scene. For one thing, he and Becky had a stable marriage and, by the time of the band's second album, a baby. For another, he avoided the smack scene. More important, Tyner seemed more interested in the quasi-religious elements of what was going on. "The Five was ritualistic from the git," Tyner says. "I understood it from the Black Baptist church. When the Holy Ghost takes over, then the magic happens. Then the music becomes more than an arrangement of noises. It grabs you and shakes you into an awareness. If it wasn't for the music, I don't think I ever woulda bumped into God."

Most of all, though, the pragmatism of Tyner's basic philosophy insured survival at some level. "For me, existence and survival is a process of avoidance more than anything else," Tyner says. "It's a process of avoiding the things that will kill you." He sells himself a bit short, because Tyner has always acted as if it's also a matter of finding and nurturing the things that sustain you, whether that means multigenerational family life or working with returned Vietnam vets. Having lost what was certainly the greatest communal rock band, Tyner spent the past two decades seeking out and helping to form and improve other such units. As a result, he's reinvented himself as one of the most highly individualized performers—hell, people—I've ever encountered.

Tyner's language is so high-energy and descriptive, his sense of humor so dry, and many of his attitudes and opinions founded on such deeply internal and counterintuitive logic, that he often seems involved in some elaborate put-on. He almost never is. Working with some of America's least conventional bands was part of the process by which he acquired the skills, musical and recording studio craftsmanship, and basic social information he needed to reemerge.

"I've come to realize that the one who hates violence the most is the warrior," says Tyner the Art Warrior, "'cause he's the one who's got to deal with it." *Blood Brothers* is a first vehicle for Tyner to do just that. There will be live shows around Detroit, maybe a tour. There will be another record, this one exploring the theme of "how very difficult Peace is and how very painful Peace can be" and using Tyner's potential as a power balladeer.

Most important, Rob Tyner will go on making music for the rest of his life—out of need as well as desire. "I was never comfortable in the '70s," he admits. "And I *hated* the '80s. But the '90s, so far, I kinda like 'em." So he's back, on the way to what's next, proudest of all that "I came out of it with the same values that I went in with.

"But I'm a little tougher now," he adds. "Because teenage boys are coming to the door to take my daughter away."

CROSS ROADS

—*RRC #84*, DECEMBER 1990

For fifty years, Robert Johnson has been *the* great musical mystery. *Robert Johnson: The Complete Recordings* (Columbia) doesn't solve the puzzle, but it does magnificently pull together the clues: all forty-one takes of the twenty-nine songs Johnson recorded between November 1936 and June 1937; a hysterically over-detailed liner booklet (the lyrics are *footnoted*); photos of Johnson, his parents, and his environs.

None of it lays a glove on the core of the case. In those eight months, Johnson thoroughly redefined blues guitar playing and came up with songs and lyrics that form the bedrock of rock and roll: "Dust My Broom," "Crossroads," "Love in Vain," "Stop Breakin' Down," and "Traveling Riverside Blues," in which his lemon is squeezed 'til the juice runs down his leg.

The mystery's not only that he died young and was murdered. Until five years ago, it was presumed no pictures of Robert Johnson had been left behind. The only clues to his identity were his salty sexuality and his fearless improvisation.

What makes the Robert Johnson mystery consequential is the way he connected it all. In "Stones in My Passway," sexual desire and forebodings of fear and disaster are so mingled it's hard to tell where—or if—metaphor leaves off and description begins. This quality became a crucial part of Black vocal music, up to and including rock, rap, and hip-hop.

Robert Johnson seems to have picked up the guitar largely to meet girls. He became a universal artist. How? Partly physical skill, partly talent and insight, partly his incomparable mastery of blues tradition. But there is always something more and *other* going on, and it's linked to the possessed, haunted, dreadful feelings that linger even in the songs that aren't about spells and devils, sexual hoodoo, being chased out of house and home, or riven by disease from within.

Much of this is spiritual—Robert Johnson was no less sensitive than, say, his near-contemporary F. Scott Fitzgerald. But it's also tied to the material conditions of Robert Johnson's life.

To understand where Robert Johnson's blues (and thus, rock and roll, even unto the juice running down Jon Bon Jovi's leg) came from, you need to know *Blues in the Mississippi Night* (Rykodisc), a late-forties recording by Memphis Slim, Big Bill Broonzy, and Sonny Boy Williamson, among others. It's a weird disc—the liner booklet is seventy pages long and the music takes decided second place to the conversation. But that conversation is a rare, unexpurgated Black view of life under the terror of Southern segregation. It's a world where no Negro could ask a shopkeeper for a tin of Prince Albert tobacco, because there was a White man on the can; where a plantation owner built a fifty-mile perimeter road at his own expense so that no Black person would set foot on his property; where grown men hid in the back rooms of storefronts to read "subversive" northern Black newspapers like the *Chicago Defender*. It's a world in which release of these tapes could have gotten these bluesmen killed, and they begged Lomax not to reveal who made them.

As you listen to the sometimes surreal, sometimes terrified, always haunting music that Robert Johnson and his heirs produced, you need to know these stories. Their power helps explain why the Robert Johnson boxed set has become a hit—150,000 copies sold before Christmas shopping began. Robert Johnson's music retains its power because its stories are far from over—Black students are being beaten and thrown in jail in Selma, Alabama, *today* for trying to wrest control of the city's school system from a White minority government. More than half a century after Robert Johnson went down to the crossroads for the last time, the Black Belt still has the blues.

THE DEATH OF ROCK

—ENTERTAINMENT WEEKLY, JANUARY 1991

Rock & roll is dead again.

The news first came from *Billboard*, the music-biz trade journal whose chart pundit, Paul Grein, headlined his year-end column "Rock-a-Bye-Bye: Genre Left Behind in '90." Grein noted that in 1990 no rock bands reached #1 on the charts, the first time rock had been shut out for an entire year since 1963.

Of course, rock was also supposed to be dead in 1963, just before the Beatles arrived to resurrect it, and it was pronounced dead again during the disco years. But this time rock's disappearance from the top of the charts reflects bigger problems.

The current autopsy suggests that today's rock has also been strangled by definitions: what's amazing is the variety of music that's no longer considered rock. A wide range of current top hit artists—from post-Madonna singer-songwriter Sinéad O'Connor to old-fart art-rock balladeer Phil Collins, black-mood music kings Depeche Mode to druggy dilettantes Jane's Addiction—would all have been regarded as rockers in the '60s, '70s, and early '80s. Now, though, such artists are placed in a narrower category— "pop" or "dance" or "postmodern" or some other slim niche.

By such standards, any Black act less heavy metal than Living Colour (virtually the only recent Black rock act to succeed on the pop charts) couldn't possibly be rock & roll. In fact, one of the most striking similarities between rock's current alleged demise and its earlier mortal moments is that all have occurred during periods when White rock has been separated from Black music—especially on the airwaves. Rock stations, including the so-called "alternative" ones, don't program Black records, period. Apparently, if it's got a good beat and you can dance to it, it's no longer rock & roll.

So M.C. Hammer's biggest smash, "U Can't Touch This," based on Rick James's "Super Freak," a Motown hit with one of the crusher rock riffs of the early '80s, is not rock. Neither are any of the other hip-hop records that—though this might come as a surprise to people who think rap is closed to White music—sample as freely from Led Zeppelin and heavy metal as from James Brown and funk. This isn't a new problem: Rick James, who desperately wanted and deserved to be accepted as a rocker, spent his whole career failing to persuade the radio and record industries that rock was about beat and attitude, not skin color.

Old story or not, all this means that the most exciting, rebellious, hardest-rocking music of the early '90s—rap and hip-hop—can't be considered rock. Given that rap and hip-hop have more in common with the fierce and joyous spirit of the Who and Little Richard than any other brand of contemporary music does, that's a silly artistic judgment. But it's an all-too-intelligent reflection of music-industry reality, in which radio, record labels, and most record stores maintain separate categories for Black and White music makers.

This set of false assumptions is also an unfortunately accurate mirror of music-industry priorities. Nobody's saying that good rock & roll records in the tradition that descends from the Beatles and Bob Dylan aren't being made, and nobody's even saying that rock no longer makes money: Aerosmith and Mötley Crüe were among Billboard's 1990 Top 10 bestsellers, and the Black Crowes and Damn Yankees have two of the hottest albums on the charts right now. No, the real complaint, from a White-dominated music industry, is that rock is no longer king of the hill.

But who says that rock's hegemony was healthy? In the past few years, the horizons of ambitious young rockers—especially hard rockers—who want to make it commercially have narrowed. Mainly, the approaches are too often limited to using shock or silliness as an art masquerade, as with Jane's Addiction and Faith No More, or using mega-sales as their own justification, as with Warrant and Cinderella. If the best that new rock can offer is not even novelty but outright gimmickry, like Billy Idol's stud routine; if the most worthy new hero it can find is a bonehead shill like Jon Bon Jovi, whose synthesis of heavy metal and Bruce Springsteen sucks both into the vacuum of pure cliché, then maybe it really is time for rock to leave center stage.

Of course, rock's current death may turn out to be as temporary as its earlier ones, since some of the biggest rock acts of all—Bruce Springsteen and U2, Guns N' Roses and R.E.M.—will release high-profile albums this year. But if rock's continued relevance depends on the recycling of the same handful of predictable heroes, then it's not too much healthier than post-Sinatra saloon singing. Whether rock can survive and prosper in the '90s is really a question of whether those artists—and new ones—can learn to use its musical vocabulary to say something fresh.

It's not that long ago that hard-rock records accomplished that feat. You need go back no further than Guns N' Roses' 1987 debut album, *Appetite for Destruction*, which did it in two songs, "Sweet Child O' Mine" and "Welcome to the Jungle." They opened a strangely gleeful and loving window onto the fear and isolation of the blankest new generation yet, with a vow never to surrender to despair. Such records are unforgettable because they use rock to respond to the conditions in today's world, not merely to evoke yesterday's; to break down the barriers among forms and factions, not surrender to them; to open our hearts by opening our eyes to the harshest truths and to make us laugh with an acute sense of what's most ridiculous about everyday attitudes and assumptions. If rock can't do that in the '90s, it won't be missed.

SURVIVORS

Several rock bands have made major chart impact lately, though there's very little that's likely to be long remembered:

AC/DC

The Razors Edge

Last year's one really great hard-rock record, loud enough to splinter eardrums and utterly unapologetic about what aficionados will recognize as inspired—both as an assault on the basics and an affirmation of them. **A**

THE TRAVELING WILBURYS
The Traveling Wilburys Vol. 3

Their first album was not only a great gimmick but a promising exploration of easy-listening rock that never lacked bite. But without the late Roy
Orbison's galvanizing vocal presence, Jeff Lynne's bombastic production
becomes the center of the show. **C+**

THE BLACK CROWES
Shake Your Money Maker

The Black Crowes are to the early Rolling Stones what Christian Slater is to
the young Jack Nicholson: a self-conscious imitation, but fine enough in its
own right. Authentic bluesmen these Crowes will never be, but their sheer
energy earns 'em the right to trash it up. **B+**

DAMN YANKEES
Damn Yankees

Ted Nugent is in his third decade as a chart-maker, and Damn Yankees
aren't much better or worse than the Amboy Dukes, his mid-'60s garage
rock band. So there's still a market for the third-rate after all these years. **D–**

WARRANT
Cherry Pie

Warrant wanted to be stars worse than any band since Kiss. That gave last
year's debut a certain charge—and exhausted their ambition. Now they can
record a few more discs of guitar-'n'-female-bashing, then break up and join
a sexagenarian Ted Nugent in a soft-metal supergroup sometime after the
turn of the century. **C–**

BACK IN BLACK

—RRC #86, MARCH 1991

A bsolutely nothin' remains the definition of what war's good for, but the current conflagration in the Middle East at least establishes once-and-for-all why opposing domestic censorship is essential. The women behind the PMRC are married to the men who promote the Gulf slaughter: Susan Baker's husband, Secretary of State James Baker, conducts the phony diplomacy that prevents a negotiated solution; Tipper Gore's husband, Senator Albert Gore Jr., is one of ten key Democrats who voted to end the peace process and allow the bloodletting to commence. Meantime, George Bush has appointed Florida's ex-governor Robert Martinez, the man who set Nick Navarro on 2 Live Crew, as his new "drug czar." Navarro will serve as the spearhead of America's other open war, even though the Martinez reelection campaign (chaired by Jeb Bush) was partly financed by contributions from drug smugglers, according to Jeff Morley's report in *Spin*.

These connections are fundamental to understanding the how and why of attacks on free speech in America. Metallica, Robert Mapplethorpe, and N.W.A are targets of opportunity, establishing the context for criminalizing any journalist who mentions facts inconvenient to the government even if they're as mild as Peter Arnett's reports from Baghdad.

The government also needs music censorship because rap and hard rock will be the soundtrack for opposition to the war. Certainly, other musicians will also get involved. But rap and hard rock are the only media voices directly available to those who will do the dying. Not surprisingly, it was Aerosmith who made the least ambiguous anti-war statement at the Grammys, saying they supported the troops by wanting to bring them back home immediately. You have to wonder if fear of an even more militant anti-war statement was CBS's reason for keeping the Best Rap and Best Metal categories off camera.

Sound conspiratorial? A week into the war, I was contacted by a *Baltimore Sun* reporter, who wanted to know my reaction to U.S. bomber pilots listening to Van Halen to pump themselves up for sorties. "It's repulsive. I think it defiles American pop culture to use rock and roll to murder people," I said.

Reporter Randi Henderson had the guts to print that comment, as the final paragraph of her story, which also moved on the *Los Angeles Times/ Washington Post* wire service, much to my amazement. The first we knew that it had made the paper was when contributing editor Ben Eicher sent us a clip from the Rapid City (S.D.) *Journal*. A few days later, though, Eicher sent a clip from the "highly respected" *Omaha World-Herald*. It was exactly the same story—minus my comment.

More tellingly, no reporter has asked the PMRC and other music censors to back up their horror of rock-related violence by opposing this use of the music. I challenged Robert DeMoss of Focus on the Family to join me in condemning rock as a war tool at the Gavin Convention on February 15, but he declined to do so. Mrs. Baker, Mrs. Gore, and their friends also maintain silence.

The picture of America as a nation content to kill and keep on killing is exaggerated. While there is mass support for the war, it's the proverbial mile wide and inch deep. On February 18, I spoke to over a thousand people at Northeast Missouri State University in Kirksville, equidistant from St. Louis, Kansas City, and Des Moines. Every attack on the war and war censorship in my lecture was met with applause.

So Americans are willing to listen to another side of the story, especially when it involves links to the demise of free speech. Since the media is reluctant to tell that side, the rest of us need to pick up the slack. You should speak out; write, perform, buy, and request anti-war songs and videos; and pass out anti-censorship material at anti-war rallies and teach-ins and distribute anti-war material at concerts.

The people who need accurate information most desperately are the troops. So if you're in the record business, get free goods to send to the troops—and don't spare the radical stuff. Everyone should join the Military Family Support Network (MFSN) at Box 11098, Milwaukee, WI 53211 (414-964-3859).* If you don't have a friend or relative in Desert Storm you can write to, MFSN will help you adopt one.

—the Editors

---

* While there no longer appears to be a national MFSN, look for local chapters in your town.

LETTER TO AXL ROSE

—*RRC* #91, SEPTEMBER 1991

It's like the song "One in a Million." I'll get lambasted and filleted over that song. Dave Marsh will be writing about this "We Are the World" consciousness, but Dave, I don't know where you were doing your "We Are the World" consciousness, but we were getting robbed at knife-point at that time in our lives. "One in a Million" brought out the fact that racism does exist so let's do something about it. Since that song, a lot of people may hate Guns N' Roses but they think about their racism now. And they weren't thinking about it during "We Are the World."

—Axl Rose, *Musician*, September 1991

Yo, Axl: Thanks for paying attention. Turns out I developed my consciousness in Detroit (mugged twice at gunpoint) and New York (mugged twice, once at knifepoint, once by being thrown to the sidewalk), so we have that much in common. But as a fellow victim of street violence, you've got me confused. What do such incidents have to do with hating Blacks, gays, and immigrants—the targets of "One in a Million"? It's a serious question, and one to which I think you gave the beginnings of a good answer in "Welcome to the Jungle." So thanks for the mention, and I hope that someday we get to finish the discussion, face to face. Keep on rockin' and rollin'.

JUST WHAT'S BEING SOLD IN COUNTRY?

—NEW YORK TIMES, MAY 1992

Jimmy Bowen says he loves rap music. "Every morning when they play that stuff, people come running to us," Mr. Bowen, who runs Liberty Records in Nashville, told *Time* magazine in March. Asked recently to amplify his remark, he said: "For the most part, people listen to music because they can relate to the lyrics. If you live in the inner city, where murder and rape is all around you, then of course you can relate to rap. But if you don't share that life style, then you can't."

In such imagery, country music finds its equivalent of Willie Horton, the furloughed rapist whose use in 1988 presidential campaign advertisements made him a racially charged code word; the benign surfaces of these images conceal a sinister undertone. Rap, in this context, serves as a reference both to a musical style and to unspoken polarities between disparate American communities—mainly White versus Black ones. So rap joins "tradition" and "family values" as concepts that assist country music executives in niche marketing an image to an audience distressed by the embittered voices of Black youth, voices that country music excludes. The issue is all in the subtext.

Country executives selling the "new traditionalism," a supposed return of the music to its homespun values, aren't necessarily racists. They're shrewd marketing opportunists. Nor does a taste for country music make a listener a bigot. Yet the marketing of country—from record promotion and advertising to the far less tangible nuances of image-building—parlays the music's long-standing association with conservative values into a justification for White audiences to turn their backs on Black voices. Allusions to rap's negative stereotype, like Mr. Bowen's, suggest that some of country's new success is based on rejection of the rap alternative.

An expression of racism doesn't always require a robe and hood; it often manifests itself as an ethnic double standard. Imagine how the rapper Ice Cube would be denounced for a song about drunkenly disrupting an old girlfriend's wedding and threatening the groom, then setting out on a bender with his crew. That's exactly the story line of Garth Brooks's "I've Got Friends in Low Places," an anthem for country-loving teenagers. Yet Mr. Brooks isn't seen as a dangerous instigator of social irresponsibility. Unlike rappers, Mr. Brooks doesn't threaten. Ice Cube's perpetual scowl personifies (as it is intended to) the rationale behind White flight.

If that flight made a noise, it might resemble the soft, Southern-accented twang of Mr. Brooks's recordings. The anger of rap and of heavy metal, another villain often flogged by country music executives, is entirely absent from today's country, as represented by Mr. Brooks and a whole spectrum of young, Nashville-based singers. The most telling example of conservative country marketing was Randy Travis's 1991 hit, "Point of Light," a song written by Don Schlitz and Thom Schuyler at the request of President Bush for his campaign to promote volunteerism. Even a Republican rock star like Jon Bon Jovi wouldn't try to sell that to his audience.

Mr. Travis and Mr. Brooks are part of the wave of new traditionalists. But, with few exceptions, new traditionalism has less to do with honky-tonkers like Hank Williams and Merle Haggard than with sentimental domesticity and social conformity. In a music whose origins lie in the White South and whose allegiances clearly remain there, such values have unsettling implications.

Mr. Brooks's albums typify the conservatism of contemporary country. Each song presents the singer with a dilemma that he is powerless to resolve: in "Low Places," the singer is losing the love of his life and all he can do about it is pour another drink. In "Unanswered Prayers," even wanting a break from convention (divorce) appears to be sinful—God grants what we truly need, while our desires only damn us.

Resignation to one's fate and status constitutes only half of country's tradition, however. Since the mid-'50s, the problem has been how to recapture its raucous other half, which was transformed by Elvis Presley into rock-and-roll. By openly infusing country with Black rhythm, rock-and-roll integrated it, but rock also demolished country's insularity. Commercially, country never entirely recovered; unlike Black pop, it has never been (and isn't now) pop's main trend. One reason is an inability to retrieve its rough and rowdy ways without having the result wind up sounding like rock-and-roll. Until recently, that has been a marketing liability. But for much of today's pop music audience, the liberation symbolized by sounds derived from rhythm-and-blues and rap perhaps inspires more anxiety than ambition, while country's reassertion of social and musical limits seems reassuring, not restrictive.

Of course, no one listens to country, or any other kind of music, for just one reason. Anyone might enjoy country's musical emphasis on strong songs and vocals. But the fundamental problem with country's anti-rap approach is that it oversimplifies rap's appeal. In the same way, country music is trivialized when we deny that it markets racial antagonism. Country remains mired in ambiguity, especially because the issues of conservatism and traditionalism have both a musical and a marketing basis.

In the political and economic environment of 1992, it's not surprising to find extremes becoming popular. In its own way, Nirvana, last year's biggest new rock act, also uses negative salesmanship by railing against rock's old fogeys. But there's a big difference between a partisan assertion of esthetic superiority and social innuendo. As in so much reactionary salesmanship, the imagery debases what it would celebrate. After all, it's a sad comment on contemporary country if the best Nashville now boasts is a vision of what it isn't.

TIMING IS EVERYTHING

—*ROLLING STONE*, OCTOBER 1992

P atti Smith saved my job as a *Rolling Stone* feature writer, and I never even thanked her. Patti's story and my role in its early moments formed an article called "Her Horses Got Wings, They Can Fly," published in *Rolling Stone*'s first issue of 1976. The story remains the most complete account of Patti's peregrinations on the way to pop stardom ever compiled and, given that Smith, although absent many years from the pop scene, remains one of the more influential performers of the seventies, needs no further justification—certainly less than it needed in '76, when she seemed an entirely impossible Rock & Roll Queen for the Bicentennial. What's more curious is why my job was jeopardized. Blame that on Mick Jagger. I always have.

Or maybe Joan Didion and John Gregory Dunne really deserve the blame. See, they were the ones scheduled to tour with the Rolling Stones in the summer of '75. This had nothing to do with me—I'd just been hired away from *Newsday* to replace Jon Landau as associate editor in charge of record reviews. This was a most prestigious role, which had been held by only three others: Landau, Greil Marcus, and Ed Ward, all top-notch rock-crit names.

But I come from restless stock. My grandfather hunted deer for seventy-four consecutive years without ever shooting one, not out of animal-rights scruples but because he was constitutionally unable to sit still for five minutes and his gyrating alerted every beast within miles to his presence. This gene lurks within me also, and so, unlike previous reviews editors, who had made the Records section a fiefdom by holding it as their exclusive responsibility, my duties as enumerated during the discursive weekend hiring session at Jann Wenner's house in San Francisco consisted of editing the Records section and the Performance page, writing features, occasionally editing features and editing Ralph Gleason's Perspectives column.

All of this I actually did, with the exception of editing Ralph, because he died the day before I started work. I'd asked to edit Ralph because I knew him a little and liked him a lot. But there was no way to anticipate what his sudden death would mean to the magazine. *Rolling Stone* in the mid-seventies was no more somber than you'd think it was—I distinctly remember being in the offices for the fall of Saigon, the death of Elvis, and the arrest of Patty Hearst, and none of those occasions was the least bit funereal. But Ralph's death threw everybody into mourning that approached despair; we were not and could not be prepared for his passing, especially so suddenly. More than any rock star's demise, this one sank in—as deeply as mortality ever sinks in when you're young and feeling invincible, as all of us were.

When I next heard from Jann, he phoned me at home with more trauma; Didion and Dunne had reneged on the Stones assignment. Part of the editorial genius that possesses Mr. Wenner, it seems, is his willingness to run with the hot hand. He'd decided that the new kid on the block—and a salary man, to boot—made the most suitable replacement.

Oh, unhappy day! Jann meant the assignment to be a plum. In those days the magazine covered tours by the Rolling Stones with an attentiveness other publications bring to presidential campaigns. But by '75, the Rolling Stones already struck me as pretty passé; their shows were more like tourist attractions, for people without interest in rock as music, than hard-core rock & roll events. Wenner would want a celebration; the readers would expect one. My jaundiced eye and music critic's ear suggested that I'd be unlikely to deliver.

To top it off, Jann neglected to tell me that Mick Jagger harbored a (temporary, I guess) antipathy to *Rolling Stone*. For six weeks, Jagger creatively (tediously, actually, but hey!, he's Mick Jagger) evaded my daily requests for an interview. I wound up writing a story called "I Call and Call and Call on Mick," a morose account and relatively lackluster piece of writing redeemed only by Jann's last-minute amplification of my hard-boiled-detective diction.

Not only had I failed at my first assignment, but when I got back home, things had become unstable at the office. Staying in New York had been an important precondition of my taking the job, partly because I didn't want to move my family, but also because I wanted the independence that only a long-distance work relationship offers.

In 1975, *Rolling Stone*'s New York bureau was the place to be. It harbored Chet Flippo, Joe Klein, Jonathan Cott, and my own all-time favorite among the magazine's feature writers, Tim Crouse. Reporters Tom Powers and Howard Kohn were often around. The redoubtable managing editor Marianne Partridge and senior editor Paul Scanlon had been transferred from San Francisco. Jann swore he loved this team, and I do believe he meant it, 'cause he soon announced that he was moving all of the magazine's staff to Manhattan. Glum news for a guy like me, who experiences supervision as surveillance.

The Records section and the Performance page chugged along. But the editors displayed all the lack of eagerness that you'd expect when it came to offering me another feature assignment. I've always loved being a critic, but like any writer, in my heart I'm a storyteller. Quite frankly, I needed a story that could be written in my own voice to establish my credentials as a feature writer.

A Patti Smith story was being prepared by a freelancer whose identity now eludes me. Because of my early relationship to Patti (as editor of *Creem*, I actually hold the distinction of being the very first to publish her poetry), Partridge asked me to read it. The story struck me as okay but not nearly good enough. I went to Partridge. Let me redo the story, I pleaded. I promise I can get further inside it than what you've got. Partridge gave me a shot.

Feeling slightly guilty about swiping someone else's assignment, I went to work. The interviews went fine—I remember talking to Patti on a gray day in a rehearsal hall near Times Square and seeing her in the Village at a poetry reading, but not much else. Rereading the story now, what strikes me is the peripheral but crucial role Robert Mapplethorpe played in it. (Patti's celebrity had then outstripped his, though obviously not for good.)

The real point was Smith's fables of her own origins. I must have believed most of the yarn, because I set it down so faithfully. Patti's stories mesmerized everybody who heard them—in fact, I'm sure if she told me the same stuff today, which she most certainly would not, I'd put it down just as plainly. Her claims about artistic independence amounted to little more than the kind of willful myth-mongering dabbled in by every rock star since Bob Dylan. But this time, the artist hadn't adopted a coy and convenient marketing strategy. In all her tale-spinning, Patti never swerved from her purpose, which was establishing the complete integrity, rock & roll authenticity, and deep poetic purpose of Patti Smith the Artist. Patti knew she had something new to say, and her intent was to use it to inspire the masses.

About her chances of actually accomplishing this, I could afford to be dubious, since I was totally persuaded of her artistic validity. But I was wrong. "Her Horses Got Wings" is quite unconsciously set amid the then-stirring CBGB punk scene that the Patti Smith Group inaugurated. Yet it never occurred to me to view Patti as part of anything so orderly as a trend or a movement. For me, her whole attraction stemmed from being one of a kind. If I'd paid more attention to her band, whose members I conceived of—perhaps inaccurately—as helpmates only, I'd probably have been more attuned to what Patti's project shared with the Ramones, Television, and Talking Heads.

But ultimately, whether you believe that what became one of the great pop explosions could have been predicted six months or a year in advance depends, I suppose, on whether you think Malcolm McLaren was a true visionary or just a hustler who got lucky. Having watched him "manage" the New York Dolls, I've never had a doubt. One way or the other, I saw where Patti and her band came from far more clearly than where punk and New Wave were going.

Between us, Patti and I ensured that the major themes of punk and postpunk were covered, from the suspect credibility of record execs to the casual racism of the romantic bohemian narcissist.

Not surprisingly, Patti made it clear that she hated the story. "You always get it wrong, even when you get it right," she sneered backstage a few weeks later. I always figured she was annoyed about the part where I'd attacked her theory of the rock & roll boho as "the last white nigger,"* but it occurs to me now that maybe I'd hurt the feelings of Clive Davis, the head of Arista Records.

---

* A quote attributed to Patti Smith in the original *Rolling Stone* piece.—EDs

No matter. The editors of *Rolling Stone* liked it. As well they should have. *Rolling Stone* in my day was renowned as a "writer's magazine," but the actual line editors really ran the place quite imperiously. You could struggle with your copy for weeks, but a day before deadline, they'd simply say, "We have to cut four lines to make room for a photo caption." Protest rewarded only those who enjoyed placing themselves on the wrong side of a blank and beady stare. Editing "Her Horses Got Wings" gave me a memorable chill, since it was on this occasion that Partridge offered to discipline me by cutting all the articles (*a, an, the*) from my copy. I settled down immediately, not because I thought she would, but because I knew she could.

Having run this gauntlet, I was thereafter able to spend the better part of five years writing an assortment of feature-length articles for the magazine. Eventually, I wound up creating a column called American Grandstand, which was the successor to Ralph Gleason's Perspectives. (Jon Landau wrote one called Positively 84th Street for a few months in between.) By 1980 or so, I was able to do what I'd come to *Rolling Stone* to achieve, which was to function as a writer on my own. Not that I left any more willingly than most of my colleagues.

Jann doesn't know this, but a little while after "Her Horses Got Wings" appeared, I overheard him down the hall, talking to someone in San Francisco—probably Ben Fong-Torres—late one evening. He was grousing about an editorial trouble spot. "Well, you know," he said, "Marsh made a mess of the Jagger interview. But that wasn't his story. When he got to do his own, he came through." Praise spoken behind your back is the kind that counts, I figure, and so I thank him now for what I didn't dare thank him for then.

I belatedly thank Patti, too, annoyed as she may have been (and after this account, may become again). But I still figure we're even: Who do you think introduced her to the guy who wrote "Because the Night"? His idea, not mine, I hasten to add. But then, I never have been very good at seeing into the future. Sometimes, though, it's enough just to be in the right place at the right time.

SINCE I LOST MY BABY

—*RRC* #104, FEBRUARY–MARCH 1993

T he night before my daughter's funeral, some of her friends and I stayed up late making a tape to be played at the service. It started with the Stairsteps' "O-o-h Child" and ended with Bob Marley's "No Woman, No Cry," whose "Everything's gonna be all right" had become a mantra for Kristen and her boyfriend while she battled her cancer.

I never imagined that in a period when Dizzy Gillespie, Reverend Thomas Dorsey, Eddie Hazel, and Albert King had just died, I'd wrack my soul to tell the story of a twenty-one-year-old who never made a record. But Dizzy and Dorsey, Hazel and King made their marks—in the words of a Terence Trent D'Arby song on Kristen's tape, they signed their names across their hearts. You can measure how well in the wonders of their recorded works: "Salt Peanuts," "Take My Hand, Precious Lord, Lead Me On," "Maggot Brain," and "Born Under a Bad Sign" and they'll help heal your soul, and I can prove it. But my girl never got her chance.

I need to eulogize Kristen Ann Carr, because her death means I'll never write about music in the same way. Not only because my family and I have gone through such a soul-shattering experience, but because Kristen helped determine how I listened to music. From "Papa Don't Preach" and Seal's "Crazy" to House of Pain's "Jump Around" and Enya's "Caribbean Blue," she made me hear stuff I might have dismissed. And I mean, she made me— she'd lecture me about it. In this way, she wasn't my stepdaughter but a true child of my heart. (We'd lived together since she was three.) That's why the track on the tape I chose to speak for us was "Sweet Child O' Mine." But another speaks for me alone: the morning after the funeral, "I've got sunshine on a cloudy day" came over the radio and I lost it completely.

Kristen also belongs here because, however you may have received these past ten years of ranting and raving, I've seen *RRC* as an espousal of life against death. After watching my own child wage that struggle in literal terms, I know there's a way to live that message to your final breath. You do it by choosing the spirit of hope and affirmation that Kristen held so completely that she awed even her doctors.

Sarcoma, the very rare disease that killed Kristen, receives almost no study, mainly as a result of insufficient funds. Obviously, the best way to change that would be to establish a humane government. To help do the job quicker, send donations to the Kristen Ann Carr Fund, c/o Empire Events Group, 18 Sherwood Court, Holmdel, NJ 07733. But first go and find the children you love best and hug them as tightly as they'll permit.

GRAVE DANCERS UNION

—*RRC* #109, SEPTEMBER 1993

Y ou can tell jazz has entered a period of creative ferment not only by the release of hip-hop-styled albums such as those by Greg Osby and Gang Starr's Guru, but by the ongoing battle between musicians pushing the stylistic envelope and musicians who oppose change in jazz. In a lengthy interview in the August *Downbeat*, trumpeter Lester Bowie (a founder of the Association for the Advancement of Creative Musicians who's featured on David Bowie's new album and plays in several experimental bands) and saxophonist Osby (who covers Henry Mancini tunes while also a partner in the Rebel-X and Funk Mob record labels) began by pointing out that the jazz pioneers so slavishly imitated today developed by finding their own voices.

Then they got down to specifics, which can only mean Wynton Marsalis. "He's a good brother," Osby allowed, "but his dogma, his rantings, some of these things are unforgivable."

"He even accused Miles Davis of treason because Miles played a Cyndi Lauper tune," Bowie added. "In the '50s, 'Surrey with a Fringe on Top' was on the *Hit Parade*. That's part of the thing, to be contemporary, to express yourself. Wynton's trying to tamper with the music's development, and I see some kind of evil overlay on that."

Bowie knows what he's talking about. His Brass Fantasy group covers Michael Jackson while also touring with a chamber orchestra. He issued a joyous manifesto: "Cat's sitting back scared, 'I won't play in that rhythm, I don't play country & western. That ain't jazz.' I say, later for them. Jazz is hip-hop, Dixieland, anything the people playing it want it to be. 'Man, don't listen to that Argentinian shit, it might influence you.' C'mon baby, influence me!"

Ironically, the Marsalis worldview, which claims to honor jazz history, actually cuts it off by omitting the musical explosion that took place in the late 1960s. This version fails to acknowledge everyone from Jimmy Smith, history's dominant organ influence, to the freewheeling, wildly eclectic music written and performed by the likes of Charles Mingus and Pharoah Sanders. Above all, Marsalis denies John Coltrane.

He can't embrace Coltrane because the tenor saxophonist made perhaps a dozen records that challenge the structure of chords, melody, and rhythm itself, while surfing ever upward spiritually. Meanwhile Marsalis, as Bowie points out, is always the artist whose supposedly superior technique is *about to* result in an artistic breakthrough but never comes up with the goods. Marsalis has never come up with a ballad half as memorable as "A Love Supreme," reworked a standard as definitively as "My Favorite Things," or come anywhere near the crushing originality of albums like *The Avant-Garde, A Love Supreme, Impressions, Kulu Se Mama, Africa/Brass,* or half a dozen others.

Coltrane made his music using a variety of information, some of it derived from his work with the bebop and earlier masters Marsalis reveres, some of it from his stint with Miles Davis, and a whole lot of it by opening himself to Eastern religious and musical ideas. But Coltrane had another resource: he paid attention to whatever experience brought him, including his audience.

As part of the press package for Rhino/Atlantic's fine new Coltrane anthology, *The Last Giant*, a cassette of Trane being interviewed by Ralph J. Gleason appears.

"We went into the Apollo," Coltrane says, "and the guy said 'Man, you're playin' too long. You gotta play twenty minutes.' So now, sometimes we get up and play a song and I play a solo that's maybe thirty minutes. I said, 'How the hell we gonna do this?' And man, we ended up, around the third time we did it, we ended up playing three songs in twenty minutes. And I played all the highlights of the solos that I'd been playin' in hours in that length of time. So I had to think about it, you know. What have I been doing all this time?"

There are three things about this story that are conceivable only from the Osby/Bowie point of view. First, that Coltrane's quartet actually played three dates at the Apollo, the premier showcase of Black working class *entertainment*. Second, that they paid attention to commercial pop demands and learned from them. And third, that Trane was smart enough to admit that he didn't understand a good part of what was happening in the process.

The day that Wynton Marsalis and his acolytes achieve those things, they will have made major steps toward becoming great artists, instead of just a bunch of smirking prizewinners holding their brothers down.

THE PRESENT DAY COMPOSER DIES

—RRC #111, DECEMBER 1993

C ontemporary cultural history conspires to teach us that being a great man has little to do with making great art (examples abound: Elvis Presley, Frank Sinatra, John Wayne, Kurt Cobain). Frank Zappa, who delighted in overturning expectations, certainly stood that principle on its head. Zappa made music that tried to burst every convention, he satirized mercilessly, he took on political figures bigger than himself. In short, Zappa brought passionate intensity and complete conviction to everything he did. Moreover, when he didn't feel those things for a certain subject, he did nothing, always a brave choice.

Zappa formed his own record company not because he had to—*somebody* would always have been willing to support his work on some scale—but because business fascinated him (and in his wife, Gail, he had someone to run the show more competently than a record biz stooge). He fought censorship not because the censors were coming after him—his ass must have felt buttered by all the flattery he received when he testified in the 1985 Senate hearing—but because censorship is wrong, dangerous, and capable of empowering people who he knew to be evil.

Zappa wasn't a Democrat or even particularly tolerant. He believed in excellence, kept his own point of view about what constituted quality, and had no patience for work that didn't meet his standards. This led to his famous disdain for music journalism and criticism—although as I worked on censorship issues, my *Louie Louie* book, or other projects, I found that it never kept him from helping out. This hardly means his attitude was an act. To be worthy of Frank Zappa's attention, I learned, you didn't need to understand his thorny compositions, you needed to be up to something he found worthy of *his* attention.

In November, a publicist called me to find out if I'd heard Zappa's latest album, *The Yellow Shark*. I said I'd be grappling with it later (which I tried real hard to do) and asked after Frank's health. He was doing fine, she said, which I figured was what he wanted the world to think. Okay, I said, but do me a favor, will you? Tell him, he can think whatever he wants to think about rock critics, but there's at least one here who loves him.

That hasn't changed a bit. Frank Zappa may be gone from the planet, but his musical and moral legacies remain alive and potent. Janet Reno, watch your step. Necessity remains the mother of invention.

PERILS OF ROCK CRITICISM (VOL. 1)

—RRC #113, MARCH 1994

I'm beginning to believe that it's impossible to be a competent music critic. Consider:

Last week, I received about forty CDs and tapes in the mail. This may seem a strange thing to complain about, but it reflects a disconcerting reality. At an average of sixty minutes a disc, it means I need a full business week to do that pile justice—presumably one listening is just, which it rarely is. Experience tells me that a lot of important music—*The Chronic* and *Ten* are two excellent recent examples—can only be evaluated accurately over weeks and months of listening. If you try to be conscientious about your work, you may even find yourself digging out *Murmur* after a decade to see if it sounds better in light of "Man on the Moon" and the "Everybody Hurts" video. If you find, as I did, that it does, you then have to figure out how to catch up to a band as significant as R.E.M.—while still doing *some* kind of justice to those forty new records every week.

On the other hand, I can still remember one of the first packages I ever received from Warner/Reprise. (Research suggests it would have been early 1970.) It contained *Moondance, Sweet Baby James,* and if I remember right, a Randy Newman album, along with a few other forgotten items, less than a dozen albums in all. That was it from the highly prolific Warner labels—for that *month.*

Two decades ago, then it was possible not only to listen to every significant record released but to give it full attention over a fairly relaxed time span. Not only that, there was little or no deadline pressure. Because major newspapers and magazines didn't cover most kinds of pop, you could figure out what a record meant before deciding what to write about it. In today's climate, that's impossible. Most magazines and papers insist on running reviews on the day, or certainly in the week, that an album is released. You can't digest all the information Prince, for instance, will probably throw at you in that time span. All you can offer is what I call the light-switch judgment: an on/off appraisal of whether the record's surface is appealing, whether it's "consumer-worthy." Most editors, who find idea-oriented pieces vaguely unjournalistic, prefer it that way. It isn't clear to me what most writers think. Since most never knew any other system, what you get is hackery, though it's always a surprise to find what thoughtful critics (Leonard Pitts Jr. at the *Miami Herald*, Jon Pareles at the *New York Times*) can do within such limits. The review sections of most music magazines have become sinkholes of product evaluation, about as soulful and reliable as the automotive magazines (and without as much interesting art), though J. D. Considine at *Musician* writes one-paragraph reviews with wit and clarity.

But mostly, the combination of musical overproduction and deadline regimentation results in hyper-specialization. Writers who know about indie rock or New York hip-hop feel little need to know about "mainstream" bands or West Coast rap—meaning, you get the lives of Pavement and Onyx evaluated by people who don't bother paying close attention to Pearl Jam or Too Short. Often, I feel like I'm reading reviews written in the intellectual equivalent of a none-too-spacious soundproof closet, into which no noise or idea not preapproved has ever been (or will ever be) admitted.

In a music market where everyone from Bulgarian choirs to shy girls in British bed-sitting rooms to street-smart Oakland gangs to beleathered Southern smartasses to New Orleans music snobs has found a substantial audience, focus can only be found by narrowing your vision somehow. But both critic and audience pay a heavy price, especially when the terms and conditions under which writers work remain secret.

For a musical omnivore like myself, the job is truly impossible. The time I spend trying to figure out dancehall is insufficient, my take on grunge too affected by my age and history, there were probably six or eight fine country voices that got by me while that fascinating but as yet undeciphered cumbia anthology was playing, and I've never heard Springsteen's *Unplugged* EP. There are twenty albums of Mexican rock on a shelf waiting for me to make further sense of them (without as much as a school day's Spanish), but all I can tell you for sure is that if royalty advances were determined by raw R&B energy, Tex Tex would have $25 million and ZZ Top would be just getting by. Confronted by all this, I can only tell you that listening to everything is still the right way to go. You may not get there first with the new Mariah Carey review, but in the end, what you do tell people will add some perspective to what they're hearing and maybe even help keep the historical record straight. That's my version of the job, and I'm sticking to it for as long as I can make it last.

VS

By now, you probably know all about Pearl Jam's appearance in Congress. You know that guitarist Stone Gossard and bassist Jeff Ament testified before an obscure House subcommittee, and they did it wearing short pants. You may even know that Stone's orange shirt had a Peter Pan collar. You know that the Democrats kissed their asses (California's Lynn Woolsey called them "darling guys"). You know that Stone and Jeff summoned righteous wrath about their fans getting ripped off. You know that when a Republican mugwump grilled them too closely about irrelevancies, Jeff finally said he had to go to the bathroom and, without asking permission, got up and went. You may even know that a few others—including myself—also testified, and that the day's witnesses concluded with Fred Rosen, the dese-and-dose businessman who runs Ticketmaster, who presented statistics that refuted every charge anyone had made against his company.

You know that the whole thing was a hoot.

You know nothing.

Almost certainly, you don't know that Aerosmith manager Tim Collins's testimony included this quote from Steven Tyler: "Mussolini may have made the trains run on time, but not everyone could get a seat on that train." But even if you got that secondhand sound bite, you didn't hear the more important story Collins had to tell.

On January 5, 1993, he met with Rosen to try to renegotiate a "rebate" on Ticketmaster charges, which Aerosmith planned to pass along to its fans. Rosen refused, instead proposing that Aerosmith allow him to *increase* the service charge by a dollar. That dollar would be split between Ticketmaster and the band—as long as the band agreed to advertise the ticket cost and service charge as a single price, concealing the scam from view. Collins said he told Rosen "his offer was like offering a cold man ice in the winter." When Rep. Steven Horn, the Republican congressman whose questions were written by Ticketmaster's own staff people, deviated from the script long enough to ask Rosen to verify this, the Ticketmaster exec first changed the subject and then said, "I don't particularly remember the full details." Typically, the members of the committee, none of whom could pass an elementary journalism school course in interrogation, never bothered to ask Rosen the logical next question: Are there any bands to whom you've offered such a deal *who've taken it?*

But that's not the only story you missed. For instance, my own testimony included information about parking charges tacked onto Ticketmaster charges, such as those at Michigan's Chene Park Amphitheater, where seven people in a van are charged seven times as much as one person in a gas-guzzler.

I attempted to testify from the point of view of the consumer. Clearly, both the other witnesses and the congressmen were far more comfortable dealing with the ticket issue as a dispute among businesses. But, as I told the subcommittee, "the dispute [is] between Ticketmaster and growing numbers of disgruntled ticket buyers . . . When they complained to the Department of Justice, Pearl Jam . . . became the standard-bearers of that dissatisfaction."

But nobody wanted to deal with that. Even Pearl Jam, whose bravery in bringing this action has invoked the wrath of some of the most powerful figures in the music industry, conceives of a resolution only in terms of "more competition"—as if having two ticket services to gouge us would be an improvement on having just one. I proposed that ticket service charges be governmentally regulated, like other utilities, an idea that was greeted like it came from Roky Erickson's legendary Two-Headed Dog.

But as long as ticket agencies, venues, and promoters can get together—with or without the artists—to add "service charges," "facility fees," and the like, consumers are going to continue to be gouged whether by this one ticket-selling service or eighty.

Besides, Ticketmaster is just a part of the bigger cartel that is the concert industry. Several promoters around the country, including three of the biggest in the Northeast, are already operating under "consent decrees" for their monopolistic practices, and in most places the stadiums and arenas have monopolies on the shows that come through town.

But the ticket-selling monopoly is the most out-of-control member of the concert cartel, and Fred Rosen's own testimony proved it.

Rosen said that Ticketmaster's average service charge is $3.15. But that includes low-priced tickets for events like the circus. No congressman asked Rosen what the average service charge for *concert tickets* is. A statement submitted by Pearl Jam included charges as high as $7.25 for the Eagles and no rock concert charges lower than $5.75. A 1990 survey by the New York State Consumer Protection Board found that fees sometimes climb as high as 55 percent of the ticket price.

Rosen's own numbers didn't make any sense. He claimed that in 1993, Ticketmaster sold 55 million tickets for a gross of $172 million. But just two weeks earlier, the company's sales were reported in the *Chicago Tribune* as $191 million—that's $3.47 a ticket. Rosen claims that Ticketmaster earns less than ten cents per ticket. But in the *Tribune* story, Ticketmaster exec Ned Goldstein claimed the company makes a profit of about 5 percent. Five percent of $3.15 is *sixteen* cents.

Rosen claimed Ticketmaster made a profit of about $1.5 million in 1992, $7.5 million in 1993. But Ticketmaster was sold for $300 million last year, and Fred Rosen received a reported $15 million plus a percentage of the company in the deal. If such compensation, which siphons off profits, were added in, how much profit would Ticketmaster have shown? Rosen presented a chart showing that Ticketmaster's service charges rose "less than 4 percent from '89 to '90; less than 8 percent from 1990 to '91; 4 percent in '92; 4 percent in '93." That's a 20 percent increase in four years, far outstripping inflation.

Rosen told subcommittee chairman Gary Condit (D-Cal.), "I think all of us support lower ticket prices . . . Ticketmaster doesn't set ticket prices." Condit knew—or at least his staff did—that Fred Rosen has made several speeches to industry groups over the past few months railing against ticket prices for *being too low*, and claiming that this was one reason the business has a ticket scalping problem. Both the congressman and the witness also knew that *the service charge is part of the ticket price*, and that no one but Ticketmaster and its associates—the venues and the promoters—has any control over it. Pearl Jam's failure to tour this summer came precisely because the band could not fit the service charge into its overall pricing plan.

Condit did manage to bring out that, despite Rosen's bright claims about Ticketmaster's 4,200 employees, more than 2,500 of them are part-time and receive no benefits. But nobody even mentioned the current labor dispute between Ticketmaster and unionized employees in New York City. Those employees were told by a company exec that they *could* be given all that they were asking, "but we just don't want to give it to you." Pearl Jam knows all about *that*.

Rosen got away with claiming that the service charge per ticket (rather than per order) was justified because the ticket is "the unit of measure in this industry." Congress also let him get away with claiming that Ticketmaster has no quarrel with breaking down the service charge on the printed ticket—even though Tim Collins had just testified that Rosen tried to negotiate a deal with Aerosmith to prevent it.

Rosen also denied that Ticketmaster pays any kickbacks to promoters or artists. But he was never asked about so-called "overrides," which, according to the *Boston Globe*, net Boston promoter Don Law alone half a million dollars a year.

Rosen was asked to name some rock bands who don't work with Ticketmaster and he couldn't think of one. Asked to list his competitors, he kept a straight face when naming companies such as Home Shopping Network.

The kid-glove treatment Ticketmaster received from Congress (Condit described Rosen's testimony as "very candid and very open") shows the company isn't under enough pressure—yet. After all, there are class action suits filed against the company only in Massachusetts, Pennsylvania, California, Washington, and Florida. Why not in all fifty states and in every city where Ticketmaster does business?

It's up to you to give Pearl Jam some backup and contact your state attorney general and local or state consumer affairs department to register a complaint about price gouging.

If Ticketmaster isn't brought to heel, there's nothing to prevent Fred Rosen from telling Pearl Jam: "Okay, tour for an $18 ticket price. But we've got to pay for the costs of defending ourselves against your Justice Department complaint *somehow*—so your service charge is $18."

Where would Pearl Jam, or its audience, go then? Not to the Home Shopping Network, that's for damn sure.

SUICIDE NOTES

—RRC #124, JUNE 1995

Last April 5, Kurt Cobain put a gun to his head. On April 7, a workman discovered his body. In millions of heads, including my own, the echo of that shot still has not died.

For all that's been written about Cobain's death, its foreshadowings and its aftermath, what's inside that echo has barely been explored. The power that his death holds over our emotions and imagination remains, for the most part, a mystery. It doesn't come down to anything quite so simple as great songs, a great band, a great singer, or "the voice of a generation." The answer doesn't lie in poring over the details of his life, either. There was nothing simple about what drove Kurt Cobain to leave this world; there's nothing simple about what leads any person to choose death (or, in the most desperate instances, to reject death and continue living).

But if we can never know what combination of biochemistry, family background, drug addiction, neglect, celebrity, and self-hatred caused Kurt Cobain to obliterate himself, it's still worth pondering what it says about the rock world, stardom, and our own complicity in it—as fans, critics, partisans, brothers and sisters within a generation and across the gap. If we can't figure out what Cobain's suicide says about him, we should at least try to grasp what it says about us.

Alternative rock may believe that it discovered the idea that stardom is lethal, that embracing fame and fortune represents a death wish not only for the star but for everyone involved in the process, but that's a joke. The idea is there in the 1937 version of *A Star Is Born,* and before that in the story of Icarus, who soared too high in emulation of birds and the gods. But there "is" something new about the current rock scene's attitude toward stardom, fame, and its own sense of community. The night that the electrician found Cobain's body, someone who worked for him approached me in real distress. "I don't understand how this happened," he said in genuine mourning. "How do you get through to a guy who feels like a bigger and bigger failure the more people respond to him? And the more he says he's a failure, the bigger the response."

For me, that exchange became part of the echo. It determined how I interpreted his suicide note, and that note deserves more analysis than it's received. The excerpts Courtney Love read at Cobain's memorial service last April reveal a lot about the thinking that led him to kill himself. And while it would be crazy to take anybody's suicide note as the last word on why they did it, it's equally crazy to ignore it and refuse its implications.

"This note should be pretty easy to understand," he wrote. "All the warnings from the Punk Rock 101 courses over the years since my first introduction to the, shall we say, ethics involved with independence and embracement of your community, it's proven to be very true. I haven't felt the excitement of listening to as well as creating music, along with really writing something, for too many years now.

"I feel guilty beyond words about these things—for example, when we're backstage and the lights go out and the roar of the crowd begins, it doesn't affect me the way in which it did for Freddie Mercury, who seemed to love and relish the love and adoration of the crowd . . ."

At which point in her reading, Courtney Love paused and commented, "Well, Kurt, so fucking what—then don't be a star, you asshole."

Then she read on: ". . . which is something I totally admire and envy. The fact that I can't fool you, any one of you, it simply isn't fair to you or me. The worst crime I could think of would be to pull people off by faking it, pretending as if I'm having one hundred percent fun."

"Well, Kurt," she interjected, "the worst crime I can think of is for you to just continue being a rock star when you fucking hate it, just fucking stop."

Well, he did.

II

PUNK ROCK 101 UNPLUGGED

Cobain's commentary on his own demise is a muddle of half-digested contradictions that, in my view anyway, reveal a fundamental quandary that has beset pop stardom since before the advent of punk—since it began to incorporate ideas from the folk music world, really.

The "warnings" he mentioned are about selling out, a category that may or may not include commercial success. Selling out in this context really means displaying personal inauthenticity, which is the reason Cobain can express such admiration for Freddie Mercury, a star who lived his life in a closet, but one who was true to his own fakery. Punk Rock 101 teaches that the greatest sin is not meaning what you're doing; and as a perverse corollary, that if you really mean it, it doesn't matter how jive you are. So we get acts of self-destruction like the Replacements drinking themselves half to death and making it look less like fun than an obligation, Courtney Love insisting her Madison Square Garden audience join her in bellowing racist insults, ordinary fans bruising each other, even breaking bones, all in order to "prove their cred."

Such an edict represents a curious thing in the annals of popular music. It is not an idea inherent in rock & roll. Who knows if Elvis really meant what he sang in "Mystery Train" or "Heartbreak Hotel"? (He obviously didn't mean "Hound Dog" and "All Shook Up," and some people never forgave him for it, a fact Cobain might have found useful.) Who cares if Pete Townshend really wanted to die before he got old? Who is crazy enough to believe that Mick Jagger genuinely could not get any satisfaction?

Whether Bob Dylan really heard those answers blowing in the wind is another matter, though, and it was the arrival of Dylan and the folkies that begat rock's cult of authenticity. Dylan was said to be a phony when he tried to sing like Blind Lemon Jefferson on his first album; when he failed to devote "enough" of his time to playing civil rights and other movement benefits after "Blowin' in the Wind" hit, when he stopped writing and performing "protest" songs after *The Times They Are A-Changin'*, and, of course, when he began playing with a band and electric instruments in

1965. Similarly, rock bands got away with all sorts of folderol in the studio for years, but when the Byrds, the first important folk-rock band, recorded with session musicians rather than just using band members, they found themselves excoriated for it.

The roots of the folk scene's quest for authenticity are deep, going back to the turn of the century when British scholars like Francis Child first scoured Appalachian communities for the remnants of Elizabethan balladry and found a host of such songs, akin to the version of "Where Did You Sleep Last Night" that Cobain learned from Lead Belly, who called it "In the Pines." Child and others found great songs, musical treasures, and some of the greatest examples of vernacular poetic and narrative writing in the English language, material that still informs the writing of Dylan, Neil Young, and Allen Ginsberg, among others.

The authenticity issue arose in trying to make sense of what happened to these songs when they moved out of the preliterate traditions of the Appalachians (or British village life) and into the stream of urban music-making. Folk music scholars insisted for the next century—some, like Alan Lomax, still do—that Tin Pan Alley songwriters who used folk elements created "inauthentic" songs; folk music arose and was passed along anonymously and orally. There were even supposedly inauthentic instruments on which folk music could not be played—the piano, for example, supposedly existed only in bourgeois households, though a single visit to a juke joint would have blown that idea out of the water.

Such thinking suffused the folk song movement as it developed an urban "topical" or socialist realist aspect during and after the Popular Front era of the 1930s. Thus, Woody Guthrie attacked the jukeboxes that entertained America's working class, in part because such machines put live musicians like him out of work, but mainly because, as he put it in a 1947 journal entry: "A folk song tells a story that really did happen. A pop tune tells a yarn that didn't really take place." Well, after writing "Goodnight Irene," Lead Belly didn't jump in the river and drown, and I presume that Woody wouldn't have wanted him to.

Nevertheless, this ideology had real staying power, finally foundering only when it met Dylan's impossible challenges, beginning with "Restless Farewell" at the end of *The Times They Are A-Changin'*. Dylan stopped writing protest songs, I think, because the stream-of-consciousness material seemed "truer," more "real." Meaning that he hadn't changed his position on authenticity at all, which was just as well, since neither had his audience, as the folkies proved at Newport '65 by booing, and thereafter, by scrambling to catch up by immersing themselves in ever more "intimate" confessional material, until finally that whole stream came to a dead end in a welter of singer-songwriters as self-pitying as they were self-parodying, who were prominent among the artists who demanded the response punk's initial assault provided. (Dylan had by then moved on to other things, including the wearing of masks and face paint.) The most prominent Dylan followers today—Neil Young and Bruce Springsteen—have made their strangest, bravest, and most ridiculous moves in the name of being true to themselves on those same old terms.

The shaky and querulous alliance between rock and the student left in the late 1960s reinforced the primacy of "authenticity." Political movements, particularly those as rootless and disaffected as the New Left, necessarily require a great deal of suspicion: radicals need to prove their "authenticity" from time to time to demonstrate that they are not traitors, agents provocateurs, or otherwise in league with the bad guys. But the anarchist ideologies of the terminal portion of the sixties (and almost all of the post–civil rights movement Left, especially in America, became dominated by anarchist thinking) demanded authenticity of another sort: they demanded that people really meant what they said about making the personal political, and so we got, among other things, communes with enforced bisexuality run by the Weathermen, and the dropout sloganeering of the French and English Situationists.

The Situationists were onto something—no need to keep a long face any longer, there's more than enough material wealth to go around—but their elitism toward activists who did grassroots political work, as opposed to various sorts of "art" and media manipulation, scuttled whatever genuine revolutionary potential they brought to (and took out of) the crisis of 1968. It's probably more appropriate to think of the Situationists as philosophers than as political radicals, and their philosophy was a species of nihilism: the central tenet, after all, was "Nothing is true, everything is permitted."

Punk inherited all this when Malcolm McLaren and his cohorts, notably graphic designer Jamie Reid, expropriated Situationist ideas to help build the image of the Sex Pistols, and Clash Svengali Bernie Rhodes followed suit. McLaren, Rhodes, and other punk entrepreneurs essentially took Situationist and anarchist ideas into the realm of promotion, marketing, and advertising. The Pistols, in particular, employed a phalanx of PR men so numerous and so astute they might have made Michael Jackson blush, which rather makes hash of the recent article in *BAM* that looked askance at Epitaph Records for being so unpunk as to have marketing and promotion departments. Managers like McLaren, Rhodes, and even Miles Copeland, the decidedly non-anarchist CIA scion who handled the Police and founded I.R.S. Records, found such rhetoric useful for a variety of reasons, not least of which was that it allowed them to assume superiority over the acts, who were supposedly mere instruments of theory, after all. (McLaren seems to remain unaware that the Pistols were a great band, or that they had an existence independent of his enterprise, even after he got his clock cleaned in court by Johnny Rotten.)

In English pop, the punk revolution changed everything on the surface and nothing at the core; Dave Rimmer's lost classic, *Like Punk Never Happened*, a book that traces the punk kids who became Culture Club, captures the result perfectly. Unless you believe that Morrissey is the voice of a generation, punk left British rock spent as a market force and laughable as a culture, depending as it now does on cannibalizing last year's version of the recycled fads of some previous era.

But those first punk kids in London envisioned waging a revolution against the corruption that had undeniably crept into a becalmed and boring rock scene. The terms in which they expressed their disdain for hangers-on and those whose post-hip credentials didn't quite make it came straight out of the authenticity movements: "poseurs" was the favorite epithet.

It was back in the States that rock's two streams of authenticity finally come together. You can pinpoint the moment in a single song: Neil Young's 1979 "Out of the Blue and into the Black," the song that Kurt Cobain quoted in a part of his suicide note that Courtney Love did not read. Remember that when punk first began to take shape in New York in the mid-seventies,

Young seemed the archetype of the laid-back California singer-songwriter, whining "Heart of Gold" and other such gems through his nose. By 1979, though, Young had undergone a couple more of his Dylanesque transformations and he sang "Out of the Blue" twice, once in a folkie acoustic guitar and mouth harp arrangement at the beginning of his album, and then again at the end, against a grinding grunge guitar: "Hey, hey, my, my / Rock and roll can never die," he sang, making it seem like a vampire's curse, and then, a verse later, "Out of the blue and into the black/ You pay for this, but they give you that / And once you're gone, you can't come back / When you're out of the blue and into the black." As a critique of suicide, it's hard to beat.

But those aren't the lines Kurt Cobain remembered when he wrote his note. The line he quoted is the line everyone remembers: "It's better to burn out than to fade away." But those words don't appear in the grunge version at all. Only in the folkie one.

III

"IN THE PINES, IN THE PINES / WHERE THE SUN NEVER SHINES"

Rock's quest for authenticity reached Kurt Cobain as legend as much as history. Cobain was eight years old when Patti Smith made *Horses* and the Ramones stormed England; nine when "Anarchy in the U.K." came out; all of fifteen when the Clash broke up. These events took place so far from Aberdeen, the little Washington logging town that was his Castle Rock, that they might as well have happened in an entirely different generation.

What Cobain received from the first-generation punks was inspiration and a set of assumptions. If Kurt Cobain had grown up in the '50s or '60s or even the early '70s—if he was anybody from Lou Reed to Melissa Etheridge—his early encounters with rock & roll almost certainly would have represented a glorious possibility, a chance to communicate across all the gaps in our society—gaps of class, race, region, gender, generation, education, you name it. Used this way, rock & roll became not just a "way out" of impoverished working class or straightjacketed middle-class existence, but a method of absolutely transforming yourself, a means of becoming who you'd always dreamed of being, confronting your fears with the power to transmute them into assets, a chance to be a hero not only to others but in your own life; to articulate out loud a vision of the world you'd previously have been terrified to whisper into the mirror. Of such things is freedom constructed.

But for Cobain, and lots of kids like him, rock & roll offered no such hopes.

Instead, it threw down a dare: Can you be pure enough, day after day, year after year, to prove your authenticity, to live up to the music? In short, can you prove you're not a fake and keep on proving it, without respite? And if you can't, can you live with being a poseur, a phony, a sellout?

Those questions present a classic double bind: in the first place, demanding "purity" really means proving something you don't have—that you lack all corruption—and no one *can* prove a negative. Besides, the elusive notions of purity and authenticity here can barely be articulated, let alone put on display; they are like the Puritans' idea of grace, supposedly evidenced through worldly signs, here presented as a kind of hipness or "independence." But establishing such rigid qualifications immediately eliminates ease and freedom, the true hallmarks of independence and emotional authenticity. This setting really does make it easier for a professional poseur like Freddie Mercury than for a raw and amateurish, but heartfelt and insightful, artistic spirit like Kurt Cobain. So, Cobain—but not Cobain alone—groped blindly, looking for a transcendence he could *feel* but which the rules of the game he was playing—at least, the game he thought he was playing—prevented him from reaching. Yet if you don't reach that transcendence, then in ways far too lethal to enumerate, you really *are* a fake. That's the double bind, and Cobain buffeted around in it for a decade. No wonder his guts ached.

Again, there's nothing inherent about rock stardom in this. John Lennon, to choose a performer in many ways similar to Cobain in his drives and insights, never had to worry about such things. Even at his most despairing, on *Plastic Ono Band*, Lennon never descended into nihilism, because he expressed his despair in terms that implied that any such obstacle could be overcome, if only the right mechanism—political, personal, psychological, religious—could be located. Even Iggy and the Stooges, by far the darkest band of rock's first two decades (no "linger on, your pale blue eyes" for the Ig), sounded as if they believed in a way out—or, for that matter, as if the life force in their death trip songs might be so powerful it could *drag* them out of its own murderous maws. That way out might be painful, dangerous, and not a little self-threatening, but it was a pathway out of nothingness, not just another route to describing it but a means of obliterating the hollow core of the everyday and bursting through into free space, beyond all doubt. When you did that, the music promised (and early results demonstrated), the world would change, at least as it presented itself to you, because "you" had changed.

Beyond any of that, Lennon and the Stooges played rock & roll as hedonists, for whom pleasure was central, not foreign. By maintaining their links to the world of Chuck Berry, Buddy Holly, and Elvis, they somehow managed a last stand, out of which they took solace, relief—a good time. They could affect any pose they chose, from village idiot to irascible artiste, snarling snob to bemused bohemian, so long as it worked—and what worked wasn't what kept them pure, it was what let them experience this liberating sense of play. "Fake" might have been an epithet in which artists like Lennon and Iggy delighted. At the very least, "No Fun" was a situation they didn't intend to put up with.

Kurt Cobain didn't hear "No Fun" as a protest; he heard it as a description of how things were and how they would stay. In the world he was born to, he literally couldn't imagine changing things. The best he could hope to achieve was to stay outside the corruption, stay true to his principles, not sell out, never become phony, never fake it.

I'm not saying Kurt took no pleasure or solace in music. You can hear that he did all over Nirvana's records, particularly in the beautiful *Unplugged in New York*, where he sings songs he loves by everybody from Lead Belly to David Bowie to the Meat Puppets. The love Kurt had for this music—and for his own songs, too—shines bright and hard, like a crystallized essence of what he's trying to say through the petulance and recriminations of *Bleach*, *Nevermind*, *Incesticide*, and *In Utero*. (One of the greatest series of album titles in rock history, incidentally, a set of images as bloody and beatified as the stations of the cross.)

On *Unplugged*, you can hear Kurt being all the things he dreamed: un-bridled hostile, at war with everyone and everything; self-defeating cynic ("I guarantee you I will screw this song up," he says, by way of introducing "The Man Who Sold the World," and then, so far as I can hear, redeems it); little boy ("Jesus Doesn't Want Me for a Sunbeam"); and his final, linger-ing incarnation as a man not yet dead but already haunted on Lead Belly's "Where Did You Sleep Last Night."

Cobain's version of "Where Did You Sleep Last Night," an ancient song known primarily in folk and blues circles (Neil Strauss wrote a marvelous history of it in the *New York Sunday Times* last summer), may be as great a performance in its own way as "Smells Like Teen Spirit," which is only the greatest single rock & roll record of this decade. You can hear Cobain as the pure product of punk and postpunk culture in those songs, but you can also hear him struggling to break free from the clichés imposed upon him. Co-bain is looking for several things here. First of all, he's trying to find a route to community, as the only alternative to the atomized isolation that was killing him and his society. And secondly, he was trying to feel good about it, to locate that moment's respite that could only come from opening his heart to the embrace offered by so many people who had mocked and rid-iculed the geek he used to be. A terrifying possibility, but the only life raft he could reach.

Undoubtedly, Kurt Cobain came to feel trapped by the adoration of the geek-bashers, the squares, the frat boys who heard "Smells Like Teen Spirit" as a party song and saw in its bizarre cheerleader video not an anomaly but a true reflection of the world they so comfortably lived in. Trapped, in short, just as Punk Rock 101 told him he would be. When he sings "There's a friend, there's a friend, there's an enemy," he sounds like he's counting the house at a post-*Nevermind* show. But oppressive as their presence may have been, the geek-bashers and squares and frat boys aren't what pushed Kurt Cobain to suicide. How could they have done that? They lacked the imagination and the interest. If philosophical questions about how star-dom backfires had arisen for the beer guzzlers in the mosh pit, they'd have moved on. No, I don't think that Kurt Cobain killed himself to escape the intrusions of Nirvana's legions of unpunk fans.

Which brings us to the punks themselves: an answered prayer to those who lamented the corruption of rock and the rest of popular culture, perhaps, but a sect with, shall we say, certain problems of its own. In a 1979 *Village Voice* essay, "The White Noise Supremacists," Lester Bangs identified the problems as racism and sexism, and maybe fifteen years ago you could limit them to that: "Sometimes I think nothing is simple but the feeling of pain," Bangs wrote at the beginning of his essay, concluding, five-thousand-odd words later, by remarking that he had written "not because you want to think that rock & roll can save the world but because since rock & roll is bound to stay in your life you would hope to see it reach some point where it might not add to the cruelty and exploitation already in the world."

If we have learned anything since then, it's that while feeling pain may be simple, figuring out how to stop feeling it is incredibly difficult and dangerous (maybe Kurt's stomach really did hurt that bad, maybe the heroin really was the only thing that helped), and that within the bounds of hipness, it's damn near impossible to figure out how to quit inflicting it—because that can only happen when you learn to feel the pain that you're causing others, and *that* can only happen when you let go of your worries about purity and begin the very impure, perhaps unhip process of communicating your most vulnerable hopes and fears with others. In short, when you admit out loud that you can and do hurt, not in any mewling or fashionable fashion but right at the core of your being, which good little alternate rockers are supposed to shield with the true armor of their authenticity. I guess.

God knows, this defines perfectly well the dilemma of Kurt Cobain, who wore his abraded empathy more poetically than anyone since Lester Bangs himself. What I have come to love most about the grunge bands—beyond the sheer sonic fury, the slash and snap of their attack and its dark, muddy-yet-crystalline musical ambition that brings me back to my days with the MC5 and the Stooges more directly than even the punks of the '70s—is their absolute disinterest in the art of the compromise. In the past two years, bands like Green Day and Pearl Jam have completely disrupted the American concert business and, given time, they will do the same for records, radio, retail, and maybe even their audiences.

They will do this because such musicians operate out of some values that also emerge out of this very history I have spent so much time here describing and criticizing. But they don't proceed to create from this history the anything-goes decadence that gave us Culture Club and a slew of other interesting British bands who then crashed, full speed, into a brick wall because, if nothing is true and everything is permitted, then finally, making distinctions of any kind becomes an absurdity. Everybody's a fake.

The grunge bands upended that aesthetic by standing up and saying, "No. *These* things are true, and *those* things are not permitted." And in this respect, it is unquestionable that the original grunge/neo-punk standard-bearer was Nirvana, which took such risks—and standing up for what you believe in, whether that means wearing a "Corporate Magazines Still Suck" T-shirt on the cover of *Rolling Stone* or playing a pro-choice concert on the site of the first abortion doctor murder, is a risk in truth, a risk among other things of getting caught being sincere but wrong, in either attitude or action, which could cause some to label you: Fake. Phony. Poseur. So not compromising, all by itself, becomes as much a dead end as just shilling for the bucks. Proving you're not a fake doesn't make you feel real—that's what his suicide note struggled to tell us. And it was then, if at no other time, that Kurt Cobain really did become a spokesperson for his rock & roll generation.

"Nothing is true, everything is permitted." At one time, back when it became so beloved of Situationists and Satanists, this statement completely invalidated social conformity. But today everybody feels that way: Newt Gingrich, Kurt Cobain, Neil Young, O. J. Simpson, CNN, and most likely, you and me. The credo no longer expresses an undercurrent of rebellion; it's the prevailing value at the center of everything from the Contract with America to Steve Albini's production on *In Utero* to Young's sad attempt to explain away the consequences of writing "It's better to burn out than to fade away" on "Sleeps with Angels."

"Sleeps with Angels" doesn't say a thing to me, although I think it's the song that's meant to eulogize Cobain. What does connect to the tale I've been trying to tell is "Change Your Mind," a melodic rewrite of "Heart of Gold" and "Down by the River," whose lyric sounds like Neil pleading with Kurt to do the one thing that Young derives his alternate rock credentials from not doing: consider the consequences. It's Young's dilemma that touches me most deeply, maybe because nobody who's spent the past twenty-five years helping create and define the rock & roll world can help but feel some similar complicity in the Kurt Cobain story, maybe because Young struggles so palpably to convince us (convince himself?) that his ideas could not have had such consequences—and fails.

Today, "Nothing is true, everything is permitted" rebels against nothing and liberates no one—and what is rebellion without liberation except the essence of what Kurt Cobain is talking about in that suicide note? What the ascendance of this form of nihilism has given us is another heartless rebuff to a world conceived in exactly such terms: dirt to those who don't have riches, spit in the eye for the ones who ain't hip, contempt for anybody who'd actually try for connections, and above all, a suspicion verging on contempt for anybody whose empathic resonance is so great that an entire generation or even an entire nation would respond to it. The saddest, most pathetic moment in his suicide note comes when Kurt Cobain talks about how much he lacks empathy, how much he envies those who possess it—this from the author of all those songs!

And yet, he did connect. No one, not even him, could entirely deny it. People may have taken what they heard, not what Kurt wanted them to hear, but they took great things from Nirvana's scabrous and beautiful music. In that end, Kurt Cobain may have found this the most frightening aspect of his whole life and career. He thought he was alone in what he felt, and it turned out that in feeling alone, he connected to just about everybody. Such a realization would scare almost anybody; having to live with a truly penetrating awareness of how isolated and beyond solace most everybody in our world feels could scare almost anybody to death.

In this respect, Kurt Cobain's death differed utterly from 1994's other nihilist suicide, that of Guy Debord, the philosophical eminence behind Situationism and thus a grandfather of punk. Debord shot himself to death last November 30. His friends weren't surprised and nobody else paid much attention. For a philosopher who devoted his work to writing about representation and communication, it would be hard to define a greater failure. But Debord was no Icarus; he didn't soar. His theory kept him grounded. Or mired.

Kurt Cobain, on the other hand, died as something more than a star, a symbol, or even a generational martyr. He died like the painter Mark Rothko, who killed himself, it would seem, from an excess of feeling. Unlike Rothko, though, Cobain died from being a modernist (a modernist being a person "whose social history is that of a spiritual being in a property-loving world," as Robert Motherwell wrote fifty years ago) who tried to live up to postmodern values.

What I have come to believe is that Kurt Cobain did not die because he could not fit in, but because he did. Which is why I can take my solace not from Neil Young's stumbling for an explanation (much as I relate to it) or from Courtney Love's vainglorious effort to put the principles that doomed Kurt into practice (compelling as I find *Live Through This*) or in my friend Gina Arnold's bittersweet efforts to put the passion of Nirvana's fans into words, but only in the half-intelligible singing of Michael Stipe on *Automatic for the People*—a fit epitaph for rock & roll's first celebrity shotgun suicide, if there ever was one.

Stipe said later he and Cobain had been talking a lot, while planning a collaboration; I don't know what Michael tried to say to Kurt in their last few conversations, but in my imagination, he sings him a lullaby that says, "When you're sure you've had enough / Of this life . . . Well, hang on."

I don't know what really happened—in those talks or in the last days of Kurt Cobain's life. I do know that those of us left behind had better start singing such things to one another or we will find our way to the ocean, not like the water that runs down so beautifully at the end of *Automatic for the People* in "Find the River," but like lemmings.

Hang on.

THE LONG AND WINDING ROAD

—TV GUIDE, NOVEMBER 1995

The *Beatles Anthology* opens just the way it should: a shot of that famous bass drum with the Beatles logo, a quick downbeat, guitars chiming, voices ringing, and then . . . the screams!

It ends just as you knew it would: their final, perfect harmony declaring, "And in the end, the love you take is equal to the love you make."

Certainly, you're well aware of a lot of what's in the nearly six hours of TV that comes in between those two moments. *The Beatles Anthology* is, after all, the story of the most famous pop music group in world history.

But even if you'd seen every other frame in the special that ABC will broadcast this week—and you certainly have not, since some of it comes from footage of the group on vacation that had never before been developed, and a good deal of the rest has been unknown or unavailable—you still wouldn't know the core of this story. *The Beatles Anthology* is unique and invaluable because it tells the story of the group from the perspective of the band members themselves.

"What makes this special," says Ringo Starr, "is that George, Paul, and I are interviewed over the past couple of years." The interviews are sometimes quite telling. Ringo discusses his humiliation at the producer George Martin's insistence on using a session drummer at the first Beatles recording session. Paul McCartney describes the conscious decision he and John Lennon made to write a song using "reported conversation" rather than first person narrative (which became "She Loves You"). At the end, George Harrison speaks acerbically about the real consequences of being in the band: "*They* gave their money and their screams. *We* gave our nervous systems."

"Looking at your life in six hours is pretty scary," says McCartney. "It just slips by you all the time. You get a feeling of 'Wow, that's what I did. Wow! That's what he did. These are the guys, these are my friends, this is it.'

"It's very satisfying to have something like our own version. This surprising fact is, we thought we'd absolutely have the definitive lockout version—no one could ever say anything after this—[but] it's still up for grabs. We've given our version."

The way in which the *Anthology* is the Beatles-by-the-Beatles goes far beyond that. The film offers no pundits or other outside authorities. All wives, ex-girlfriends, guitar tuners, deejays, children, siblings, fans, naysayers, and fifth through five-thousandth Beatles are shut out. When we see other stars, mainly early rockers and R&B singers, they're present for musical reasons. No music film has ever been more lucid about the process of songwriting and music-making. Every musical point is amply buttressed by complementary footage of the Beatles in action. It helps that the Beatles used TV more avidly and wisely than any other pop group before the age of MTV, coming to the medium on its own terms (the bits of variety-show sketch comedy here are truer relics of another age than even the oldest songs), but always bending it to their own benefit. Where Elvis seemed a pawn of Ed Sullivan, the Beatles seemed to be doing *him* a favor, as can be seen when Sullivan nervously introduces the group at Shea Stadium.

The psychological stresses of the Beatles' fame are also presented in a way that's extremely clear, thanks very much to the use of footage from the film *Let It Be*, which started out to be a documentary about the making of a Beatles album and ended up chronicling their dissolution. By giving us so much background, the *Anthology* gives a much clearer depiction of why the group came apart than *Let It Be* could. As the Beatles give up their stage work, which had knit them together since the early days on Hamburg's Reeperbahn, the music gets weirder and the interpersonal tensions begin to tear at the fabric of their solidarity. "You can't really put it on anything else, bar time," says Ringo, and he means the time of their own lives, the fact that by 1970, when the Beatles finally came to a halt, each band member had married and developed a lifestyle and interests of his own. They were no longer teenagers or even young adults. Ringo was almost thirty! And he may have taken it hardest of all: "When we split up, I didn't play Beatles records for years because it was like . . . life."

It's that sense of life, which only the group itself and its most intimate associates experienced, that the *Anthology* portrays. The film's speakers are Paul, George, Ringo, the late John in a variety of film clips, and producer Martin. There are cameos by former roadie/now Apple president Neil Aspinall, and the group's legendary press officer, Derek Taylor; the voice of interviewer Jools Holland is occasionally heard asking a follow-up question. And there are, of course, a few people who interact verbally with the band during the documentary footage—for instance, the hapless journalist who asks Harrison, in a scene from *A Hard Day's Night*, what he calls his hairstyle. "Arthur," replies the Beatle. (Harrison, by the way, informs *TV Guide* that he currently calls his hair "Cyril.")

The four Beatles define a fifth presence, which is the group itself, something that each of them has always held separate. "Many things about the Beatles as individuals have been left out because there was so much about the Beatles as an entity," says Harrison. "I feel I could make a documentary about myself, which would have very little to do with the Beatles." True enough: there's some coverage of the band's Maharishi experience in India because it happened to all four of them and couldn't be avoided, but about George's involvement with the Hare Krishna group (which resulted in the temple changers' recording a single for Apple), not a peep.

The rest of the group feel similarly distanced. "It's not me I'm talking about, it's this beast—the Beatle Beast—with four heads," says McCartney. Ringo, predictably, has the most positive take on that. "The great thing about the three of us hanging out struck me like a bolt of lightning one day. They're the only people in the world who don't treat me like a Beatle."

Ringo's summary of the group, in the final moments of the *Anthology*, is "We were four guys who really loved each other." That, he says, explains why the Beatles, uniquely among pop celebrities of their stature, have remained relatively sane and healthy into middle age. None of them looks as rode-hard-and-put-away-wet as Mick Jagger, let alone Keith Richards; none has frozen into a thousand-yard stare like Bob Dylan; none has the addiction problems of Elvis Presley (although John and Ringo each had one to conquer). "We were stuck with each other," says Ringo. "And that wasn't a bad thing. It was the lifesaver. There were four of us and there were four brothers. We were the Four Musketeers. And everybody saved everybody else at some point."

The *Anthology*, then, is celebration, not journalism. But it's a celebration without pomposity or unnecessary self-aggrandizement. For instance, the vitriol with which the band's early music, style, and demeanor were greeted is entirely passed over. It seems simply to have been of no consequence to the Beatles themselves, though Ringo does confess himself hurt that Elvis allegedly wanted to help the FBI get the Beatles thrown out of the U.S. Avoiding all that makes the band seem less self-important than tackling it head-on would. (The music *has* lasted; thirty years later, the Beatles are not only still remembered but remain revered and influential.) Anyway, the show isn't a whitewash: drugs, the discarding of early members Stuart Sutcliffe and Pete Best, John's "The Beatles are probably bigger than Jesus right now" flap, and the internecine wars that led to the band's breakup are all covered quite honestly.

The sad part is that Lennon, the most articulate, sarcastic, iconoclastic, uninhibited Beatle (one is tempted to say "public figure of our time") can't give his mature insights. John is missed not only because we wonder what he'd think today of his youthful deeds, but because so many of the Lennon quotes that are here come from his early solo period, when he was engaged in nonstop idol-smashing, often stated in the most acerbic terms. Yoko Ono says John's segments strike her as representing "a lot of fun moments with his sense of humor showing. I didn't feel he was being harsh." But to an outsider, John seems more sour than he did when he gave print interviews before the release of his last album in 1980, and even Yoko acknowledges that, today, he might be "a more gentle person."

On the other hand, John's absence also provides an opportunity for the others. Harrison and Starr have never had their perspective on the band so thoroughly represented. One consequence is that Harrison, in particular, seems more accessible than ever before (only on film, unfortunately; while McCartney and Starr sat for interviews with *TV Guide*, Harrison responded to questions only by fax). Ringo, meanwhile, sober since the late '80s, comes across as the band's sage. McCartney, for better or worse, has never ceased being the glib Liverpudlian mop-top, if you can imagine such a character with salt-and-pepper hair. None of them, not even Harrison for all his dour perspectives, displays a sense of cynicism, a feat Taylor, the saner-than-thou hipster who's worked with them forever, attributes to their very provincialism. "Mick Jagger said years ago, 'The Beatles are *so* provincial.' But undoubtedly it's worked in their favor. In the back of their minds, there's always been a sense that people back home would very quickly see through the [London] b.s. So they never really got into show business."*Anthology* producer Chips Chipperfield says he's been working on the project for almost four years. Actually, though, the show's a lot older than that, dating back to Aspinall's projected *The Long and Winding Road* film from the early '70s. Ringo says that a version of this film was, in fact, assembled, but was rejected because "it was mainly airplanes landing and taking off." After that, Beatles projects of any kind became nearly impossible for the best part of a decade, due to the legal and personal squabbling among the band members. The lawsuits and attendant ill will were resolved around 1989, and soon after, Chipperfield and director Geoff Wonfor went to work.

Yet, why finally release the *Anthology* now? An obvious answer might be that the Beatles somehow need shoring up. But Taylor says stoutly that the band's recorded catalogue sales are all strong "at front-shelf prices," and last year's *Live at the BBC*, while it did not dominate the charts, sold well, too. So what's in it for the Beatles?

"I think it's just 'Oh, hell. We're all fifty; let's do it,'" says Taylor, although he and Aspinall acknowledge an economic incentive, and not only for the Beatles. The Beatles have coordinated the broadcast with the release of a double-disc companion CD called *The Beatles Anthology Volume 1*; it will be followed by two others (in February and May), finally mining the rock world's most valuable back catalogue.

Maybe, though, the main reason for releasing *The Beatles Anthology* now is less mercenary. Maybe, having constructed a video universe with themselves at the center, the Beatles looked upon it and saw that it was good. Maybe they saw what I did, which is that it's not only their music that holds up well, thirty years later, but also their legend—a story that deserves retelling because in it, we discover some valuable things about the way in which humans who do love one another can function creatively and prosperously.

What was the Beatles' message, after all? "Yeah, yeah, yeah," says Harrison, and he's only half-kidding. As Taylor puts it, "That you could be yourself, and you should be, too. And make sure that the self you want to be sets some kind of standard for people around you." For six hours this week the Beatles set exactly such a standard. If anything, it's a message the world needs to hear now even more than it did in 1964.

STARFOLKING

—*ADDICTED TO NOISE*, FEBRUARY 1998

When I was fifteen years old and discovered Bob Dylan and the blues for myself, I went to the local library to see what was available to learn from. They had a copy of a multivolume Atlantic Records series called *Sounds of the South* (now available, under just that name, as a four CD box set). I don't think that the library had all the volumes in the series, but they did have the one featuring Mississippi Fred McDowell, to this day one of my favorite rural bluesmen. The album's liner notes vividly detailed the discovery of McDowell, which seemed to have been quite unexpected—that made perfect sense to me, because Fred McDowell's great talent was for making all the music he played sound surprising, something that remains true, in my ear at least, after more than thirty years of listening to him.

I did not pay any attention whatsoever to who his discoverer was.

If the name had registered, I would have honored it. Indeed, I might have been quite astonished, for one of the records I actually went out and purchased around the same time—again as part of becoming a Dylan fan—was the Elektra three-LP box of Woody Guthrie's Library of Congress recordings, much of which was given over to a dialogue (a kind of fake radio interview) between Woody and the producer, Alan Lomax. It was Lomax who recorded the Atlantic *Sounds of the South* set.

About a decade later, my friend and fellow critic Paul Nelson, who had spent the folk revival as an editor of the *Little Sandy Review* and *Sing Out!*, two of the most important folk magazines, recommended I buy a set of three Folkways box sets, *Anthology of American Folk Music*. The music, now available in a six-disc Smithsonian Folkways box set, astonished me. I had known some of it from my boyhood, but the "Sugar Baby" of Dock Boggs and the "Frankie and Johnnie" of John Hurt and the "Kassie Jones" of Furry Lewis were nothing like the songs I'd heard my neighbors and parents sing, nothing like the versions I'd heard over the radio. I didn't want to say the versions on the *Anthology* were more authentic, necessarily. They were better, and a lot of them were sung by people who clearly had a lot fewer inhibitions than anybody I'd grown up around, and by fewer inhibitions, I don't mean Iggy and the Stooges. I mean an absolute ability to stare death in the face, to look at bizarre events and convey them in the spirit of the everyday, to tell the wildest jokes you'd ever heard and almost—almost—conceal the threat within them. My favorite track on this album was Rabbit Brown's "James Alley Blues," which did all of this.

After I expressed my slack-jawed enthusiasm for the set, Nelson told me some stories about Harry Smith, the man who compiled the old-timey and blues records it contained. But the story about Smith was only an amusement; the amazement remained "House Carpenter" and "Two White Horses," "Spike Driver Blues" and "Oh Death," "John the Revelator" and a "Boweavil Blues" that had either nothing or everything to do with the jolly Fats Domino tune I knew by heart from the virtual dawn of rock'n'roll.

The reissue event of 1997 was the Smithsonian's repackage of the *Anthology*, which is just as it should have been. There is no greater storehouse of American vernacular music, and the new annotation—by Greil Marcus, Jon Pankake (Nelson's old partner in the *Little Sandy Review*), John Fahey, and several other folk performers—add valuable dimensions, reflective of how the material came to be created and assembled, how it has been used since the set was first issued in 1952, and how that use has affected our culture.

The *Anthology*'s rerelease nearly overshadowed the release by Rounder Records of *The Alan Lomax Collection*. Most of the first seven volumes there—all the best stuff in my opinion—is identical to what's on the *Sounds of the South* set, which was virtually ignored when it came out on CD in 1993, despite an adept new annotation by Robert Palmer.

I wonder if the attention would have been great had *Sounds of the South* been retitled something like *Alan Lomax's Sounds of the South*?

It's a question worth wondering about because, with the exception of the annotation itself and the extraordinarily detailed commentary in Marcus's *Invisible Republic*, almost everything I've read about the Rounder series and the Folkways box has been about not the music but Alan Lomax and Harry Smith. So much so that the dolt who writes for *Entertainment Weekly* had Harry Smith making the field recordings himself, rather than collecting and compiling from 78s. Smith was in diapers and grade school when the bulk of the tracks on the *Anthology* were recorded.

Every bit of the attention paid to the Lomax set was to Alan Lomax. I didn't see anybody singing the praises of Fred McDowell at all, even though, you'd think, they did hear at least once the stunning exuberance of "Freight Train Blues" and "Shake 'Em On Down."

This certainly wasn't the case the first time around. What resulted from the reissue (really rediscovery) of the sides collected on the *Anthology* was an outburst of people performing the music, not making their own mix tapes—in other words, an uprising of people who wanted to be like John Hurt and Rabbit Brown and Buell Kazee and Bascom Lunsford, not a bunch of people who wanted to be Harry Smith. The consequence of the release of Lomax's field recordings was similar, leading to the first of many "blues revivals."

But the fifties and sixties were only the beginning of today's celebrity culture. In "James Alley Blues," Richard "Rabbit" Brown may have made the greatest blues record in a lot of minds, including mine; hell, he may have made the greatest record of all time. But he can't be a "star," because what do we know about him? And what else do we know about him? Enough to fill out one side of a Matchbox LP (*Country Blues—The First Generation*), with four other tracks, the best of the rest being "Sinking of the Titanic." Annotator Paul Oliver, one of the world's great blues scholars, tells us that Brown grew up in James Alley in New Orleans, but he can't tell us his age, just that he was probably "well into his forties," when he made the five extant recordings for producer Ralph Peer. How do you fashion a star out of that?

We know much more about Rev. J. M. Gates, the most prolific and arguably the best of all the Black preachers; his "complete recorded works in chronological order" run to nine Document CDs, all copiously annotated. Gates had a profound effect on the history of Black preaching, his raspy voice, quaking with an intoxicating mixture of inspiration and flat-out fear of God, finding its way into the mouth of even Dr. Martin Luther King, through the influence of Rev. C. L. Franklin (whose masterpiece, "The Eagle Stirreth Her Nest," is a reprise of a Gates homily). Gates's best-known recording, "Death Might Be Your Santa Claus," was even smuggled into the rock'n'roll laboratory by Mott the Hoople (who lifted the title but nothing else, so far as I've ever been able to figure—I'm not so sure that Kaleidoscope's recording of "Oh Death" in the late '60s derived from Gates). But the guy made "Oh Death" in 1927 (the first time; he recorded it as often as Chuck Berry recorded "Johnny B. Goode") and he stopped making discs in 1941. We're not even sure what year he died, let alone how, although it pretty certainly was a death as romantic or sordid as those of Robert Johnson, Bessie Smith, or Billie Holiday. There's no star material there, either.

Gates was a star of sorts—the Document liner notes claim that about one-quarter of all the pre–World War II sermons recorded by Black preachers were done by him. But only in a narrow community of Black people, perhaps even a narrower world of Black Baptists (for an enumeration of the myriad other theological possibilities available in Black society at that time, see Washington Phillips's immortal "Denomination Blues"). Rabbit Brown would have counted himself fortunate to have one-tenth as much recognition.

What that means is hard to grasp today. What it certainly does not mean is what the *Village Voice* claimed in its Pazz & Jop poll issue, that the recordings of the *Anthology of American Folk Music* spoke to "subcultures," just like today's alterna rockers. Not at all. When Ry Cooder travels to Cuba to make a record with the musicians he calls the Buena Vista Social Club and brings that record back home to play for the likes of you and me, that is subcultural. But when those musicians play *in Cuba*, that's just culture. When a contemporary singer-songwriter adds a hammer dulcimer to her album of original songs, that's subcultural. When my old high school teacher Patty Looman records her albums of mountain airs on hammer dulcimer (*Mountain Laurel Melodies* and *Nothing Fancy* are the two I have; they're available from 228 Maple Ave., Mannington, WV 26852) that may be one or the other, in a way depending on who is listening, or maybe who she thinks she is playing for. But when Looman makes her music in her native West Virginia for an audience of her neighbors, that is *culture*. Nothing sub- about it, because it doesn't think, or feel, in terms of some other culture to which it is subordinate. This isn't a matter of better or worse: I prefer the subcultural recording Junior Kimbrough made with Jon Spencer to the ones he made with Robert Palmer producing, though Palmer's are the ones that better reflect the music in its true cultural context.

All of the records on the *Anthology of American Folk Music* were recorded in this spirit, and that's true, even though, as Marcus rightly argues, all of them were made by people—artists and producers alike—who wanted to reach out beyond the mountains or valleys or details where they spent their lives to a broader world. Nevertheless, that broader world had not penetrated very far into those areas. Hell, in the Michigan where I grew up, you could still find all sorts of culture that had not been affected hardly at all by what we now think of as "mainstream" culture. You didn't have to go any further than my grandfather's fishing cabin. If you talked to my neighbors from Kentucky, West Virginia, southern Illinois and Indiana, Georgia and Tennessee, you'd be talking to people who were surprised by the advent of Elvis only because somebody had actually allowed such a character out of the yard, not because such a guy existed.

That kind of culture, existing in isolation from the Ted Koppel world, exists only at the most extreme margins today. A hammer dulcimer picker here, a maker of Cornish pasties there, a quilter in a cabin off in some holler or a rancher singing old corridos in some Southwestern arroyo.

The sounds such people made when they lived in communities where the local culture *was* culture sound so exotic today that we can barely bother with the details of even something so supernatural as Clarence Ashley's haunted "House Carpenter." At the panel I chaired at this year's Folk Alliance conference, someone complained of not hearing any traditional songs, and that is always a surprise to me, too. By paying diligent attention, I heard two versions of "John Hardy," but when people stayed up all night to sing, the tunes they picked were from Aretha Franklin and Motown and James Brown.

This is part of a folk music dilemma, and not for the first time. The most comical of all the paeans to Alan Lomax came from someone in the Sunday *New York Times* who claimed "Lomax would record anything."

Bullshit.

Alan Lomax wouldn't touch what was then known as "Negro rhythm and blues" or its White counterpart, rockabilly. The result is that not only his but our connection with the music he collected and the material Smith compiled is distorted. We think there is a hard distinction between "folk" and "commercial" music. We think that there are people involved in music who are "only in it for the money." (I've been doing this work since 1969 and I've never met such a person, not even in the figure of someone who would put their name on the copyright of "Goodnight Irene" without having written a line or a note of it.) We think that the men who make the music are the men who compile the discs or seek out the singers. To return to my current hobbyhorse, we think that music is a thing, not a doing. What made "I'll Be There" and "Since You've Been Gone" and even "I Got You (I Feel Good)" folk songs that night in Memphis was the fact that folks chose them to do with balalaika accompaniment, but even without it. That has everything to do with what we inherited from Bascom Lunsford and John Hurt. It has damned little to do with Harry Smith or Alan Lomax, except maybe as part of the prayers with which they accompanied their endeavors.

Nevertheless, as the Folk Alliance always reminds me, the connection is only distorted, not severed. Because you can't sever it—you cannot have Kirk Franklin without Aretha Franklin without C. L. Franklin without J. M. Gates. You cannot have Marilyn Manson without Black Sabbath without Cream without Eric Clapton without Freddie King without B.B. King without Fred McDowell and his peers. That is the triumph of yesterday's music, and the glory of today's. The problem is, as long as we're focused on the wrong end of the previous era's equation, how do we get to tomorrow's?

THE HERO AND THE BLUES

—*ADDICTED TO NOISE*, MARCH 1998

Oh, the church bell tollin'
Ooohhhh, the hearse come drivin' slow

—Howlin' Wolf

I need a haircut but I probably won't get one very soon. It was never my favorite thing to do, and not just because of the castration complex, thank you, Sigmund. Not even just because after the Beatles and the Stones, long hair and rock 'n' roll were for a long time synonymous. Like most rock-drunk kids, I longed for my hair to grow "down to my feet so strange / That I look like a walking mountain range," as Bob Dylan sang in "I Shall Be Free No. 10," the earliest indication I had that he was actually a rocker in folk singer drag.

Of course, I tried to grow my hair as long as the authorities—high school officials and my parents—would allow. The school had rules, but they weren't very clear: your hair might not extend past your collar or your earlobes or some area as ill-defined as the major-league strike zone before you got a call to go see the principal. I took his threats to expel or suspend me pretty seriously, because it was worth my hide to have any such thing happen. Between travel and work, my father was out of the house about fourteen hours a day, but he'd notice that.

It was a dangerous thing, to attract my father's attention. He was 6'3" and, depending on how strictly he was dieting, went anywhere from 190 to 250 in his prime. He was forty in 1967, which is the year I'm thinking about, and still in good enough shape to handle a scrawny seventeen-year-old who'd gotten out-of-bounds. His fists were about the size of the hocks of a sizable hog, and when he swung them, they made a sound just about like what you'd get if you took a ham hock and swung it against a countertop—a series of wet thumps. I thought I was pretty much in the clear that fall, a high school senior who knew he had enough credits to graduate and could basically go to classes mainly to read books, write, nap, and dream. I already worked forty hours a week, partly because I did not trust what relying upon my parents for a clothing allowance would have left me looking like, and what I looked like, to me, was already bad enough. But the other reason I worked so much was that work was a place out of reach of those fists and their wet thumps.

So I dressed somewhat as I chose and began to avoid the barber even more religiously. It seemed to go over at the house, no worse than taking up smoking had. In fact, my old man had not spoken to me since the spring—I mean, not "Good morning," "Good night," or "I've fucking had it with you, you little shit-ass." Stupidly, that made me feel secure, almost (almost) manly.

Then one bright winter morning, I stepped out the side door into the driveway and an avalanche of pain. I don't remember how many times he struck, but I do remember the conclusion, which was being picked up and thrown as hard as he could heave me against the garage door. In full view of every other teenager on the street, waiting at the end of the block for the school bus.

In the stillness, as I picked myself off the ground (a foolish move, but if I weren't a fool, I wouldn't be available right now), his voice echoed like a gunshot. "Get your fucking hair cut. Today." He got in his car and drove off. I went into the house and trembled with shame. It wasn't that he'd beaten me—he'd always done that, intermittently, not every day like you read about, but just when he needed to inflict some pain and I'd given him an excuse—but that everyone had seen it happen. My mother understood this and let me sit and stew a while before she drove me to the barbershop.

This is why there is no picture of me in my high school yearbook. I refused to have my picture taken looking like that. There is no explaining exactly how I got away with that except that I was at least as stubborn as my father, and did not think that I had a great deal more to lose. It was around this time that my friend Jim came into our living room, one lonely Friday night, and found me with a shotgun lying across my lap. It wasn't there for the reason he thought it was, but he talked me into sticking it back in the closet.

I wasn't going to shoot myself, I'm pretty sure of that. I was contemplating shooting somebody else. There were a lot of rifles and shotguns in that house, and it seemed to me that, sooner or later, someone was going to try that on somebody. As soon as college started, I arranged to move out. My father didn't talk to me that day, either. I wrote all this, which is as true as I can make myself remember it, while listening to *Safe House: A Collection of the Blues* (Relativity), which was compiled by Andrew Vachss, who takes a credit larger than any of the artists, and deserves it. He deserves it because, as a lawyer and writer, he lives a brave life, and because this "soundtrack" to his latest novel, also called *Safe House*, says all the things that nobody's writing can ever capture about lives like the one I lived in my teenage years.

As a lawyer, Vachss has a practice that consists entirely of children— human beings under age twenty-one—who, for the most part, have been battered or molested, although that is not, I suppose, always what they are in trouble for. As a novelist, he has used his skills to blow the whistle on a society that thinks it ought to turn a blind eye to pulverizing children out of their hopes and ambitions and warping them into misshapen caricatures of what any person ought to have the chance to be. Some of this stuff is about people who rape babies; some of it is about abuse in a more elastic sense. All of it takes the revenge I was looking for that night in my living room and puts it to good use. No one in the English language—not Hemingway, not Hammett—has written prose as spare and vicious as Andrew Vachss. Not even Jim Thompson and Stephen King have been able to conjure greater scenes of everyday horror. I doubt if there is a movie producer in Hollywood who'd have the guts to put on the screen the highly pictorial and dramatic stories Vachss creates. I could not have begun to think about writing about Vachss and his work and what it has meant to me without telling you the scariest truth I know about myself: I was willing to kill my own father to get him to keep his fucking hands off me. And I was right. Right to want to do it and right to let someone stop me.

Vachss has written a dozen novels and books of shorter fiction, all as terrifying as they are gratifying. When people talk about there being too much violence in our culture, I lash out at them because the truth that these books contain is one of the things I fear losing. In the world according to Andrew Vachss, it's not just that the good guys win; it's the immense amount of pain the bad guys are put in while they lose. Yet, at the end of every one of these stories, the reader is given to understand that the meaning of the world is not an endless cycle of vengeance and remorse, but family, friendship, love. Burke, the blues-loving Nowhere Man who is at the center of most Vachss stories, fries child-molesters without a blink, but when a child himself shows signs of being abused, his first option is trying to redeem the kid, to allow or persuade him to understand that he can break the cycle, all by himself, by not becoming a monster like the people who taught him what evil consists of. The very fine short story that takes the place of liner notes in the soundtrack album is a perfect example of how he works this. I think the reason that Vachss loves blues so much—and this selection is so well-chosen that even singers I don't prefer go down smooth—is that they operate on exactly the same wavelength.

Safe House takes Burke into comparatively new territory. It's about men who brutalize women, by which he means beating, raping, and stalking. It's also about the world of White supremacy. You might think the connection is far-fetched, but I don't. The same pastoral farming village that produced my father also produced Terry Nichols, who helped Timothy McVeigh kill all those people in Oklahoma City.

You might think that all this is also awfully far from the blues. I can't think that. When I was at my most stupefied, in the most pain, it was blues records—the music, above all, of Muddy Waters and the great, early Paul Butterfield Band; of Little Walter and the Animals; of Mississippi Fred McDowell and the Rolling Stones—that dug me out from under. I listened to soul to dream, and hard rock when the frustration made my throat too tight. I listened to the blues to survive. Some of the records Vachss has chosen for *Safe House*—Howlin' Wolf's "I Asked for Water (She Gave Me Gasoline)," the Paul Butterfield Blues Band's "I Got a Mind to Give Up Living,"

Otis Spann's "Some Day"—are among the ones that gave me such succor back then. They didn't tell me what the liars always said, that it wasn't so bad, that my hurt was something I deserved, that patience would let me escape. They told me the truth: it was way more than bad enough, the kind of thing no one deserves, and that there might not be enough patience or no escape, so the only thing worth maintaining was my dignity. And they issued one promise: Dignity was possible, no matter what happened. Not guaranteed, but possible. Or as Andrew Vachss expressed it in his one nonfiction book, *Another Chance to Get It Right*. For him, every child—every human life so far not surrendered to "the meanness in this world"—is that chance.

In this sense, every line Andrew Vachss has ever written is pure blues.

Did I say he was brave? Hell, he's a hero.

LAMENTATION FOR A PUNK

—*ADDICTED TO NOISE*, MAY 1998

"By the time the funeral ceremony was set to begin at eight that night, the temperature had dropped to three above zero . . . Three thousand people jammed into the Tabernacle Baptist Church; another seven thousand waited outside in the cold. 'A few white people were seen among the mourners,' a reporter noted, 'and a few celebrities, but basically the crowd was formed by the little people off the street . . .'"

—Daniel Wolff, *You Send Me: The Life and Times of Sam Cooke*

There is something immensely gratifying about what we have seen from the American press in the past week. A major figure of American popular music has died and the press has not focused on his gang associates, his drug habits, his inability to finish high school, the role of money derived from running drugs and whores in starting his career, his perpetual philandering, his reported suicidal frenzy when he lost the girl of his dreams, his vicious misogyny, his ruthless and asinine public attacks on the press, his callous behavior toward his first wife, his rocky relations with his children, his associations with politically dubious characters (some of "them" criminals), or even the records he had made in recent years that were artistically hideous attempts to do nothing more than line his pockets. Instead, the coverage has been about the music he made, on stage and on record, the tremendous effect it had on the public, both in its musical tastes and its sense of what constituted good style, the innovations he wrought as a singer, the creative achievements of his life outside music in film and TV, his recent good relations with his family, his loyalty to his friends, and the continued devotion of his fans long after he had lapsed artistically.

Frank Sinatra deserved all this, in my opinion. He was a great singer, overrated in the way that only the very greatest can be overrated, which is to say, no he wasn't the only singer of the pre–rock'n'roll era, and no he is not "inarguably" the greatest of all those singers, and yes, I still think Tony Bennett and Nat "King" Cole, Billie Holiday and Louis Armstrong ran ring-a-dings around him, but that's just me and *"de gustibus."* I couldn't even bring it up if having it rammed down my throat over and over again didn't stick in my craw.

Why can't Sinatra be a great singer? Why does he have to be the "only" great singer?

I presume the answer is the same as the answer to why all those negative attributes are explained away. Sinatra had ties to gangs who wreaked more killings and sold more dope than the Crips and Bloods combined; his addiction was to alcohol not illegal drugs; his politically dubious cronies included the anti-Semitic president of the United States, not the anti-Semitic leader of a comparatively powerless Black group; his exploitative records were done "in good taste"—as if bad music coming out of the throat of a singer whose voice has the elasticity of an eighty-year-old rubber band could possibly be in good taste. In short, Sinatra couldn't be just a great singer; he had to be the only one because, after him, all the rest were tainted, by being Black or Southern or radically disaffected from the conventional mores of our time that allow us to pretend, when it is convenient, that Black ghetto kids forming gangs that run drugs in their communities is more dangerous than the Mafia controlling entire American industries, that more people have their lives ruined by coke, heroin, and marijuana than by booze, that Louis Farrakhan is the bogey man and Richard Nixon just went astray, that the music that operates by the standards of Afro-America is mere commerce, while that which operates by the standards of Euro-America (with its various thefts from Afro-America concealed and denied) is indelible art.

Frank Sinatra didn't particularly piss me off. He wasn't any more boorish than Marilyn Manson or Rick James, his pretensions weren't any greater than those of Marvin Gaye or Carlos Santana, and shit, we probably had a lot in common: we grew up kind of poor, we both like a drink or two, and most of all, we love music, especially great voices and great songs. My standards are different than Frank's, but that's back to *de gustibus* I think. As a matter of absolute fact, and you could ask my wife, when I found out Sinatra had died, I was halfway through listening to *Frank Sinatra Sings the Select Johnny Mercer*, with its great versions of "One for My Baby (And More for the Road)," the song that inspired "Louie Louie," "That Old Black Magic," and "Blues in the Night." At breakfast the next morning, I gave my daughter a copy of *The Capitol Years*, which may not be all the Sinatra she ever wants, but is pretty much all she'll ever need. I still get a cold chill of excitement every time I hear the guy sing, "I get no kick from champagne . . . ," and while I think the sentiments are basically provincial bullshit, the place now being run as a Jesuit high school with a vindictively psychotic novitiate as its principal, at the end of a Yankee game, nothing sounds better than "New York New York."

It's just that Frank Sinatra is being presented now as a hero, and he could never have been a hero of mine. Yes, he acknowledged that Billie Holiday was the greatest singer he ever heard and the greatness of many Black artists, and he sang "The House I Live In" and hosted that New Deal film on tolerance. Yes, he eventually agreed to appear on stage with Elvis and sang songs by the Beatles and Billy Joel, and allowed Bob Dylan to salute him and even hung out for a while with that other ultimate Jersey boy, Bruce Springsteen. In the beginning Sinatra may even have been a symbol of pride for an oppressed ethnic group, Italian Americans, looked down upon with hatred and disdain.

But sometime after that, he allowed himself to become a symbol, a different kind. Sinatra was in a sense the model for the Angry White American Man. More than anything else, this accounts for his alliance with Nixon and later that ultimate enemy of tolerance and equality, Reagan—and for his loathing of women as public figures, and his hatred of the media (which 95 percent of the time kissed his ass, just as it kisses the ass of most of the Angry White American Men who complain about it most avidly, from Rush Limbaugh on up to actual humans). The beginning of Sinatra slipping into this symbolic role came in the mid-1950s, when he became part of the effort (I am tempted to say "plot") by the Tin Pan Alley establishment, led by the ASCAP songwriters (who barred virtually all Black and working-class songwriters), to discredit the new musical synthesis by claiming it was the pure product of payola and other forms of bribery and chicanery. One of the things that has been forgotten is that, in the process, Sinatra lied to Congress. In 1956, Sinatra told the House subcommittee chaired by Emanuel Cellar that his recording career had faltered beginning in 1950 because Mitch Miller, his Columbia producer at that time, had shoved down his throat "inferior songs" published by BMI (which was open to all sorts of people, including the Black, Southern, and working-class writers who were fashioning rock'n'roll). Miller, who also hated rock'n'roll and refused to sign R&B acts to Columbia, later showed the committee that in their three-year association, Sinatra had recorded fifty-seven sides, of which five were published by BMI.

"Rock'n'roll smells phony and false," Sinatra (or a ghost using his name) wrote in *Life* in 1957. "It is sung, played, and written for the most part by cretinous goons and by means of its almost imbecilic reiteration . . . it manages to be the martial music of every sideburned delinquent on the face of the earth." Although I suppose this remark—and he made plenty more along the same lines—was "tasteful," to the extent that he didn't join the Alabama White Citizens Council in labeling rock'n'roll "animalistic nigger bop," you don't exactly need a slang dictionary to figure out that this was an important undertone of what Sinatra was saying. Nor was his statement just some quaint "old fogey" mistake. It was another blatant lie. Sinatra knew the history of American popular music; he knew what had been happening in jazz and R&B as big bands shrank to small combos and "jump blues" evolved into R&B and that evolved into rock'n'roll. He knew that Nat "King" Cole had been beaten up by the same White Citizens Council that made that statement and that the music industry was rife with naked racism—the great *Billboard* editor Paul Ackerman, a gentlemanly Southerner, was receiving complaints about "nigger music" because he refused to suppress or denounce the new styles and its crossover appeal to White audiences.

At a moment of tremendous social and music importance, when he could have made a difference, Sinatra wasn't even silent. He actively joined with a batch of liars who had in part made their living for decades off swiping Black styles to which the bulk of the American public was denied access. In the end, it was left to Cole's wife, Maria, to make the only statement to the House subcommittee that accurately portrayed the new music as a direct development of persistent tendencies in the music of Black America.

I doubt if very many of his sycophants are conscious of this history—one of the biggest, the unctuous New York disc jockey Jonathan Schwartz, who does a weekly all-Sinatra program, surely knows, since his father, songwriter Arthur, was ASCAP's lead fabricator—but to omit a discussion of Sinatra's relation to the powers-that-be in the music world at the time of the most momentous change of his life is to efface his real history. I know that in recent years many rock critics have taken up the Sinatra banner, which I believe they've done because they want to show that they know it's not just about guys who write their own songs and that they understand that American pop music had a beauteous history before Elvis and Ray Charles and Ruth Brown. That's fine with me.

But I assure you that when James Brown, a titan who humbles Sinatra (who was not a writer or a bandleader or an instrumentalist at all, let alone a great one, as James is), dies, his obituaries will focus as much or more on his prison record as on his mind-bogglingly diverse contributions to music. I know that if Chuck D (God forbid) got hit by a car tomorrow, his obits would mention Farrakhan at least as prominently as the Bomb Squad. I know that Keith Richards's life will be seen, in most obituaries, through the lens of his addictions. Ike Turner's immense talents as musician, arranger, talent scout, and record producer will probably be entirely ignored in favor of accounts of his abuse of women. And so, if fair's fair, then let's remember the real Frank Sinatra, who stood up for hoodlums, took great pleasure in performing in the casinos where they laundered their drug profits, belittled women and bullied the press, and, oh by the way, once made an album called *In the Wee Small Hours*, that is one of the greatest ever recorded.

May you live one hundred years and may the last voice you hear be Snoop Doggy Dogg's.

THIS MACHINE KILLS
PRECONCEPTIONS

—ADDICTED TO NOISE, JUNE 1998

"Does Whitman, Sandburg, or Pushkin, either one, actually talk in the lingo, brogue, and ways of talking through of the kinds and breeds of the working people I've met and dealt with?

And the only answer I can say is, no . . . They praise, describe, they pay their thanks and their tributes to my people, but not in words my kind of people think.

So I've got to keep plugging away."

—**Woody Guthrie, August 5, 1947**

One afternoon in the early 1950s, Fred Hellerman of the Weavers and Harold Leventhal, that group's manager, went to visit their friend Woody Guthrie.

Guthrie was hospitalized because of Huntington's disease, the inherited neurological disorder whose symptoms gave him what were then thought to be psychiatric problems. "Aw, don't worry about me none," Woody told them. "I'm worried about how are you boys doing out there." It was the height of McCarthyism, so the question had a special intensity, folk music being a passion of the left, then as now.

"Why, we're fine. But we're worried about you," Fred replied.

"Naw, I'm way better off 'n you," Woody insisted.

"How do you figure that?"

"Well, out there, if you guys say you're communists, they'll put you in jail," Woody replied. "But in here, if I say I'm a communist, they say, 'Argh! Just another nut.'"

Hellerman told me that story in the course of speculating on what might have become of Woody if he'd stayed healthy. Woody composed dozens of famous songs, told barrels of oft-repeated tales, wrote one important book and a couple of minor ones, inspired a generation of singer-songwriters and urban folkies, and left behind a huge archive that is only being sorted out now. All that, and his creative life basically ended after about 1952, when the Huntington's symptoms became so bad that he was more or less permanently hospitalized. That was the year Woody Guthrie turned forty.

If Woody Guthrie had been healthy, he would have been more famous in the early '50s, when the Weavers first hit with "This Land Is Your Land." Not much later, he'd also have been blacklisted, perhaps even have been sent to jail for contempt of Congress like Pete Seeger. As one of the first people who studied the Guthrie archives (in the course of editing the 1989 Guthrie book, *Pastures of Plenty*), I find it virtually inconceivable that Woody could have collaborated with the "anticommunists," who actually included every crypto-fascist, bedrock racist and anti-Semite in Congress and its environs. In the first place, Woody wouldn't have had much incentive to rat out his comrades: he didn't care that much about his "career," which then consisted mostly of playing for the few unions that hadn't purged their Reds, and he had far too great a sense of personal honor, and anyhow, the greatest of all his social commitments was opposition to fascism, foreign and native. Beyond that, becoming a fink was a lonely man's game. Communism in New York—and New York was where Woody associated with communists—was a kind of community. If Woody Guthrie believed in anything, it was community, the power and solace of groups of people, pulling together. That was what he found compelling in the Dust Bowl migration and in the unions, in the mobilization for World War II, and the drive to create a "People's Songs" movement when the war ended.

If Woody had lived, he'd soon have been confronted with the most vital American issue of all: race, in the form of the budding civil rights movement. No doubt, he would have written songs to celebrate and support the bravery of Rosa Parks in Montgomery and high school kids in Birmingham, to mourn the murder of Jimmie Lee Jackson by troopers in Selma, and to commemorate the marchers who strode across the Edmund Pettus Bridge in the wake of Jackson's death.

I say this with confidence because some of those kinds of songs did get written, and the people who wrote them—Bob Dylan with "Only a Pawn in Their Game" and "Oxford Town," Phil Ochs in "Here's to the State of Mississippi," Richard Fariña with "Birmingham Sunday," and lots more obscure—considered themselves "Woody's children." Dylan, the greatest of them, even wrote Woody a song on his first album.

But of course, few of "Woody's children" and certainly none of the best of them stuck with the "pure" folk music—the acoustic guitars and songs taken from either the Anglo-Celtic ballad tradition or the lore of labor unions and other struggles, sung gently either in grad-school English or some affected "authentic" regional accent, at a pace and to a tempo that ensured that the words stayed in front and the beat, if there was any, led to nothing more than hand-clapping. All this gave way in short order to electric guitars and ferocious backbeats, songs written out of personal experience, late night rendezvouses with an often-fraudulent destiny, songs about the struggle of inner life with infrequent referents to the material world, let alone to the palpable injustices it contains.

If Woody Guthrie had stayed healthy, he might have hated this stuff; he might have been standing next to Seeger and Alan Lomax when they tried to cut off the power to Dylan's electric show at Newport in 1965, and he might have taken the ax out of Pete's hand and actually used it. Woody could be pretty doctrinaire; he hated jukeboxes because he thought they put "real" musicians out of work, and he mistrusted the pop music of the '40s and early '50s as deeply as that segregated, snobbish stuff deserved to be mistrusted.

I'm not so sure that response is the only possibility though, and in fact, with the release of *Mermaid Avenue*, the new album by Billy Bragg and

Wilco, I'm starting to think that if any of the older folkies could have had a positive response to the emergence of folk-rock, Woody would have been the man.

Mermaid Avenue consists of fifteen songs drawn from the Guthrie archives. Like most of the roughly one thousand songs contained there, these songs consist only of lyrics; Woody either had the music in his head or planned to locate a traditional tune that would fit their meter. There is every kind of song there, from stuff Woody took right out of the headlines and back pages of the newspapers to meditations on the fate of the universe, comic pieces about his connection to American history to statements about the totality of his love for his wife and kids, faux English ballads to "supersonic boogies." Car songs, children's songs, nonsense songs, songs meant to cure the world of what ails it, and songs where Woody Guthrie himself seems on the verge of being crushed by that very ailment. Songs that are plain junk, and songs that are among the best things he ever wrote. (In fact, one of the few that leaked out over the years from this pile was "Deportee," which is definitely top ten among his works.)

We can't really know why these songs weren't ever recorded or taught to someone who could teach their intended tunes to us. Woody didn't get to record very much (although the archival material taken from the Folkways archives is on its third volume, with another to come, and with no sign that it's thinned out), and he sang live mostly at union rallies and other political gatherings. That meant he had little occasion to sing something like the yearning "California Stars," which feels like something Don Henley should have done, or "Way Over Yonder in the Minor Key," which is a story weird enough to be an outtake from *The Basement Tapes* or *Nebraska*. Or "Christ for President," which is a proposition weird and detailed enough to be an outtake from *Never Mind the Bollocks* or *London Calling*.

Bringing It All Back Home and the Byrds' *Mr. Tambourine Man* might have liberated this material, let Woody Guthrie's image blossom into one of America's undeniable great humanist artists, rather than remaining a stick figure of left-wing agitprop, which is how he's usually seen.

Mermaid Avenue explodes that old folkie image, while at the same time proving how genuinely prophetic Guthrie's social vision truly was: "She

Came Along to Me," a metric journal entry, is probably the best popular song about the power of feminism and the possibility of human collective action ever written. (I'm in the market for all the alternatives you'd like to submit.) "Hoodoo Voodoo" is a rock'n'roll rave-up ahead of its time, and "At My Window Sad and Lonely" and "Hesitating Beauty" could have come from the Dylan of "Boots of Spanish Leather" and "Don't Think Twice," which is to say, the Dylan that inspired the confessional singer-songwriters like Joni Mitchell and James Taylor.

I don't know if anyone would ever have associated "those" songs with Woody Guthrie's influence—although I suppose Bob Dylan might have. "Song to Woody" addresses Woody not as a committed protest songwriter, but as a ramblin' hobo. But it also honors him as an existential visionary:

> *Hey, hey, Woody Guthrie, I wrote you a song*
> *'Bout a funny old world that's a-comin' along*
> *Seems it's sick an' it's hungry, it's tired an' it's torn*
> *It looks like it's a-dyin' and it's hardly been born*

Without *Mermaid Avenue* and its inspired old-new songs, those words seem like just Dylan's odd take on Guthrie. With these songs ringing in your ears, they seem to speak the simple truth.

I wondered for weeks while listening to this music almost obsessively where Woody's vision left off and those of Bragg and Wilco's Jeff Tweedy and Jay Bennett (whose guitar playing here seems to encompass the whole history of blues-based rock'n'roll) began. "She Came Along to Me" rides along on Bennett's Harrison-like guitar breaks, Tweedy's vocal on "Sad and Lonely" has the cracked desolation of Dylan's best love songs, and the drolleries of "Walt Whitman's Niece" and "I Guess I Planted" rock right out of Dylan and the Hawks, the Byrds. I could probably give you a specific contemporary rock reference point for every arrangement that's here. But was that music implicit in Woody's words, or was it just the information in Bragg's and Wilco's heads that made them envision it this way?

It's only now, trying to explain it to myself, that I realize it doesn't matter. What makes this music work is the collaboration—its triumph is that you can't tell where Woody leaves off and Billy and the boys begin. The

Woody Guthrie I love, the one that helped inspire me like so many thousands of others to try to live a life steeped in justice, equality, and music, believed in the magic that happens when people embrace one another in loving kindness. Even in his horniest song here, "Ingrid Bergman," what happens when Woody gets the girl is this:

If you'll walk across my camera,
I will flash the world your story / I will pay you more than money, Ingrid
*   Bergman*

Not with nickels, dimes or quarters,
But with happy sons and daughters, / And they'll sing around Stromboli,
*   Ingrid Bergman*

You don't have to share Woody's passion for Bergman as the most desirable movie star ever (although as it happens, I do) to see in those words a prayer, and to hear in the way that Billy Bragg sings those words, that prayer is realized. Records as miraculous as *Mermaid Avenue* bring all such dreams to life, by granting a sense of harmony to what had seemed discordant. Never again will Woody Guthrie seem like just some crackpot commie politician, an apostle of agitprop with no interest in art. Here, his artistic stature is not so much restored, as discovered. But that's not all. These songs don't just tell us a lot more about who Woody Guthrie is and what legacies he left us; in the end, they fill in the blanks in the eternal pursuit of the history of ourselves.

STRANGE FRUIT

"Woe, woe unto the false prophet that prophesies out of his own heart. This is a sin against the Lord. We must understand this. We must get ourselves together soon because there will be nothing left."

—Albert Ayler, liner notes to *New Grass*

"Jazz has had a peculiar history, another peculiar institution, if you will. At just the moment when it assumed the mantle of the most creative music in this society, the whole electronic world erupted, rock and radio gave birth to the amazing amalgam of poetry and music with which we have been blessed these past few years, and jazz seemed to diminish, somehow . . . What was really happening was that the centers of gravity, the major forces of thrust in jazz were changing. The concepts were shifting around; the very purpose of jazz's existence was being redefined."

—Ralph J. Gleason, "The Death of Albert Ayler"

A great new sound reaches us, always, as a miraculous gift. Yet this miracle need not be new; it need not even be unfamiliar, though this is extremely difficult to imagine, let alone appreciate, in a culture sapped from so many decades of being slugged with the shock of the new.

Two recent events reminded me of this. The first time, what I heard was literally nothing. My daughter and I, with four dogs between us, had driven to extreme northern New Hampshire, just south of the Quebec border, to spend a week hiking logging roads and reading beside a deep cold lake. I brought very little music with me, just a small packet of CDs, and left those in the car the whole time. We were about a mile up the first trail when I stopped and said, "Listen." "What?" said Sasha. "Nothing," I replied. "There's nothing to hear." She said she could hear some leaves rustling and a few insects but I couldn't and when I got back to my own backyard a week later, the backyard around midnight sounded like the subway at rush hour. In urban areas, even the insects call to one another at a much higher volume, or in greater numbers. Maybe they have to. Out in the forest, though, even a forest as brutally cut over as this one, something much closer to silence can be discovered.

If you live my life, with the central activities being listening and talking from the moment you arise until you fall in bed, silence is to be cherished. I don't mean that I would welcome becoming deaf. Deafness is not silence. Silence, as I relearned in that instant in the woods, is not nothing, but something deeper. Musicians know this much better than mere professional listeners, and the best of them use it to great and sometimes even cosmic effect—a profound respect for silence is at the heart of the greatest music made by Miles Davis, and Mahler and, for that matter, Frank Zappa and Bruce Springsteen.

A little before we left on vacation, my friend and colleague John Floyd and I were discussing, via email, great wads of noise we knew and loved (or loathed) and I mentioned that, in many ways, my relative lack of interest in rock's great dissonants came from an early immersion in free jazz—the kind of music the MC5 and John Sinclair force-fed Motor City heavy music maniacs by performing regularly with the likes of Sun Ra and His Solar-Myth Arkestra and Joseph Jarman, Leo Smith, Roscoe Mitchell, and others from Chicago's Association for the Advancement of Creative Musicians (AACM). Thirty years ago, I meant, I knew this music, or at least a significant stream of it as well as I knew Bonzo Dog or the Kinks or "Let It All Hang Out" or "Hey Girl"—that is, ranked somewhere between a passion and a matter of curiosity. In the face of that, most punk and metal screamers strike me as just . . . having a lot they need to listen to.

It was the ambition of some of the greatest musicians of my era in

Detroit—the MC5, the Stooges, the rising P-Funk mob, and, I think, even Ted Nugent—to forge a grand synthesis out of all such sounds—jazz, soul, rock, nature. I mentioned to Floyd that I thought that the album that came closest, ever, to achieving that synthesis was Albert Ayler's *New Grass*. "But," I added, in one of those grand pronouncements no one, let alone a critic, should ever make, "the prejudice against it is enormous. Jazzers describe it all the time as the worst jazz album ever made. So it'll never get reissued. And my LP copy is old and scratchy and, anyhow, it has a terrible mix."

Barely a week went by before John Floyd sent back a message that he had been in New Orleans, where he came upon a Japanese reissue of *New Grass*. It's a 20-bit remaster from MCA Japan; John paid $29.95 at Tower NO and I paid $27.95 for the copy I located a few days later at Virgin in Times Square. It was a pure bargain.

John immediately praised it as one of the best albums he had ever heard. He grasped the parameters of Ayler's ambitious synthesis instantly, not only because he is so perspicacious about music, but also because, if you're mostly a blues-rock-funk-punk-noise-etc. guy, what *New Grass*, recorded in September 1969 (a month before *Kick Out the Jams*, a year before *In a Silent Way*), sounds like, mostly, is the future, which is to say, right now.

New Grass opens with Ayler screeing and scrawing on his tenor sax, as those who'd heard his earlier jazz albums would have expected; then he delivers the recitation, whose central message appears at the top of this piece, accompanied by what amounts to a free jazz chamber group. Ayler is deathly serious about this—he really believes, as a musician recording in 1968 should have believed, that the sounds he is about to make illumine a pathway toward human liberation.

But when the second track, "New Generation," begins, the screes and scraws have vanished. Instead, a honking R&B sax riff, followed by bass and drums straight out of the James Brown book and classic Stax/Volt horns, shock you with something that's not new but absolutely as familiar as it is out of context. When the singers coming in, singing a basic set of gospel-soul lyrics that conflate the worldly with the spiritual, the yearnings of the flesh with the yearnings of the heart. Rose Marie McCoy and Mary Parks aren't the Sweet Inspirations, but they aren't bad at all, and the message they deliver is about Albert Ayler's truest rebellion, not so much because of the words they sing ("It's a new generation moving on down the line / It's a new generation grooving it all the time"), but again, because of the context. Albert Ayler is clearly taking a side and the side he's taking is that of pop music. "Sun Watcher," the third track, has a bass line swiped straight off a Dyke and the Blazers record.

One of the best things about the MCA remaster is the way it emphasizes this pop feeling, without doing anything to detract from the free jazz blowing (and beats) that are also all over the place. The Japanese edition blends the voices with drums and horns to create something that sounds even more like a soul record. Producer Bob Thiele's original soundscape was too spacious and clattering; it sounded like a jazz guy condescending to tinker with rock in search of a payday. To me, Ayler's music never sounded like that for a single bar, although you can read in any number of jazz histories, particularly the English ones, that Ayler was "encouraged by a record company" to make such records as this. But that's silly. Thiele and his Impulse label didn't record any other artists exploring jazz-rock-soul fusion.

Of course, it is not appropriate for a practitioner of an Art Music to have come over to rock and soul out of passion. In the *Rolling Stone Jazz Record Guide*, the very astute Bob Blumenthal calls *New Grass* "disturbing," and declares that "Ayler's true motivations . . . are as clouded as the circumstances that led to his being found in the East River (tied, according to some accounts, to a jukebox)."

There you have it. The ultimate paranoid jazz parable for what comes from "selling out." Ayler did disappear in 1970 and his body was dredged out of the East River, though the circumstances of his death were more likely despondency over the state of his life and career than a sellout. As Gleason pointed out in his obituary, free jazzers like Ayler, Archie Shepp, and Cecil Taylor couldn't get gigs at the Monterey Jazz Festival, amongst many other places where their inferiors made a whole lot more cash than Ayler could have hoped to glean from making *New Grass* and its successor, *The New Wave in Jazz*.

If you really want to grasp what Albert Ayler's last desperate days were like, read the 1962 James Baldwin novel, *Another Country*. Its central character, a jazzman, kills himself, but the reasons have absolutely nothing to do with the music; the music is the purest thing in his life. There is absolutely no evidence—there is certainly none in the music—that Albert Ayler hated himself for the music he had made.

It's just as likely that it kept him alive as that it killed him. But we don't want to hear that about Albert Ayler any more than we want to hear it about Kurt Cobain. Nevertheless, what his friend and collaborator, trumpeter Don Cherry, told Ben Sidran about him remains true: "Albert Ayler was one of those persons that really had—and to the end—there was something that he had to do and his life was dedicated to doing it. And when you heard his sound, it would make you feel you were in the church. It was real what we call gospel sound, but he was a jazz player."

I have no idea which records Cherry was thinking of specifically when he said that—he goes on to talk about their first recording session, in Copenhagen in 1962 with Cecil Taylor—but there is probably no better way to define where the magnificence of New Grass comes from. It's probably also the single biggest thing that jazz-rock fusion of the '70s missed. Even the Miles Davis electric recordings don't come this close to the pure funk of street level Pentecostalism and, without that, no form of rock can mean much. Ayler also understood song form far better than any other free jazz writer of whom I am aware.

For about ten years, I didn't have a copy of New Grass. Then the sound of New Grass, especially "New Generation," with its lines about "a new generation / Screaming it loud and clear," somehow re-insinuated itself into my head. On a trip to Maine in 1995, I found a battered LP in a Portland used record store, so my recollections of it are fresh. Nevertheless, the return of this old friend is a magnificent gift, and I recommend it to you as highly as I know how. I do not think it is very likely that the people currently running the Impulse reissue series in America will put it out here—I remember asking when Ayler's Live at the Village Vanguard came out on CD a few years ago and getting back the sort of blank stare you always get when someone thinks you ought to be locked up.

Which I am perfectly willing to be if I can take music this glorious with me.

Speaking of songs that insinuate themselves in your head, Eric Predoehl, their liberator, is now offering a complete copy of the 1963–1966 FBI files of the Bureau's investigation of "Louie Louie." I read this stuff and was inspired to write a book, if only to show how fucking stupid about culture (amongst many other things) the government actually is. Eric, who got the files in the course of researching his documentary film *The Meaning of Louie*, will send you the file for $25. Visit his great "Louie"-oriented web page: https://www.louielouie.net/blog/?page_id=2807. Neither the file nor the site has the "real" lyrics to "Louie Louie," but the file has the dirty ones. Thank you, J. Edgar.

AND THE LAW WON

—ADDICTED TO NOISE, DECEMBER 1998

A small confession: I have never downloaded an MP3 file. There are two reasons, one of which will be eliminated shortly, when I acquire a hundred-odd additional megs of RAM and about fifteen more gigs of hard drive. But even then, I have my doubts. There are, at a guess, four hundred CDs sitting here in various states of being listened to—most awaiting their first play. I would a lot rather go through the Impulse box set of the John Coltrane Quartet a second time, or finally get around to playing that disc of the Searchers' greatest hits, or devote more time to figuring out Goodie Mob and Kelly Willis.

This doesn't mean I've never heard MP3s. In the stack are three or four CDs burned for me by friends of material available on the net. I am quite sure I am in deep violation of the copyright act by possessing these, and if the RIAA's Hilary Rosen would like to send her pet FBI agents over to the house, maybe we could discuss this latest act of criminal behavior. Hell, in *Rock & Rap Confidential*, we run our record reviews under the heading "This Month's Home Taping Tips," so I'm sure to be jailed someday for advocating the violation of this most important of all music-related laws anyhow.

Of course, almost nobody in the MP3 dispute understands the copyright law. That'd be the last thing the record companies as represented by their RIAA lobbyists and enforcement agents would want you to do. To understand the copyright act, anyhow, you have to know some history, which means someone would have to teach it to you, which is probably already illegal or soon will be.

As a dedicated miscreant, when copyright issues come up among the sophisticates who work in the music industry, I like to pose a simple question: "When did the first copyright act applying to music become law?" The answer is 1909. Before that, all musicians starved to death.

They didn't? Well, then, there must be some other ways for musicians to make a living. As a matter of fact, the vast majority of people who make music for a living, in America as in the rest of the world, do not own any copyrights, and the vast majority of those who do derive no significant part of their income from them. You can copyright a song by sending about ten bucks and a cassette of the song and some forms to the appropriate office in Washington, D.C. It doesn't mean anyone's gonna pay to hear it, though.

You could get into worse trouble if you actually made a record for one of the FBI's record companies. Almost certainly, you wouldn't own a copyright then. You might, if you had a great negotiating team, still own part of the copyrights for your songs. Maybe not. You would certainly not own the copyright to your recordings. The record companies own those, and pay you a slim percentage of whatever portion of the proceeds they admit to receiving. You can audit them periodically, but not at the pressing plant.

If you doubt me, take a look at any of the official RIAA record company albums you own—or if you don't own, go to the record store and look. Either way, a magnifying glass will be a big help. I keep one on my desk so I can decipher dates and credits, and I suppose that, sooner or later, CD players will come with them as spare parts, kind of the way they give you cables and radiation warnings now.

Before 1909, there was hardly any copyright "enforcement" in America when it came to anything—music, books, newspapers, or magazines. In Article I, Section 8 of the Constitution (the world's slipperiest document, as even Arkansas crooks now know), Congress is empowered "to promote the Progress of Science and useful Arts, by securing for limited Times to Authors and Inventors the exclusive Right to their respective Writings and Discoveries." As music is generally regarded in our society as useless, it's no surprise it took so long to come under legal control.

But even sixty-five years after the Constitution was written (on one of Ken Starr's parchment legal pads, while he was interrogating a slave impregnated by Thomas Jefferson, I think), the United States honored no international copyright conventions. When Charles Dickens arrived for his first American tour in early 1842, he engaged in obsessive lobbying to get the U.S. to recognize such rights. At his first big gig, a dinner in Boston, he made a speech in which he insisted that recognizing foreign authors' copyrights was crucial to America someday becoming a true civilization, in which every writer could aspire to the Dickens condition (enormous wealth and fame, copyright or no copyright), or words to that effect.

The next day newspapers screamed that Dickens had been guilty of bad taste and charged that he had "created huge dissonance where all else was triumphant unison," wrote Dickens biographer Edgar Johnson. Marilyn Manson–like, Dickens refused to shut up. A week later, in Hartford, where he was willing to visit despite the absence of an NFL franchise, he smarted off by saying, "I would beg leave to whisper in your ear two words, International Copyright."

Fred Kaplan, a more contemporary Dickens biographer, outlined the Dickens position, and its antithesis: "He argued that literature was property to be protected by rules of equity and that a native American literature could flourish best in circumstances that encouraged American publishers to pay American authors rather than have foreign authors free. The opposition maintained that literature, like all imaginative creations, should not be regulated by law and commerce, that undercapitalized nations, without public libraries, needed inexpensive access to ideas and entertainment that they could not generate themselves or afford to purchase at high rates, and that the free availability to publishers of an author's works did more to advance his reputation and long-term earnings than the restricted circulation created by the higher price of books on which a copyright royalty was paid. American opinion, across every interest group, including authors, was divided . . ."

You can see why the RIAA wouldn't want American schoolkids taught stuff like that. A world in which things like music are not property does not exist and should not be imagined. Otherwise, the singers and musicians might travel in limousines and the guys who distribute their records might be traveling around in beat-up vans with no heat and leaky radiators. Can't have that.

Anyhow, it took a while, but the Dickens side won. Songs became property and when they did, all that was sonic melted into air, the chairs got up and danced the boogaloo, and the songwriters (like most other creators) started losing more to copyright than they generally gain from it. As you will recall, the Constitution provided protection to "Authors." (The Inventors stuff is mostly about patents, and I'm already confusing you enough.) But copyrights today are not owned by Authors—especially not music copyrights. Or to look at it another way, the flesh and blood people who used to control their songs as best they could have been replaced in the process by the fictious people called corporations. (You thought I was kidding about the chairs, too, right?)

The best split a songwriter gets from a publisher—other than himself— is 50/50. So half that copyright money already goes to corporations. Which ones? When MCA/Seagram merged with Polygram, it became not only the world's largest record company, but also the world's largest music publisher. All the other big record companies also have publishing firms. All of them also do their best to strong-arm young acts who want record contracts into giving up the "publishing half" of their tunes to those publishing firms. Since this has been going on for at least fifty years, and is common knowledge to anyone interested in getting a record deal, I don't suppose the RIAA can have me arrested for revealing such proprietary information here. Or even for remarking that since the copyright in the recordings is held by the record company, the Authors of the performances protected by the copyright law revision in 1976 get shafted exactly the same way—in fact, their situation isn't any better than it was in 1975.

This is why it always gives me such a laugh when Rosen and other industry propagandists start bellyaching about how stuff like MP3—like cassette tapes and DAT before it—is gonna ruin their ability to protect creators. Creators are not protected in the music industry. They are usually raped. The notion that the record industry, of all institutions, stands for the fair payment of people who do creative work is so blindingly false that you have to laugh.

For instance, how is it that when they want to, the record companies can sell you twelve CDs for a dollar (or is it a penny)? They do this through the record clubs—which they happen to own. They are able to do it because they don't pay the artists. Hell, they usually manage to stiff the poor songwriters whose songs they "don't" own—75 percent of the compulsory royalty rate was the standard in the ancient (published 1979) music biz guidebook on my desk at the moment. Artist royalties are a fraction of that—and of course, the giveaways don't count at all, because that comes under the "free goods" exclusion in the standard contract. Record clubs sometimes sell millions of records. The corporations make "all" that money. The creators make none of it. I think, personally, that when the FBI comes knockin', I'm going to ask that they investigate stuff like that.

Fact is, we don't need no stinkin' record companies. There was music for approximately one hundred centuries before the first record company came along. It is one of the cultural universals—in no place on the planet that I have been able to find is there no music. In only a comparatively few places is the music distributed by means of record companies that have the fictitious legal status of "creator." Artists themselves often believe that their world would crumble if they didn't have copyright protection. But they don't know—since history is illegal—that their creative forebears believed passionately that there were other, better ways to organize things. We could, if we wanted to, use the internet to make music—a human necessity—available to everyone with a computer, which would be a start to making it available to everyone. In order to do this, we would have to guarantee musicians a decent, maybe even a high, standard of living. In order to do that, we would have to do the same for everyone else.

The resources are there to do it. There are empty buildings in the very places where people don't have housing. There is food rotting in the very nations where people are starving (including the United States). Old computers get tossed in the attic instead of being upgraded, or cannibalized, and recirculated. We could do it. We'd have to get rid of stuff like the copyright laws and the RIAA and the FBI. But we could do it. And you know what? The existence of the internet, at its finest, indicates that we "want" to do it. Maybe not you—but me, and the kid who will break the code on the RIAA's Official Expensive MP3 Files (dumbest idea since DivX), and a ton of others. In some ways, we're already doing it. I'm sure it will gross out a lot of people, but there are those of us who are up here in cyberspace for something other than the chances to be bombarded with ads.

Here's the coolest part, though. If we do do something like that, someday, artists—all of them, not just the thin slice that runs from Mick Jagger to the Goo Goo Dolls—would be one hell of a lot better off. They might not travel in limousines. But I bet we could fix up those vans.

NO HIDING PLACE

—OXFORD AMERICAN, SEPTEMBER 1999;
DAVE MARSH AND DANIEL WOLFF

America's most powerful singer and songwriter is over seventy years old and lives quietly in Birmingham, Alabama. Her daily life centers on her family, her church, and her Deep South community, which she, unlike almost all her contemporaries from the golden age of gospel—Mahalia Jackson, Sam Cooke, James Cleveland—probably never left.

Perhaps she's simply husbanding her energy for better purposes, in the manner of her nearest regional and demographic analogue, Eudora Welty. Maybe she long ago gave up on getting an honest count—from record companies or reporters or, for that matter, history. Maybe Dorothy Love Coates just lives in a place where none of this matters. Listening to her sing, in a voice that still has the tremendous dramatic force of her youth, you could believe it might actually be that simple. Or maybe it's even simpler than that. Maybe, as Coates tells us in the words of one of her most powerful songs: "I've got Jee-ee-sus, and that's enough!"

By Coates's definition, that's a lot. In her music, the African American tradition of the social gospel comes to full, fierce life. Her pursuit of justice has remained consistent and scathing over the last half century. Appropriately enough, when she did surface recently—in the movie *Beloved*—she led a chorus of local women trying to exorcise the ghost of slavery through song. That is one way to summarize her life's work: a gospel warrior trying to win souls for Jesus and, at the same time, right some of history's wrongs.

As she says in another of her greatest records:

I went to the rock to hide my face
But the rock cried out, "No hiding place down here!"

Coates was twenty-three in 1951, when her group, the Gospel Harmonettes, signed with Art Rupe's Los Angeles–based Specialty Records. She was twenty-seven when Rosa Parks was arrested in Montgomery and the subsequent boycott of that city's bus system began a new, militant phase of the Civil Rights Movement. The next year, the NAACP was banned in her native state of Alabama. Meanwhile, Mahalia Jackson and Roberta Martin and the great quartets like the Dixie Hummingbirds and the Soul Stirrers toured the country, separate and unequal. This was a kind of true underground music world, composed of church rallies—or "programs"—known only to the faithful, and "hit" records played on a select few radio stations, surfacing mostly after being plundered by pop, rock, and r&b acts.

The great majority of soul and r&b stars were church trained, or at least church-experienced. Singers like Lou Rawls, Wilson Pickett, and Aretha Franklin were minor gospel stars; Sam Cooke was a major one. The list is so long that it would be easier to name the postwar Black singers who didn't have a gospel background. "How much of r&b comes from gospel?" an interviewer once asked Bobby Womack, who has dwelt in both worlds. "All of it," he replied without hesitation—or much exaggeration.

This most dynamic of all forms of American music attracted a strong cult following among knowledgeable nonbelievers, including such important early recording impresarios as John Hammond and Jerry Wexler. Nevertheless, as Womack and dozens of others learned, if you wanted to make some dough in this life, gospel was not the place to do it. The hours and living conditions were ridiculously bad, the circle of acclaim narrow, and mammon beckoned at every turn. Even those with the tremendous level of commitment necessary to stay in the gospel world found their work crossing over . . . without them.

Coates's songs were the basis for a number of secular hits. The best context for listening to her gospel standard, "(You Can't Hurry God) He's Right on Time," is alongside the Supreme Court's 1954 *Brown v. Board of Education* decision and the incredible upsurge in gospel-based r&b that began at the same time. Except you're liable to find that the song won't stay in that context. Dorothy begins, "You can't hurry God," and as the Harmonettes answer, "You just have to wait," we've jumped from 1954 to 1966, from the Supreme Court to the Supremes. The difference in the gospel song and its love child are striking. Holland, Dozier, and Holland wrote the #1 hit "You Can't Hurry Love" on the other side of the major, nonviolent civil rights demonstrations.

Motown's calculated sound was trying to bring us together—on the dance floor, anyway—with a strategy that might best be summed up by a line from the song: "It's a game of give and take." Diana Ross's slinky whisper is hanging on for the possibility of love. The broad-shouldered, stern-faced Coates is waiting on—and, with a shout, working toward—justice. With the Civil Rights Movement still before her, she's asking that old question: Do the Christian God and the African American church pacify or inspire? The gospel song is about patience weighed against activism, acceptance as opposed to all-out defiance. And the greatness of "He's Right on Time" is that it doesn't resolve the contradictions, but holds them on both shoulders, like wings, and announces that He *will* come, and in the meantime, justice is something we have to work toward.

It's no coincidence that the golden age of gospel corresponds to the golden age of the Civil Rights Movement. The power of the churches that produced the gospel singers and their ideas powered the Movement, too, uniting the Black community and reaching out beyond that community to White people of all faiths. Coates's home church is Birmingham's Sixteenth Street Baptist, where, on a bloody Sunday thirty-six years ago this autumn, a bomb blew four little girls into bits and Civil Rights mythology. Sixteenth Street Baptist was chosen for the bombing because it was a kind of ground zero for the Birmingham movement, just as the Birmingham movement was a kind of ground zero for the Civil Rights struggle as a whole, an Omaha Beach where the forces of the enemy finally began their retreat. Of all the musicians and singers, pop and gospel, who got involved in the Movement (and there were a great many), Coates wrote the most and the best songs and may well have sung at more Civil Rights meetings than anyone else.

The greatest recordings of Dorothy Love Coates and the Gospel Harmonettes evoke the passion, conviction, fear, and sorrow of that era—and of a timeless struggle for heavenly justice here on earth.

Listen to her best-known songs, and you get a picture of exactly what that struggle entails. In "I Won't Let Go," it's a shouted list: "Working, toiling, praying, hoping, trusting, believing, waiting, watching." The depth of the commitment is in the very title of "Ninety-Nine and a Half Won't Do" (which is the basis for Wilson Pickett's soul hit of the same name). A couplet from "He's Right on Time" provides an overview:

I don't know how or when He'll come
But don't let Him catch you with your work undone!

The social gospel is not only the great lost cord that knits together the New Deal and the Salvation Army, the Civil Rights and antiwar movements. It also helps illuminate the full impact of gospel music on the world of rock and r&b. That impact may *seem* purely stylistic, because its most obvious manifestations are. There's clearly a direct line, for instance, between gospel and the kinds of quartet harmony that drive group singing from doowop to the Beatles to Boyz II Men. At this year's Rock and Roll Hall of Fame ceremonies, Eric Clapton and others drew out the connections between their guitar playing and that of such gospel-derived players as the new inductees Pops Staples and Curtis Mayfield. The indelible high "woo" that can be traced from Little Richard to Paul McCartney to heavy metal and beyond stems directly from the leaps made by the great Marion Williams of the Clara Ward Singers. Sam Cooke's raspy sweetness, which made its way to Rod Stewart and D'Angelo, maybe even to Lauryn Hill, had its origins in Cooke's gospel group, the Soul Stirrers, and its original lead singer, R. H. Harris. Then there are all those songs, from "Mystery Train" and "Stand by Me" to "I Believe I Can Fly," that have gospel origins.

Coates's extraordinarily concise and moving songwriting ability is inspired by the work of Memphis minister William Herbert Brewster. Author of "How I Got Over" and "Move On Up a Little Higher" and a community organizer in the days before Dr. King—when, in Brewster's words, "there

were things that were almost dangerous to say, but you could sing it"—
Brewster was pastor of East Trigg Baptist, one of the churches where young
Elvis Presley studied the ecstatic moves of his gospel heroes.

It may be that this performance quality had the greatest effect on early
rock 'n' roll: moments of ecstasy—running the aisles, knee drops, the rend-
ing of garments, leaps past all good judgment into true conviction—that
eclipse any benchmarks of popular stagecraft, whether James Brown or Iggy
Pop or P-Funk or, for that matter, Kirk Franklin.

Less often acknowledged are the other ways in which gospel has left
its signature. The most crucial lies in its vision of community. In his book
A Change Is Gonna Come, Craig Werner traces that gospel impulse to Bruce
Springsteen's "reason to believe" (in his case, most often called the power of
rock 'n' roll) and the hope of a better tomorrow that runs through the work
of artists like Public Enemy, Tupac, and Wyclef Jean.

This vision of social change may not be something you usually associate with gospel singers, since that style grew up in the Black Pentecostal
Church. Its goal of putting people in direct and ecstatic touch with God
would seem to jump past the importance of change in the material world.
But any study of Black churches will show that there's a strong gospel current from Dr. Martin Luther King Sr. and the Reverend C. L. Franklin, Aretha's father, to the Reverend Jesse Jackson; from the Golden Gate Quartet
to Kirk Franklin's avowedly "revolutionary" choir. For people ensnared first
as slaves and then as sharecroppers, religion might only be able to promise
salvation in the next life, but it had to offer the possibility of hope in this
one, too. That's why the Civil Rights Movement had to center itself in Black
churches. That's why it could.

Most White nonbelievers cannot, or will not, see this connection between gospel and rock because of that two-syllable word (which in Coates's
case sometimes extends to four syllables): *Jesus*. The irony is that many
rockers and rock fans are happy to ascribe the visionary spirit of their music
to Robert Johnson and his deal with the Devil. But a compact with Jesus,
made not at some midnight crossroads but just up the road in a church in
broad daylight, makes them cringe.

Why is it, then, that nonbelievers rarely have the same kind of trouble
with the Christian convictions of, say, Flannery O'Connor, Walker Percy, or

W. H. Auden? Their Catholicism and/or Anglicanism may strike many intellectuals as odd, but it's not alien. It is a mostly cool, somber, and meditative belief. On the other hand, the religious side of James Baldwin continues to alienate many of those same readers. Once a boy preacher in churches much like those where Coates has plied her trade, Baldwin espouses a faith that is hot, sweaty, flamboyant, and demonstrative. The whole point, with both Baldwin and Coates, is to transgress the mind/body dichotomy and bring the spirit out of the mind and into the house.

Because nonbelievers see this as simplistic (or simply too close for comfort), they often overlook the craft and intelligence involved. Both Coates and Baldwin use their belief in nuanced ways that go far beyond street-smart. The manner in which Coates reveals biblical tales of sin and redemption to be stories of oppression and liberation has its antecedents in the slave era. As James Cone demonstrates in his book-length analysis, *The Spirituals and the Blues*, there is "a complex world of *thought* underlying the slave songs." Both Coates and Baldwin interweave threads of gospel and unmistakable commentary on the community and the world, and Coates's sense of narrative is arguably even sharper and more pointed than Baldwin's. She is a master storyteller, remaking familiar narratives such as "Hide in the Rock" and "Strange Man" with great precision and insight. And no one has used the vernacular voice with such deft shadings since Zora Neale Hurston. Not being able to hear and respond to that degree of talent simply because of subject matter is as intellectually stunted as not appreciating Mark Twain because he writes about sweaty, smelly urchins.

If you can get past the word *Jesus*—its existence at all, let alone its centrality and the atomic emphasis Coates places on what she calls "the great Emancipator and the heart regulator"—you get to hear Dorothy Love Coates sing. She is not just a finely nuanced writer; she is a once-in-a-lifetime vocal performer. Her voice has a hint of gravel in it at all times, which makes it definitively earthy, whether she is whispering or shouting. And she does both, often. Like all the great gospel singers, she has an emotional range of expression next to which all other contemporary singers pale. But even when Coates just bears down and almost recites—so slowly that you don't miss a hint or an implication—her voice is a transfixing vehicle, sweet and sharp at the same time.

Once you're ready to hear her testify about Jesus in that voice, you come face to face with seminal classics like "That's Enough." And once you hear that song's mood of stout defiance, its almost military cadence, and Coates's biting portrayal of her role in society ("There's always somebody talking 'bout me / Really, I don't mind"), you realize that singers and songwriters like Bob Dylan have been listening long and hard to this tradition. Years before he became a putative Christian himself, Dylan wrote "Blowin' in the Wind" (based on the Negro spiritual "Many Thousands Gone," also known, not insignificantly, as "No More Auction Block"), and the Old Testament-based "When the Ship Comes In." Dylan—who, like Springsteen, has used Coates's niece Cleo Kennedy as a backup singer—has never stopped reaching for biblical language or looking for an elusive spirituality in his music, and his persona as the prophetic outcast owes much more to the church than to the blues. He'd be the first to point out to you the absurdity of that hoariest of clichés, "The devil has all the good songs." Whatever it was Satan gave Robert Johnson, it couldn't have been the conviction that "He takes care of my enemies when they try to get tough." And that's not a quote from Marilyn Manson; it's one of about a dozen good lines Coates tosses off in the course of "That's Enough."

The blues/gospel division has never been as absolute as critics would make it. Thomas Dorsey, who has been called the father of modern gospel, went back and forth between the divine and the secular. Before him, during the Second Great Awakening of the 1840s and '50s, the stringing together of prayer, Bible stories, and hymn tradition produced a new kind of religious song that one scholar has called "the distinctive badge of the camp meeting movement." Son House, Charlie Patton, Skip James—the great bluesmen who contributed so much to what we now call rock 'n' roll—all played God's music as well and, like Clara Ward or Aretha, passed back and forth across the dividing lines misrepresented as inviolable. In that context, calling Coates's amazing vocal delivery "bluesy" is to retreat to the familiar; you could as accurately call Tom Waits a gospel singer.

The solitary confessionals of despair and longing that mark songs like Dylan's "Blind Willie McTell," Springsteen's bleak stories of desolation, and the most doleful ballads of Van Morrison are part of that need for each person to recount the tale of his or her individual woes. Call it the blues impulse—Ralph Ellison did. But the joyous spirit of rock 'n' roll, which encounters and transcends those woes not individually but as a group, is the gospel impulse. You have heard that conviction expressed a thousand or a hundred or a dozen times, depending on how old and picky you are, from John Lennon screaming out his definition of God ("A concept by which we measure our pain") to R. Kelly's conviction that not only can he fly, he's about to. You recognize it because the rock and r&b and hip-hop that form our musical lingua franca owe their very soul to gospel music. The stuff that drives you (as the MC5 put it) "crazy out of your mind into your body" comes as much from the churches as the juke joints.

Dorothy Love Coates recorded perhaps her most piercing, mesmerizing song, "The Strange Man," in the spring of '68, about the time that Dylan was making *The Basement Tapes* and *John Wesley Harding*. Coates's gospel matches any dream of St. Augustine or wheels-on-fire vision. And in its attempt to exorcise the catastrophe of the end of Dr. King's dream and, at the same time, hold on to the possibility of grace and salvation, it ranks among the great acts of faith set to music.

In the first two verses, Coates tells biblical stories: the woman at the well and the adulterous woman about to be stoned. Both praise the person who has saved their lives, but neither knows his name or understands how he has recognized her. They don't know anything about the "strange man," except that

When he spoke, my soul caught on fire
And I'll remember this day till the day I die.

In the third verse, Coates tells the story of her own conversion, a testimonial deep and personal. The truth of it leaves her voice next door to a sob:

I felt that same power, Lord
My soul caught on fire
I'm just glad he stopped by in Alabama
The Lord stopped by, one Tuesday evening
Blessed my soul and gone.

The shock of the story becoming contemporary is transfixing. The agony and heartbreak, the reference to Alabama, are not coincidental. Coates is singing not only about her own version, but also about the miracles she has seen wrought by the Movement, and particularly by the work of her friend and compatriot Dr. King. She's seen her hometown—"Bombingham"—transformed; she's seen grace rolling out of her very own church like righteousness in a mighty stream; she's seen her people, denied the very smallest human dignity, rise up toward full citizenship. And that very spring, she saw it end with Dr. King's assassination. She had known all along that what was happening there, in the beloved community they had created, was temporary, because she knew all things on this earth must pass. But her voice bears testimony to that glimpse of what a just world might look like. They had done not only good work but God's work; and it was not only right but righteous.

All of this is contained in the way she sings the story of "one Tuesday evening in Alabama." She doesn't sound free; she sounds like her heart will break. And yet she sings it with all the tremendous power in her body. It's a testimonial of faith—whether or not you think faith comes from God. Frankly, at the moment when Dorothy Love Coates testifies, if you could believe in her God, you damned sure would.

It's this impulse that has shaped Coates's persona, in song after song, as a gospel beacon: a defiant, guiding light. That's why the congregation will urge her to take her time as she announces, "The mean things you say don't make me feel bad," and then roar their approval when she adds, "And I can't miss a friend I've never had." She works within a tradition of what W. E. B. Du Bois, in *The Souls of Black Folk*, called Negro folk song. Without that tradition, the confessions of our greatest contemporary singer-songwriters become nothing but so much whiny self-pity. With it, they become stories we all can share. "It has been neglected, it has been, and is, half despised, and above all it has been persistently mistaken and misunderstood," DuBois wrote, "but not withstanding, it still remains as the singular spiritual heritage of the nation and the greatest gift of the Negro people." Dorothy Love Coates stands as living proof that those words, written nearly a hundred years ago, are no less true today.

THE MAN IN THE GOLD LAMÉ SUIT

W hy did the Rock and Roll Hall of Fame host a seminar and tribute concert on May 15 to honor a performer who never had a hit? Phil Ochs was more than just the singer-songwriter who remained politically involved after Bob Dylan went electric and became exclusively self-reflective. He was a great writer, brilliant comedian, and a serious journalist who said he wanted to merge Elvis Presley and Che Guevara. If Ochs was the most left-wing songwriter of the era, he was also the one who showed up at Carnegie Hall in a gold lamé suit to play with a country-rock band.

This makes Ochs, in many ways, the man who imagined the true future of rock'n'roll. Ochs, more than anyone else, even Dylan, serves as the role model for the activism of Bruce and Bono, Jackson Browne and Bonnie Raitt, even Rage Against the Machine and Public Enemy. Unfortunately, none of them were present at the concert, although such old friends as Judy Collins and Tom Paxton did turn up. More important, gifted new singer-songwriters like Tom Prasada-Rao and Greg Greenway showed that the Ochs spirit continues to bloom.

Ochs was the right kind of role model, too, and not because he was in any way perfect as a man (a manic-depressive who committed suicide) or artist (his voice was reedy and thin). "He was a man who never found a comfortable fit with his times," our mutual friend Dick Waterman wrote me recently. "He seemed to be simultaneously both far ahead and far behind." Ochs nevertheless achieved great things, because he was so intensely committed to learning about the world and sharing that knowledge in the most creative ways possible. "I know that if he was still alive, he would find the way to comfort the inflicted and inflict the comfortable . . . Can't you just hear Phil singing, 'The gravy train I'm boardin' is called The Vernon Jordan?'" Waterman added.

At the concert, Janis Ian served almost as Phil's ghost. She sang an updated version of "Love Me, I'm a Liberal," with new lyrics that skewered Clinton and Lewinsky, and just as important, she played vicious rock'n'roll guitar, including a quote from Jimi Hendrix that was as nasty as it was tasty.

THEY CAN'T KILL ROCK AND ROLL BUT THEY'RE TRYING

—PLAYBOY, MARCH 1999

T wenty-five years from now, who will be inducted into the Rock and Roll Hall of Fame? Paul McCartney, Bruce Springsteen, and Billy Joel, the 1999 inductees, built their careers over missteps and time. Paul McCartney became a star in a band whose first several releases failed in North America. Today, the Beatles would not be able to buy an American record contract. Springsteen's first two albums flopped, with sales of less than 200,000 between them. Then he refused his record company's demand to go to Nashville and record with a different band. These days, that would sink him for being a prima donna. After his first album, Joel went to California to play piano in a cocktail lounge. He managed to find another record contract a year later. Today, he'd be marked "No Sales." Those were hardly glory days, but at least the music business of the sixties and seventies paid more than lip service to the idea that talent takes development. Today, the music industry snatches artists as young as fourteen or fifteen, has them generate a hit or two, then tosses them aside when their sales falter. Who needs to foster a bunch of superstars who get paid for their work and often take their time making it? And who knows how to sell a performer without teen appeal anyhow?

Changes are coming. Internet delivery systems such as MP3 files make it possible for musicians to market their work without any record label distribution. Devices that allow you to download CD-quality music off the internet already exist; they're portable and not terribly expensive. When these devices become commonplace, you can bid most of the $12 billion music industry—retailers, distributors, under assistant West Coast promotion men and their bosses in executive suites—a sweet goodbye.

"Record companies as we know them will soon be gone," Keith Richards said recently. "There are too many other ways to distribute music, and once those are established there will be no place for record companies and their pigeonholes. They can take that as a threat if they like. It will be a big change. But as an artist I love change. Who needs 'em?"

Radio, once the voice of a culture (if not a community), is now a jumble of sounds tailored to specific demographics. Listenership is at a fifteen-year low. Record stores offer a dark circle of marketing hell, where a bewildering array of choices is presided over by a sales force that knows nothing about music. At MTV, one-hit wonders are selected, hailed, and forgotten as teen appeal takes its predictable toll in turnover. Switch to VH1, and Celine-Shania-Mariah will numb you. Concerts have become little more than lighting effects and gimmicks—the foreplay of marketers who want us to go directly to the T-shirts, hats, and jackets at concession stands.

All this amounts to the homicide of popular music. With the exception of hip-hop—whose demise has been predicted as often and as futilely as rock and roll's ever was—*Billboard*'s album sales charts look the way they did four decades ago, before Elvis. Veteran rockers show up once in a while, along with an insurgent band here and a clever solo performer there. But their tenure is as brief as the one-hit wonders, only sadder. "We have cannibalized ourselves," says Kenny Laguna, a veteran songwriter, producer, and artist-manager who's now head of Blackheart Records. "When I felt awareness of industry or cultural doldrums before, I could always prognosticate the solution," says Atlantic Records executive Tim Sommer, who signed on Hootie and the Blowfish, among others. "Nirvana had to happen after the eighties, and most of us saw it coming. But I have no idea what's going to save rock and roll now."

The recent crisis among the big five record companies supposedly stemmed from dubious investments in talent. That crisis has ebbed, but hasn't disappeared. Focusing on just the problems of the five (recently six)—Sony, Seagram, Time Warner, BMG, and EMI—doesn't tell the tale. Despite a huge increase in the number of albums released during the past four years, sales are stagnant.

Without the impetus of CDs, which in the late eighties and early nineties prompted boomers to repurchase entire sixties and seventies collections, sales might have been flat for longer than that. Debt affects the decision-making process at each stage. Over the past decade, the major record labels have bought up most of the smaller labels, often overpaying for elusive market share: Virgin Records, whose artist roster consisted of Janet Jackson, the Rolling Stones, and not much else, went for $1 billion.

Now the big labels have begun to eat one another: the $10 billion purchase of Polygram by MCA/Seagram won't be the last such deal. Mergers and acquisitions siphon off money that once was used to promote, market, and otherwise support developing talent. Since the deals are fueled by borrowed money, there's intense pressure for quick results. The labels don't have time to work a new artist for two or three records before bringing home a big, long-lasting score. They don't even have time to work on new superstar releases for more than a couple of weeks: if a superstar's music meets resistance from radio programmers, you can kiss that album's commercial prospects goodbye, even if the maker received an advance that would make Michael Jordan blush.

Radio programmers are under the same pressure. Records used to be played because relatively independent disc jockeys and radio stations were swayed by a combination of promo man sweet talk, listener response, and outright payola. But a wave of mergers spurred by changes in FCC rules about station ownership means that in any given city there may be twenty radio stations, but only two or three owners. The owner in Boston either tells the stations in Tulsa and Tacoma what to play, or tells them to stop playing music altogether to avoid competing with more profitable stations elsewhere. Although playing records may be the cheapest way to program a station and may create a heritage of listeners, music may not be the most immediately profitable format. The *Wall Street Journal* reports that some FM stations are leaving music for the kind of talk that now dominates AM.

Talkers who play any music at all have power. "In the sixties, to break an artist, you knew what you had to do," says Universal executive Steve Leeds, whose music credentials go back to Murray the K. "You went to Ed Sullivan. Today, the only thing that approaches Ed Sullivan is Howard Stern." On his daily show each week, Stern plays about as much music as Sullivan did.

Texas venture capitalist Tom Hicks wields even more clout than Stern. He has exploited the government's new ownership laws to generate more profit than ever from the broadcasting license. His Chancellor Media Corp. is a network that rules markets across the country. Stations used to battle one another to capture audiences, wrestling over exclusive releases and artist interviews. Segmenting, however, is the rule today. Audiences are narrowly defined by gender or age, and the playlists reflect this niche marketing. With playlists so refined, Chancellor and CBS make sure that those who don't want all Alanis all the time or the *Titanic* theme in titanic doses will stay away in droves.

Hip-hop, which tends to draw diverse listeners—most of whom don't have money to spend on sports cars—is anathema to this kind of radio. As a result, fewer bands and singers and fewer kinds of music are heard.

In the unlikely event that a record gets made and played, there are fewer places that sell it. The country has only three specialty music chains, and I think chances are good that two of the three superstore multimedia chains—Tower, HMV, Virgin—won't make it far into the twenty-first century. Unable to match Best Buy's loss-leader price strategy, most mom-and-pop record stores that traditionally served small communities and special markets have been driven out of business. But despite the deck being stacked in their favor with lower prices for volume purchases and advertising supplements from the labels, many chains have gone bankrupt, too. Back in the day, artists got around the lack of record company support and radio airplay by hitting the road. But a dozen or more of the country's top concert-promoting firms, including Bill Graham Presents in San Francisco and Don Law Co. in Boston, have been merged into a single company, SFX. To control the nation's important summertime markets, SFX has to use its remaining cash to buy exclusive rights to superstar tours—guaranteed sellouts such as Jimmy Buffett or the Rolling Stones. What that means is ever higher ticket prices and fewer opportunities for mid-level and baby bands.

"In the good old days, I didn't need MTV or contemporary-hit radio. All I needed was a great performing act," says legendary booking agent Frank Barsalona, whose Premier Talent agency virtually invented the live rock business, building superstars such as the Who, Van Halen, and U2. "Today you can have a great performing act, but it doesn't mean a thing if you haven't got MTV and contemporary-hit radio. And there are fourteen levels to go through before you get on the radio."

In the past, acts released albums in coordination with extensive concert tours; radio stations focused on albums, not just hits; and bands sold millions in specialty stores before the chains ever became aware of them. When acts such as Springsteen or Rod Stewart then caught on over top 40 radio and at Kmart—usually three to five albums into their careers—superstars were born. Steady touring and the development of recording skills also meant the performers had achieved an artistic identity and a marketable image that gave them a chance to last.

Now the pace has quickened, so musicians looking for a big score have to make it fast or not at all. One reason is music video. Each video costs in the neighborhood of $250,000 to produce. Pop music's tremendous profitability stems in part from how cheap it is to make a hit. A typical superstar album costs, in actual production, perhaps half of what it costs to make a video for just one of its tracks. Video sucks up the money that once went for tour support, which helped an act develop a sustaining presence. Almost always, the artist goes in debt to the record company for the costs of video and promotion. That money gets paid back out of record royalties. (P.M. Dawn's first album sold more than 500,000 copies without earning any royalties.) Acts that depend on video appeal have a short half-life: try to name a prominent MTV performer from five or six years ago who's still around.

Big record companies need to do tonnage, which usually means selling immediate hits to young people. A band such as R.E.M. needs marketing and promotional attention over a longer period to find the bulk of its audience. Almost every performer who has had a long career is in bad shape commercially. One record executive told me his company did a study of all the bidding-war acts—that is, the veteran performers who finished their contracts and went shopping for new ones. All of them, he claimed, had lost money. So why do labels keep making those deals? Record companies want R.E.M. or U2 on their rosters to help attract younger bands. U2's 1997 album, *Pop*, flopped about as badly as a superstar album can—because the industry was expecting big sales—which means it sold over 5 million copies worldwide, but not enough to earn back advances.

Nevertheless, late last year, U2 signed a new contract for a $50 million guarantee with Polygram that apparently didn't want to look vulnerable on the verge of its purchase by Seagram. In 1996, R.E.M. signed an $80 million contract with Warner Bros. and then watched each of its next two albums sell half of what its previous one had. This kind of story can be repeated with Bruce Springsteen, David Bowie, the Rolling Stones, or George Michael.

It's possible that this is artist-driven. Maybe we're just waiting until the next Beatles or Elvis Presley or Louis Armstrong comes along. But it's been a long time since such a galvanizing artist has appeared. Kurt Cobain has been dead five years.

And then there's the possibility that the next big thing has already given up. The savior we crave has either gotten lost in the jumble of music industry politics, or has decided to keep the day job and just go on making music for neighbors and whoever finds the website.

The exception among the superstar deals is Madonna. Since re-signing with Warner Bros. several years ago for a reported $30 million to $40 million, she has managed to keep her sales high. More important, she has developed her Maverick label into a vehicle for new acts such as Alanis Morissette, Candlebox, and Prodigy.

Morissette is an interesting test case for whether a long-lived contemporary star is still possible. *Jagged Little Pill*, her debut album, sold more than 16 million copies. She has made some of the more notable videos in recent MTV history. She also toured extensively, expanding her audience beyond her initial teen base. Maybe executives will remember that there is something better than an instant hit.

There are other exceptions. Pearl Jam spit the bit on superstardom, canceled tours, refused to make videos, and then went back to playing live and recording on a smaller scale. They're still a platinum act, but they've built something that may last for the long haul. Prince declared that his deal with Warner Bros. was slavery, then turned his back on big labels altogether and started independently marketing his albums—with a focus on the internet. Phish, Dave Matthews, Korn, and Ani DiFranco have all prospered with a decentralized approach that emphasizes live shows and generally ignores radio play. These acts, and musicians such as Bob Dylan and Neil Young, work steadily and hard and release records often enough to keep their names out there. Record companies are well aware of the alternatives. "If you play the game, the machine will chew you up, bum you, and spit you out," says Universal's Leeds. "Or you can just chug along and have a long career, but never have that huge success. It's going to be hard to find superstars with careers that span decades."

Record companies regard the internet with a mixture of worship and fear. Its promise is prerecorded music delivery without the expense of warehousing, shipping, and sacrificing half the money to retailers. Its threat is to make music just another kind of information swap. The biz has been a lot more aggressive in defending its current turf than in pursuing internet opportunities. Palm-sized devices for playing music that download wherever you go, not just at your computer station, are already on the market. There is no history of the courts preventing such a technology from reaching consumers—influential movie companies couldn't stop the VCR.

Thousands of websites offer MP3s, most without anybody's permission. The industry thinks this is illegal. Some artists agree, others (Pearl Jam's Stone Gossard, for instance) don't. In an effort to join them before being beaten, the industry and the executives of the five major labels said they will work with tech companies to prepare a standard for delivery of music over the internet by the end of this year.

But if Keith Richards is right, will it matter if the record companies become extinct? If the labels can declare artists expendable, regardless of talent, why shouldn't the public be able to declare the labels expendable, regardless of how music has been circulated for the past century? The fact is, the most passionate music makers have operated in ways business can barely detect. Rap acts and rock bands alike are born on the street, folk singers still have their network of clubs and coffeehouses, and best of all, this music circulates on mix tapes as often as on official record and tape releases. In entire cultures of music—rap, techno, and just about every kind of hard-core dance music—the deejays who play the records are more important than the musicians and singers who make them. Who needs a concert promoter if you're staging a rave for 5,000 people—probably a bigger audience than Buddy Holly ever saw in his life—somewhere off in the woods? CDs sound just as good if they're made in somebody's basement or garage and pressed for a company whose headquarters is an apartment house in Philadelphia, not a skyscraper in Manhattan.

In short, there's going to be music. There was music for millennia before there were record companies. Musicians will find a way to get paid. They always have, back to the troubadours. Given current record company economics, music makers might be paid better in a world without the business.

If what you want is music, there is great stuff out there in every style, from jazz to heavy metal. Some of it is old, but an amazing amount of it is new and exciting. To find it, you have to want something other than a little noise to accompany you while you're stuck in traffic, and you have to do a little work. Finding it requires some of the grit and rebellion that said rock and roll would never die.

If you're not willing to go that far, it's okay. The record business is the business of instant gratification. It'll have a new version of the Spice Girls any day now.

BABY PLEASE DON'T GO

To the Teeth," the title track on Ani DiFranco's new album, is so spare it's almost bare of ornament, yet it's perhaps her richest piece of music. "To the Teeth" completely engages DiFranco's voice because of the lyric, a tirade against "the culture of violence" in general and guns in particular. Typically, DiFranco's rage never explodes, it just smolders and sputters. But that just turns her anger into a stern belligerence that's especially powerful when she reaches the end and declares that if believers in the Second Amendment continue to assert what she calls a "fool's right," she's gonna take all her friends and "move to Canada / and we're gonna die of old age."

In conventional terms, "To the Teeth" can only be heard as a stack of noble sentiments, in which Ani DiFranco presents the "truth" about our popular culture. About the way that playing video games like Doom and watching movies like *The Crow* and listening to music like Marilyn Manson's "causes" high school students to mow down their classmates and teachers. About the way that growing up around weapons "causes" kids to murder their parents with them.

"Look at where the profits are / that's how you'll know the source / of the big lie that you and I / both know so well," DiFranco demands, and that's not a bad idea. If there is a culture of violence, someone is making a lot of dough off it. DiFranco thinks she has a remedy.

"In my humble opinion, here's what I suggest we do," DiFranco says: "open fire on MTV / open fire on NBC / and CBS and ABC / open fire on the

NRA / and all the lies they told us / along the way / open fire on each weapons manufacturer / while he's giving head / to some Republican senator."

Those last lines present a striking image, but the concept that Republicans are more pro-gun than Democrats is simply not true. For instance, Senator Joseph Lieberman issues regular proclamations damning the very institutions that DiFranco also wants to destroy. Lieberman never denounces weapons manufacturers. But that's not because he's a Republican in search of a blowjob. He's a big-league Democrat who holds Bill Clinton's old post as head of the "centrist" Democratic Leadership Council, which pretty much runs the Democratic Party these days. Lieberman did vote to proclaim October 21 as a National Day of Concern About Young People and Gun Violence, but he has yet to say one word about who makes and sells the guns. This may have something to do with the fact that Lieberman was elected from Connecticut, where large gun manufacturers have long made their corporate homes. But it has nothing to do with which party he's in.

In fact, there are *no* prominent Democrats who share Ani DiFranco's wrath against gunmakers. Vice President Albert Gore cast a tie-breaking vote to pass the Senate's most recent anti-gun bill, but as a senator and congressman, he voted against gun regulation. In 1990, Gore voted against banning assault weapons and prohibiting the sale of large capacity magazines. On his presidential campaign website, Gore addresses the guns and kids issue by proposing tighter restriction on gun ownership. Nary a word about the gunmakers. In the 3,000 words of blather on the subject at *his* website, Bill Bradley squeezes in a paragraph about a few Saturday Night Special manufacturers, but not a word about the major gunmakers. As for Bill Clinton, his seven years in office have been marked by a dramatic increase in overseas arms sales by the U.S. government—in essence, a multibillion-dollar subsidy to large weapons manufacturers.

All this may be beside an even larger point, which is whether it really is a good idea to disarm the American people. "To the Teeth" reflects the standard left-liberal idea that disarming the public will bring an end to the violence in America. I'm reminded of a BBC show when Steve Earle was confronted by a British fan who called out for "gun control." "It's too late for that in America, son," Earle drawled incisively. It would take a very violent war to dislodge the arms that are already out there—presuming the people going after the guns would go after all of them, not just those that belong to people they want to kick around.

I remember too well the incineration of the Branch Davidians and David Koresh. Their "crimes" consisted of weapons possession (legal) and sale (legal), practicing an unorthodox religion (constitutional) that involved race-mixing (probably still legal) and, in the case of Koresh, being a mediocre rock musician (not a hangin' offense, even in Texas). In the current political climate, "gun control" is only a thinly veiled code phrase that really means "people control."

The "culture of violence" probably does exist, but it isn't just a matter of TV networks and the NRA. We live in a country where commentators drool over the spectacle of immense tonnages of modern weaponry being used to level nations unable to strike back. We live in a country where almost a hundred prisoners have been executed in 1999, and there are 3,006 more men and women awaiting execution on death row. Every presidential candidate, including Gore and Bradley (not to mention liberal darling/New York senatorial candidate Hillary Clinton), is an avid supporter of the death penalty, an institution so barbarous that 105 countries have outlawed it. And, of course, we live in a country where the police who routinely kill people—often by shooting them in the back—are celebrated as heroes, as a linchpin of an officially approved "culture of violence," a culture opposed mainly by musicians who themselves are under constant attack for "violent" lyrics.

The answer to the problem of guns and violence in America isn't to reject bad behavior and flee the scene. The answer for Ani DiFranco and the rest of us is to stay here and fight it out for the heart of our nation and to show people who their true enemies are, to wean them from a culture of violence to a culture of peace that isn't tainted by the hidden agendas of politicians. You can't do that by melting the swords into plowshares. Not yet. The path for reaching that goal may still be as unclear to me as it is to you, but I do know that striking out down the road where a government like the one that rules this land has all the arms will only lead us like lemmings into a sea of blood.

The 2000s

I think it's simplistic to say that file sharing allowed the free distribution of music, because it fails to take into consideration the people who are getting robbed more than usual. Did the record companies deserve what happened to them? They did, and they do. They saw someone take something worth about three bucks and wanted to grant that kid the stature of a thief. If they really want to play equal justice before God and man, then the record executives' asses are pretty far deep into trouble. They don't believe that because they don't believe they are people who get judged the same way—because they're rich people. And of course, in our society, that's the truth. I could do without that truth.

The record industry wasn't interested in a discussion. It was interested, primarily, in cleaning what it saw as its stables. And it was interested in making more money. I don't think musicians in a capitalist system have ever been paid fairly. And by fairly I mean, in part, paid the way their goddamned contracts say they'll be paid. Those are themselves a fraud of sorts.

I intended to do things to a level of vicious satire and irony; I didn't care who this embarrassed, including me. I had subzero patience for things I didn't like. It has a great deal to do with my fondness for underground comics. I just thought: if this stuff can't be funny, and if it can't basically denude everybody from Mick Jagger to little baby Jesus . . . I wanted people to have to figure out when I was being serious.

If you just tell everybody what's serious, first you're going to bore people. Secondly, people are definitely not going to know what you're talking about half the time. You were going to be forced—because this is America; maybe it's the world—to be sober. Don't smile. And the music I loved wasn't like that. The girls I loved, the people I loved, thought the whole shebang was as fucked up as I did. And that it was funny.

—*D.M.*

SEX AND LOVE AND ROCK'N'ROLL

—RRC #176, OCTOBER 2000

I don't think a day has gone by since it first previewed that someone hasn't asked me what I thought of Cameron Crowe's *Almost Famous*. I used to work for *Rolling Stone*, and before that I edited *Creem*, a job that the film gives the guru character, Lester Bangs. This set of connections supposedly gives me a stake in the film. It doesn't, but that wouldn't mean I don't have one.

I don't know if this is my favorite rock film ever—it's too close to home to know—but I do know it's as close to what I feel about the music and the scene as anyone has come. Not that it's "true." Philip Seymour Hoffman does a great job of incarnating Bangs. That little bent-shouldered dance! But most of the ethical advice he gives is contradicted entirely by Lester's actual behavior (he got as close to rock musicians as he pleased, took every junket offered, and he didn't b.s. editors, he just missed deadlines and then turned in copy that defined the subject for good).

What makes *Almost Famous* important to me is the way it understands rock and the scene as a matter of nurture and what it shows about the role of women in the rock scene in the late '60s and early '70s. Nurture is as ubiquitous here as drugs usually are in music movies. Billy, the boy reporter and Crowe doppelgänger, finds it first in the nest of a mother who's driven out his older sister, and then gets more when he is discovered by Penny Lane, who describes herself as not a groupie but a "band aid."

Kate Hudson's Lane is a character type whose portrayal is long overdue. She's not a groupie, though having sex with musicians is part of her life. But women like Hudson, who were real enough, didn't just offer sex and decoration. Penny says she means to bring out the deepest she can find in the bands she loves, and in a variety of oblique ways, you can see her galvanizing the scene. More important, Crowe's characters are continually shown taking care of each other.

What Billy learns on the road with the band Stillwater isn't how to be a journalist or how to survive in show business. It's about the ways that needy people forge links with one another, how they pay the debts those links create, and what happens if they welsh on the deal. What makes *Almost Famous* intelligent, even beautiful, is what it says about how people struggle to express love for one another and conceal it from themselves. That's also what takes it to the heart of rock'n'roll.

In this sense, *Almost Famous* is akin to *Singles*, Crowe's 1992 film set in the Seattle grunge scene. In both cases, the point of being part of the scene is how it reminds people of their dependence on one another. The way some of them struggle against that and the confusion and frustration that their resistance creates reinforces their sense of the comfort and excitement created by the bonds of the music.

I admired Cameron as a journalist because he liked what he liked—other than Neil Young, it's hard to think of a critical favorite he wrote about. More often, he got close to bands like Led Zeppelin and the Eagles that critics like me and Lester hated. He could make you see why he liked them, not by writing a "think piece" (Bangs's advice to Billy), but by showing how it was to be around them as a fan. In this respect, it's perfect that the musical epiphany in *Almost Famous* comes from a record I loathe, Elton John's "Tiny Dancer." *You* don't have to believe a note of it. The point is that they believe every line. It ain't Billy Wilder. But it'll more than do.

HOME TO ROOST

—RRC #181, APRIL 2001

A ll through March and April, the number-one–selling country album in the United States has been the bluegrass-based soundtrack to the film *O Brother, Where Art Thou?* The record also is charting in the mid-teens on the pop album chart.

The most important bluegrass artists of all time—Bill Monroe, the Stanley Brothers, Jimmy Martin, and Flatt & Scruggs—never cracked the top 100 album chart at all. Ralph Stanley, the star of *O Brother*'s soundtrack, has been making solo records for about thirty-five years without ever charting either an album or a single.

Yet country radio programmers recently told the *Washington Post* they consider this music "poison." Virtually nothing from the album is being programmed, not even the stuff by the Soggy Bottom Boys, which is a hit on Country Music Television.

Country radio asks and receives an allegiance from its hitmakers that no other format can command. In return, it consistently rewards mediocrity. Mediocrity is exactly the difference between Jessica Andrews's personable 1999 debut album, *Heart Shaped World*, and her current *Who I Am*, whose title track is the current #1 country single. *Who I Am* is so generic that I felt like the title really ought to be *Who Am I?*

Andrews at country's #1 does count for something, but the real story is told by the pop album charts, where only sales count and radio airplay is not a factor. There, *O Brother* is perched at #14 as I write, gazing down at the Andrews album at #56.

Maybe country programmers talk themselves out of it because *O Brother* also includes some Black gospel performances, or because they agree with me that the best thing on it is Stanley's unprogrammable "O Death." But what about the Alison Krauss/Gillian Welch duet "I'll Fly Away"? What about the novelty potential of "In the Highways" by the preadolescent Peasall Sisters?

Those can't be played even though they might work because they might not. Mistakes are fatal to the careers of program directors, even though an environment in which mistakes can't be made is fatal to everything else.

Every one of America's country radio stations is being programmed in an environment that forbids taking risks. That's because the buying and selling of radio stations in the "deregulated" world brought to you by Al Gore—a politician largely created by wads of Nashville cash—has created huge loads of debt and an army of brokers and bankers demanding it be "serviced" (a euphemism at both banks and brothels).

This situation doesn't exist only in country radio. All across the radio spectrum, you can hear almost nothing but nothingness. America's radio is at war with America's music. But the music—all kinds of it, especially the stuff that can't get airplay—is getting healthier and healthier. Learning to live without commercial radio is forcing people to make smarter records and to be aggressive in seeking alternate paths to their audiences.

This is the final measure of *O Brother*'s triumph. To have broken the stranglehold of the programming morons in the most reactionary bastion of America's music world and gone all the way to #1 may not be the story of the year. But as a harbinger, it may be the story of the decade.

WHERE THE GRAPES OF WRATH ARE STORED

—*RRC* #185, OCTOBER 2001

The government's choice of "The Battle Hymn of the Republic" to close the National Prayer Service the first Friday after the WTC attack shocked me. I was more shocked when it closed the peace-mongers' Mass we attended that Sunday.

Could I have been the only one who heard that stirring melody and sang in my heart, "John Brown's body lies a-molderin' in the grave / But his soul goes marching on"?

"Don't they know who John Brown was?" I asked a friend. "He was a terrorist—maybe the first terrorist."

John Brown took rich slave owners hostage, he planned a military action solely to disrupt civilian business-as-usual in our slave society, and many people, including his own children, died as a result. In Kansas, he committed brazen acts of murder—he'd have said war—against slavers. Although the Civil War didn't break out until 1861, it was Brown's 1859 attack on Harpers Ferry that showed what kind of war it would be. That's why the Union soldiers took as their anthem a song whose first verse was "John Brown's body lies a-molderin' in the grave . . ." and which drove its point home with "John Brown died that the slaves might be free." No matter what other pretexts modern historians and politicians come up with, Civil War soldiers knew that this was what they were fighting for. Their embrace of

John Brown ultimately means the embrace of Brown's strategy of arming the slaves to kill their masters, a strategy eventually adopted by the president of the United States.

Soldiers set the "Battle Hymn"'s words to a camp meeting song with the "Glory, glory hallelujah" chorus. When Julia Ward Howe, a respectable abolitionist, heard it at a Union Army camp in Virginia a few months after the war began, the lyrics included verses like "They will hang Jeff Davis from a sour apple tree." The camp chaplain suggested, according to the story on the *Atlantic* magazine website, that Howe might write "new verses more appropriate to the Civil War effort." In fact, the suggestion must have been quite the opposite—come up with something less bloody and less committed to the war's most radical agenda: overthrowing the slave power and freeing all Black people.

Howe's verses, published in the *Atlantic* in February 1862, became the official version. So, 140 years later, the most powerful people in our nation proclaim "The Battle Hymn of the Republic"'s meaning to be: "He has sounded forth the trumpet that shall never call retreat / He is sifting out the hearts of men before His judgment-seat." This after having spent the previous week condemning religious fanatics. (John Brown was a religious fanatic who believed slavery was a sin worse than murder.)

Singing the "Battle Hymn" at the prayer service reflects the complete ignorance of context typical at all levels of a society where knowing history is an oddity if not a downright impediment. I've since decided it's far better for us to be reminded that American history contains its own terrorists than to have "God Bless America"'s gruesome rendition of Manifest Destiny ramrodded into our brains whenever we're in earshot of a radio.

The first time "God Bless America" became a hit, around 1940, Woody Guthrie grew annoyed at its jingoism and wrote one of the very first answer songs: "God Blessed America for Me." Soon, though, he came up with a better chorus and title: "This Land Is Your Land." He wrote some great verses, too, and the best is the last: "One sunny morning in the shadow of the steeple / By the Relief Office I saw my people / As they stood hungry, I stood there wondering / If this land was made for you and me." Nobody's singing that one at prayer services, not while greed remains good, the unemployment rate climbs back to double digits, and asking questions is grounds for suspicion.

But if, having blasphemed against the orgiastic patriotism of my own day, I am entitled to a prayer here, let it be that some other songwriter becomes equally inspired and that that inspiration arrives soon.

WHO ME? YEAH, YOU

—*COUNTERPUNCH*, NOVEMBER 3, 2001

Maybe when the Recording Industry Association of America (RIAA) hires new employees—millionaire former congressional stooges like lobbyist Mitch Glazier or mealymouthed PR flacks or even receptionists—they learn a theme song. The Coasters' "Charlie Brown," most likely, so they can moan, "Why's everybody always pickin' on me?" whenever the record label cartel's front group gets nabbed cheating. Cheating is what the RIAA's hired to do: cheat artists out of royalties; cheat artists out of reasonable contracts in California; cheat music listeners out of their right to control the recorded sounds they buy; cheat the public out of its right to debate changes in the law that benefit only the cartel and its fellow corporate copyright owners.

In another dead-of-night deal, Glazier and company tried to sneak one of the cartel's "anti-piracy" clauses into the already hideous anti-terrorism bill. This change actually just confirmed what the cartel believes is its right to steal more than ever; it would leave you defenseless if record companies decided to invade your home computer and wreak havoc because your hard drive contained material it considered illegal.

The RIAA, which lies about as well as a six-year-old holding a baseball in front of a broken window, insists that it just wanted to insert another of its famed "technical corrections." The last one repealed a key clause of the copyright act, robbing performers of all hope of ever recapturing possession of their work. It proved so embarrassing to the cartel that the RIAA itself was forced to campaign to repeal it.

The new one, again stuck in without a smidgen of public debate and, in essence, on the backs of the thousands murdered in the 9/11 attacks, pissed off everybody but Tommy Mottola and Doug Morris. One Republican legislative aide referred to the RIAA's "vigilantism," and Virginia congressman Rick Boucher, who's about as hostile to big business as I am to Bruce Springsteen, read the recording lobbyists the riot act in an interview with *Billboard*'s Bill Holland: "I think it's time the RIAA respect the legislative process. Nobody goes behind the scenes as much as the RIAA does, and I think it's a disservice to the legislative process for them to continue to do this."

Unfortunately, even though the RIAA vigilantes lost, the legislative process failed to stop the anti-terrorism bill from repealing much of the Bill of Rights. To speak only of those issues directly germane to the music world, the bill says the government no longer has to get a search warrant to invade your home; it virtually repeals privacy rights for computer users; it makes all business and most personal records subject to government scrutiny, violating even doctor-patient privilege. As Senator Russ Feingold said just before he became the only senator to oppose the law: "Under this provision, the government can apparently go on a fishing expedition and collect information on virtually anyone." (I urge you to read Senator Feingold's entire speech.)

But there's worse. Under the new law, cops need only define a song like "Cop Killer" as "advocating terrorism" to get rid of it and put its maker in jail. This makes the threats the FBI once flung at N.W.A over "Fuck Tha Police" much more tangible.

The FBI had pleaded for such powers for decades, so it's going to use them. And since the FBI maintains an "anti-piracy" squad that operates at the beck and call of corporate copyright holders, these powers are effectively granted to the RIAA, anyhow.

Maybe we'd all better learn "Charlie Brown."

A PLEA FOR
BYRON PARKER

—COUNTERPUNCH, DECEMBER 2001

I am writing this with an outrageous request.

Next Tuesday, December 11, my friend of twelve years, Byron Parker, will be executed by the state of Georgia. I am engaged in a last-minute search for allies to try to save his life. What follows is an attempt to tell you why I believe that life is worth saving.

This is not a case of "innocence." Byron is guilty of the crime he committed, and the victim was an eleven-year-old girl. There are many questions about how the cops and the court system treated him—for instance, he was sentenced to death on the basis of a rape that never occurred, which the courts acknowledge, without releasing him from the death sentence. But he did kill her and he deserved jail time for it.

I tell you that, in those terms, because that is how Byron tells it. He is deeply ashamed of what he did and for the past sixteen years, while he has been imprisoned, he's worked to understand why he did it. In the course of that, he's earned a GED (no death row prisoner in Georgia has ever done that; Byron had an eighth-grade education), taken college-level psychology and writing courses, and undertaken a great deal of introspective discussion with prison counselors, ministers, attorneys, the few of his fellow inmates with an interest in such things, and friends, including me.

Early on, Byron's writing talent was noticed when he wrote a letter to

Bettie Sellers, Georgia's poet laureate. (I have a copy of an essay Bettie's just written about Byron, and I will be happy to share it, if you want to read it.) Later, television writer and novelist Karen Hall discovered the same thing, and it was through Karen that I met him. I believe Byron is so talented that, if he had had half a chance as a kid growing up, he could very easily be famous today as a writer. But such chances are slim if you grew up poor, and like everyone else on death row, Byron is poor.

It never occurred to me to ask Byron why he pursued his education, why he poured heart and soul into writing, but a couple weeks ago, he told one of his attorneys: "I came in here and I saw everyone just wasting their time away," he said. "I thought, 'Each of these guys killed somebody. And now their lives are going to waste, too.' And I decided, right then, that the life of the little girl I killed was not going to be lost for nothing."

I don't know what greater evidence of rehabilitation could be offered than these things. I *do* know that there is virtually no chance that the Georgia Pardons and Paroles Board will offer Byron clemency. There will be a hearing on Monday the tenth and I will testify at it, but the process is a sham. Since the death penalty was reinstituted almost thirty years ago, not one person has received clemency in Georgia. The chairman of the clemency committee says there never will be—but he hasn't the guts to say it in public.

Not only is the clemency procedure in Georgia phony, it is corrupt. Two members, including the chairman, are under investigation for kickbacks from prison contractors. The person who will decide whether they are indicted, perhaps imprisoned, for these crimes is the state attorney general—the very person whom the board would have to defy in order to issue a clemency order, for Byron or anybody else. A third member of the five-member panel is being sued for sexual harassment—he is represented by the attorney general's office.

Byron and I will never realize our dream of hitting the streets and listening to Lynyrd Skynyrd records together. (Capital prisoners in Georgia are not allowed to listen to music except on a very limited number of radio stations; I did play Robert Johnson's "Crossroads" over the phone to Byron one night.) The most clemency will mean is life without possibility of parole.

I would settle for that for my old friend, not only because I know that all lives are worth sparing, that two wrongs never make a right, and that it is obscene to pretend that one death can compensate in any way for another. Not to mention that I would be terrified if someone wanted to judge the rest of my existence on the basis of the worst single act I ever committed.

There is another reason to want Byron to live. Byron's path has been the right way to deal with murder—to achieve a real emotional and psychological and intellectual understanding of what cannot be undone, to make atonement by living a life of worth and value and inwardly dedicating that effort and that life to his victim. Were he to be granted clemency, it would serve as an example to future prisoners.

So I will testify to the clemency board on Monday, hoping against hope that they will prove me wrong about them.

It would help me—it would help Byron—immensely if I had some support, if I could read off some names of people of respect and renown who have heard Byron's story, at least this much of it, and share my principles. If you could see your way clear to trusting my judgment on this, I would not only be eternally grateful, we might just save a life—if not Byron's, maybe the next guy's, because one thing a crooked system must fear is people like yourselves paying open attention to it.

Holler if ya hear me.

THE *TITANIC*
SAILS AT DAWN

—COUNTERPUNCH, JANUARY 2002

To attack the business at a time when we are facing serious challenges that undermine the entire base of the industry is like arguing about the size of your room and the price of your ticket when you're on the *Titanic* and you're about to hit the iceberg," said Miles Copeland at the Future of Music Conference.

As a *Titanic* passenger, let me point out that it's the perfect time to change captains. The people who steered us into the iceberg won't be the perfect ones to help us survive the collision. Can you imagine standing at the rail, listening to the cry: "Moguls and A&R men first!"

Miles Copeland is the son and namesake of a notorious CIA ferret who boasts about his role in overthrowing democratic governments in Iran and Egypt. Thus, one might argue, Miles Sr. personally instigated the war presently being prosecuted by the son and namesake of another CIA veteran. But we can't blame Miles the Younger for that (even though I've always been curious about who might have traveled with the Police on all those Third World tours Miles managed). Anyhow, I don't hate Copeland, I love him for bludgeoning every ideological point his confederates are too chickenshit to say out loud.

Our Miles Copeland, former manager of the Police and current owner of Ark 21 Records, is a propagandist for virtuous entrepreneurship. His task is mainly to ensure that the real issues—who owns what; what the owners have done with their "property" (the stuff you think of as music); whether anyone except the owners gets a say in how things change—never get discussed. Copeland does this by insisting that the bad guys are greedy artists and thieving consumers.

This isn't a full-time job because most of the time nobody would dare raise such questions in public. When they are raised, the subject is very skillfully changed. There's no need to suppress the rude person who raised the question—more likely, that person will be exalted. So Ani DiFranco is lauded not for subverting the music cartel's scam but because Righteous Babe Records became a profitable business. She becomes not a rebel but the very paragon of entrepreneurship.

In the wake of being forced to change the cover of the Coup's *Party Music* album, which showed the World Trade Center in smoke, rapper Boots did everything he could to make his political position clear. He talked about American crimes in countries like Sudan. He even said, "Our fans know that we advocate a violent overthrow of the system."

When this appeared in *Rolling Stone*, it became "we do not advocate," which the *Rolling Stone* reporter attributed to being "edited under an extremely frenetic atmosphere." In my day, this would have meant Jann Wenner was on a binge, but back then, even the tyranny of the loaded owner/editor didn't change the stuff within quote marks. Perhaps today's *Rolling Stone* fact-checkers simply couldn't believe that anyone would say such a thing.

The *Wall Street Journal* wrote a story about Boots, but it wasn't about *Party Music* or his desire that "people hear it and get involved in movements and campaigns." It's about Boots becoming a media celebrity in spite of his politics: as a guest on *Politically Incorrect*. Maybe they could invite Miles Copeland, too. After all, *Party Music*'s lead track is "5 Million Ways to Kill a CEO."

1,000 MUSICAL KISSES

—AUSTIN CHRONICLE, MAY 2002

S omething transformed Patty Griffin this spring. You could hear it in her show at Jovita's during South by Southwest, where the local singer-songwriter debuted her new album *1000 Kisses* with a performance that hushed the crowd, except for rapturous response between numbers. Her phrasing's freer, her on stage demeanor more confident. She radiated enthusiasm back at her fans. Coming offstage, she glowed like a gymnast who had just nailed a difficult landing.

Griffin no longer records for A&M, the arm of Universal Music Group for which she made four albums, two of which got released. She's much more comfortable on ATO, which is owned by Dave Matthews and distributed by BMG. She's also stopped trying to prove she's a rocker, although she convinced the hell out of a lot of us with her second album, 1998's *Flaming Red*. *1000 Kisses* establishes a new guise for Griffin's old persona and is a tour de force for a singer's singer, which would be true even if "Rain," "Making Pies," and "Be Careful" weren't among the best songs she's written.

Griffin's songs are so good, in part, because they're crafted to be sung, a departure at a time when many vocals get croaked out as afterthoughts to tunes written as hangers for clever but cumbersome lyrics. It's not that Griffin sacrifices sense to sound—she's too good to have to make such choices—it's just that her music is so, well, musical. Her performance on "Be Careful" turns those two words into an anthem, and not with a shout. Griffin sings them so delicately that the listener can't avoid feeling the consequences of careless behavior with fragile souls.

When she brought *1000 Kisses* to Joe's Pub in New York City last month, the process had gone even further. Griffin has often seemed as insular on stage as off, wrapped in her own world, turning and stretching through songs as if possessed by a Natalie Merchant dervish. Not now. She's slowed her signature song, "Flaming Red," from punk belligerence to pop purity and surrendered to the transformation.

Or maybe that's backward. Maybe this intensely personal song that she once issued like a threat (even to Dixie Chicks audiences when she toured with them) can calm down because she's found greater mastery of her music. Either way, there was Griffin, tossing her long red locks—not lost in herself, but instead locked into sounds that shone through her.

It was much more compelling visually than her insular movements ever were. She looked free and vivacious. A friend of mine who's seen many of Griffin's shows put it best: "She never let herself be beautiful before."

LIVING WITH GHOSTS

Griffin hasn't changed all *that* much. Her songs remain gems of down-hearted observation, sung in a voice that still defines sad. Or maybe just lonesome. Yet before she's anything else, even before she's a writer who earns the admiration of her peers and income from Dixie Chicks covers, Patty Griffin is a singer.

"Songwriting tends to come out of what I need to sing—the sounds that need to come out of my body," she says. "It's the feel of the thing, the way it feels to sing."

What kind of singer is more of an issue, and has been since *Living with Ghosts*, Griffin's first A&M album from 1996. The LP's songs were first recorded with elaborate arrangements by producer Nile Rodgers. "The production was beautiful, but I feel like I played a really smart part in it," says the singer. A&M hated it, but loved the demos, so Griffin proposed using the demos as the album, which with some slight touch-ups (mainly redoing vocals) was what they did. The result married intimate, intelligent songs to intimate, intelligent vocals.

Ghosts built Griffin a reputation, but it also created the illusion that she was a folkie. The follow-up, *Flaming Red*, opened with a punk flare-up that seemed designed to negate the idea that she was a folk singer. It was recorded by a rock producer, with band arrangements that gave it an updated classic rock feel.

"I always felt like I was a rock singer," says Griffin. "It was all I listened to. I felt like, 'Don't call me a folk singer.' I never meant for those songs to come across like that. It kind of stuck you out in the field with all the daisies.

"Now, I don't care."

Griffin never sounded like a folk singer, any more than she ever sounded like she didn't care; if her approach reminds me of anyone, it's Terry Callier, who's essentially an acoustic soul singer. What Griffin sounds like is Southern, a pretty good trick for a girl who grew up in Maine and began her musical career in Boston, where she went at eighteen. There, she woodshedded around a scene that included bands like Morphine, performing solo in clubs, and made a six-song cassette that was sold at her gigs.

Wherever she grew up, though, her singing makes her sound like she was born in Dixie, which, to begin with, means bluesy.

"The South, musically, makes a lot of sense to me," she says. "There's a twang in my voice, and there's always been a twang in my voice. I think that's the French-Canadian stuff actually. I have that soul. I can't really help it."

On *Evangeline Made*, Ann Savoy's recently released tribute to Cajun culture, Griffin sings "Pa Janvier, Laisse Moi M'en Aller (Pa Janvier, Let Me Go)." She chose it because she liked singing it best of the tunes Savoy offered, but "Pa Janvier" turns out to be the oldest song in the collection, with roots that trace back to France. More important, the musical style traces back to French Canada, of which Maine was long a part.

When Griffin first visited Louisiana, she was taken to a Cajun graveyard and saw a good many headstones with the name La Fay. La Fay was the last name of her maternal grandmother—apparently a crucial figure in Griffin's life. "Poor Man's House" on *Ghosts* was written about her grandparents; at Joe's Place, "Mary," from *Flaming Red*, was dedicated to her grandmother, although it's ostensibly "about" the Blessed Virgin. *1000 Kisses* is dedicated to her grandfathers, however.

In Boston, the fledgling singer married musician Nick Cobb and worked day jobs as a pizza waitress and a Harvard telephone operator. She also studied guitar with John Curtis, who wound up booking gigs for the two of them, and wrote incessantly, which garnered her friends like Ellis Paul, with whom she sometimes played. One of her songs, "I Write the Book," was included on *Legacy II: A Collection of Singer Songwriters*, put together by High Street, Windham Hill's folkie subsidiary. Good luck finding a copy.

By 1994, her marriage was ending, but her career had picked up. "Fly Away" was recorded by Southern Rail, a bluegrass group. Somewhere in there she went to Florida, where she was further scarred by waitressing, and then back to Maine. Eventually, A&M heard her demos, gave her a deal, and sent her to New York for the Nile Rodgers mismatch. She toured solo with *Ghosts*, moved to Nashville, and finally settled in Austin, where she lived for a time with Troy Campbell, now a singer-songwriter, once leader of the great Loose Diamonds.

Identified today as a kind of alt-country singer-songwriter—Americana, in a pinch—Griffin has sung on albums by Ray Wylie Hubbard, Eliza Gilkyson, Emmylou Harris, Jon Dee Graham, and Julie Miller; she fits right in with the legends. She's also developed a fascinating live collaboration with Michael Fracasso, one of the few artists who can match her vocal prowess. He's the opening act on her current tour, which ought to lead to interesting encores. Griffin has opened up a lot since she got to Austin. Singing with Fracasso was Griffin's idea.

"She came up to me backstage and said, 'Can I sing with you?'" recalls Fracasso. "I was so flattered."

Their duets began during Fracasso's SXSW 2001 set at the Cactus Cafe, and continued up through the ensuing tour, where most nights they sang "Dirty Old Town," the Ewan MacColl song that's become a staple in Fracasso's show. Again, the judgment involved seems to have centered on singing: her voice blends beautifully with Fracasso's. Together, the two have become a centerpiece of the songwriter soirees Griffin occasionally holds in her backyard.

Then there's the growing catalog of songs Griffin has had covered: Emmylou Harris did two on *Red Dirt Girl* and one on her duet album with Linda Ronstadt; Reba McEntire, Bette Midler, and Martina McBride have also found Griffin songs that work for them. Most notoriously, the Dixie Chicks did "Let Him Fly" on *Fly*, which sold 9 million copies, leading to the absurd rumor that Griffin is set for life economically. The currency of this gossip provides an excellent demonstration of how little Americana rumor-mongers know about music biz economics.

What's really important about all those associations, other than giving Griffin income and exposure, is what they say about her stature among her peers. Gilkyson put it well:

"People work their whole careers trying to find the creative sweet spot that makes music genuine. But Patty doesn't have to try to tap into the wellspring . . . She *is* the wellspring."

MAKING PIES

Unfortunately, that's not the well most of the big-league music industry draws from. The music business does draw from part of Patty Griffin's well—songwriters *can* make a living. Griffin is a great songwriter. Her melodies are graceful, easy to sing without being simplistic. Her lyrics plumb sometimes frightening depths.

Griffin is a tough-minded social observer and a romantic visionary, a combination that seems naturalistic in songs like "Moses," "Not Alone," "One Big Love," and "Be Careful." In this, she resembles no writer more than her favorite, James Baldwin, albeit without eccentricities of rhythm. As for songwriters, there's some of John Lennon's wit and rage in her, some of Springsteen's Catholicism and gift for compressing character and narrative. She expresses feminism with more clarity and less hostility than Joni Mitchell managed, although songs like "Forgiveness," "Christina," and "Nobody's Crying" show the influence of *Blue*.

Some of her songs are fierce. "Tony," the song about her gay schoolmate who committed suicide, has a furious sense of tragedy, especially because Griffin so strongly identifies her despair with his. It's comparable to "Chief," from *1000 Kisses*, about a damaged Indian character from her hometown, a less sentimental sequel to "Ira Hayes." It's still somewhat amazing she wasn't condemned by the Catholic Church for a couple of the songs on *Flaming Red*, and I don't mean "Mary." I mean the ones that can be taken as assaults on the pope and pedophile priests. Her class outrage animates "Poor Man's House" and the new "Making Pies."

These are the kind of songs that good singers want to record, and for the writer that means both recognition and a living. The record business is another matter.

At A&M, bad luck beset Griffin at every turn. The debacle that was the first version of her debut led to great critical success, and the ensuing solo tour began building a fan base and admirers in the press. *Flaming Red* increased both. If she had been operating in the classic rock era, the label would have been primed for the third album, ready to give a big push to establish her on radio and support her touring to further develop her career.

That's impossible right now. As great a performer as she may be, Griffin's not going to be heard on Top 40 radio unless she suddenly begins making rhythm-oriented records, and her videos aren't going on MTV as long as she remains an adult woman. Touring with the Dixie Chicks was a coup, but not in a way that the record label chose to exploit; most likely, major labels being as retarded in reality as reputation, it didn't know how to exploit it.

Meantime, A&M, already absorbed by Polygram, lost its identity after Polygram's sale to Universal Music, and its autonomy was further squashed when Seagram, Universal's owner, merged with Vivendi. All those deals generate, first and foremost, debt that must be serviced, which means that cash flow, not career development, becomes paramount. Hothouse flowers can be forced; the careers of naturally blooming artists like Griffin bud slowly. Time, let alone patience, isn't something the big labels can afford or will cultivate anymore.

Griffin went into the studio to make her third album, *Silver Bell*, with these realities hanging over her. Instead of A&M being poised to capitalize on the gains she'd already made, she was facing a last chance. In fact, after the merger with Universal, there was no A&M at all. Its artist roster became part of Interscope, headed by former record producer Jimmy Iovine. Iovine has a long and (once) deserved reputation as a music guy.

Though Griffin delivered the album in 2000, Iovine and his staff kept putting off its release. All their meetings with her seem to have been cordial, but when an artist tells you in July that an album you expected to hear in September isn't coming out until January, you know they're in trouble. Griffin was, even with the record label publicist in the room swearing all was going according to plan.

It's mystifying why Interscope chose to string Griffin along for so many months—it may even be a reflection of Iovine's appreciation of her gifts. But it wasn't until last March—the very week of SXSW 2001—that Interscope told Griffin she was being dropped from its roster.

That Saturday night, offstage at Fracasso's Cactus gig, Griffin reported ebulliently, "They finally gave me my release. I'm free now." She had never sounded happier. We agreed to get together the next day at a barbecue.

When she called the next day to say that she really wasn't up to socializing, the mood swing struck me as perfectly logical. People had been abusing her music, which means abusing her, and now she was free of them. That was good. In the new climate of the record business, it might even mean opportunity. By the same token, the future was gray, the complications numerous. Her manager, Ken Levitan, did strike a deal that let Griffin use some of the songs from *Silver Bell*, but only "Making Pies" on *1000 Kisses* is from that set.

Talking with a friend who's worked in the music business since he left college ten years ago about Griffin's situation, my inclination (or at least, my conversational strategy) was to rationalize in favor of the record company. They had no idea how to sell this music. He shushed me.

"If you believe in *music* at all, you don't discard artists like Patty Griffin. She'll sell records someday. And even if she doesn't, she deserves to make records. They're jewels in your crown."

Griffin's free agency didn't exactly spur a bidding war. She credits Levitan with suggesting that she make a "humble acoustic record" on her own, an idea she liked.

"I had all these songs floating around that weren't pop enough for Interscope and also some songs I loved to sing, even though I didn't write them. And I am a singer."

Griffin accepted an invitation from guitarist Doug Lancio to come up to Nashville and record in his home studio. She cut the whole of *1000 Kisses* there—except the title track. The band included her current live group (Lancio, cellist Brian Standefer, keyboardist and accordionist

Michael Ramos) plus bassist Dave Jacques. Mix engineer Giles Reaves added a batch of percussion; a few others stuck their hand in, notably Emmylou Harris on "Long Ride Home."

The recording took a week, at the end of April 2001. They did two days of vocals, three of overdubs, and mixed. The album was done. According to everyone but Michael Ramos. He called Griffin and told her there was a Spanish ballad she absolutely *had* to sing. Griffin, who doesn't even speak Spanish, told Ramos she'd come over, but "I'm not going to do the song." Then she heard it.

She might have written the lyric herself. In translation, it says: "Encountering your love I lost my faith and that gave me my reason to live. I lost my heart on the 1,000 kisses that I left on your lips. It might be a sin and it might be insane, but I have to keep loving you until my heart comes back."

"Mil Besos" fit so perfectly that it became the title track of the album. It will stand as one of the great crossover performances of her generation, a song she sings with control and passion. It is one of the hallmarks of her art that Patty Griffin doesn't seem to care whether she wrote the song or not. She inhabits it, either way.

1000 Kisses also finds Griffin transforming Springsteen's "Stolen Car" into something that makes sense for a woman to sing. Her rendition of the blues standard "Tomorrow Night" came from Bob Dylan's *Good as I Been to You*, but her performance is closer to the legato version from Charlie Rich, or Lonnie Johnson's (whose signature song it was), or even Elvis. Like Rich, Griffin is a connoisseur's singer, blessed with a rich voice and the intelligence, judgment, and grace to put it to perfect use.

In fact, anyone who thinks the new Patty Griffin album is lackluster because she wrote only two-thirds of it totally misses the point. By the time she's done with these songs, she owns all of them.

MIL BESOS

Armed with *1000 Kisses*, Levitan soon found Griffin a new record company: ATO, the label started by Dave Matthews in the wake of his superstardom and distributed by BMG, a major. ATO is the real deal, not an indulgence; it's already had success with David Gray. And the label's belief in Griffin is palpable. As she was finishing her set at Jovita's, label chief Michael McDonald (not the singer; a longtime member of Matthews's posse) whispered, "I *love* watching people's minds being blown."

The album came out April 9. By then, Griffin was already on tour. She'd put together a new live group, calling it an ensemble since she doesn't think you can really call it a "band" with a cello and accordion but no drums or bass. It fits her better than the rock group, though, because the musicians are much more supportive of her needs. Then again, she knows more clearly what those needs are. A drummer might just get in the way of the "sounds that need to come out of my body."

They are playing small rooms, traveling by bus. Next week, they get back to Austin for a show at Stubb's. Talking about the tour last week, Fracasso seemed exhilarated, because the crowds have been so enthusiastic and attentive. It's hard to imagine being anything else. This band and these songs showcase all that is brilliant about Patty Griffin and her music. They frame her talents perfectly, letting her rock some, croon a bit, and close with "Mil Besos" as a tour de force that simply leaves you gasping for breath. When things click that well, the performers know it, and it sustains them. Often, it pushes them to new heights.

Patty Griffin won't necessarily be a well-kept secret anymore. For all the heights she reaches, her music is fully accessible. And part of the world may be catching on. In its second week in the market, *1000 Kisses* topped *Billboard*'s Heatseekers chart, the highest charted release by an artist who hasn't had a hit album yet. It lingers there, in the lower reaches of *Billboard's* Top 200 album chart, and is one of the bestselling albums on the internet chart. This isn't the top, not yet, but it looks like Patty Griffin will find her place in the tradition that formed her.

In fact, a good guess would be that in the future, people will lose their hearts to Patty Griffin, and keep loving her music until their hearts come back to them, even if it's 1,000 songs—1,000 musical kisses—later.

SHELLEY STEWART, RADIO, AND THE BIRMINGHAM CIVIL RIGHTS MOVEMENT

—COUNTERPUNCH, JUNE 2002

S helley Stewart retired with fanfare from WATV-AM last week. The wire service story focused on his long tenure as a Birmingham disc jockey (originally known as Shelley the Playboy) and talk show host, his membership in the Black Radio Hall of Fame, his ability to attract a White teenage audience at the height of the civil rights movement in the most violently racist city in America, and the Ku Klux Klan describing the records he played as "jungle music." It mentioned that Stewart co-owned WATV and that he is working on a memoir.

It told less than half the story. A quotation from what looks like the proposal for *The Road South*, the memoir, begins by recounting Stewart's father murdering his mother with an ax, he and his siblings eating fried rat for Sunday dinner, and winds up with him owning the station and a $40 million company.

The Road South material mentions Stewart "scorching the airwaves with incendiary social commentary and information vital to Martin Luther King Jr. and the rising civil rights movement." Now we're getting somewhere.

Diane McWhorter's Pulitzer-winning *Carry Me Home: Birmingham, Alabama, the Climactic Battle of the Civil Rights Revolution*, the most detailed report on the Birmingham civil rights movement, establishes Stewart and fellow WENN-AM DJ "Tall Paul" Dudley White as indispensable to the Birmingham movement attracting activist students. Between playing James Brown records and making fun of racist cop Bull Connor getting busted on morals charges, Stewart and White provided the crucial information that led kids into the movement. They "were happy to go on the radio and announce 'hot luncheon' at the [Gaston motel, movement headquarters] for some of their friends—beauty queens and football stars they had gotten to know at school dances. Twenty or thirty high school big shots and church youth leaders showed up for a strategy meeting . . . Their assignment was to start a 'whisper campaign' on upcoming workshops and youth rallies."

The Klan had seen it coming: they cut down the WENN radio tower in 1958 in an attempt to get Stewart off the air. That didn't work. The more effective corporate methods of choking off radio's power hadn't been invented yet.

On May 2, 1963, Black kids all over Birmingham heard Stewart announce, "Kids, there's going to be a party at the park. Bring your toothbrushes because lunch will be served." As McWhorter notes, this was a coded call for a mass demonstration; you need your toothbrush when you go to jail. Eight hundred kids, some as young as six, skipped school and the principal of the Black high school locked the gates. More kids swarmed over the fence. "It's really coooold," said the WENN announcer at one o'clock. (The temperature was above eighty.) That signal set more than a thousand kids out to march and be arrested. As a result, the movement, which had withered, found new life.

Another day, Stewart and White told the kids to bring their raincoats. The weather didn't call for it, but trench coats provided perfect cover for banners and picket signs.

This reveals not only the inspirational world of the civil rights movement, which galvanized communities like Black Birmingham for righteous action. It also shows what was possible when radio could still be used for human purposes, not just to make money.

McWhorter reports that on May 2, the White station manager, who'd heard the code words on the air and guessed what they meant, just gave Stewart "an indulgent smile." I don't know what the White kids thought.

Maybe they were just waiting for the next record to spin. It could have been Ruby and the Romantics, singing one of the biggest hits that spring, "Our Day Will Come."

Our job, it seems to me, is to try to make it come again. Remembering what Shelley the Playboy and the kids of Birmingham set in motion, and how they did it, is a place to begin.

SING A SIMPLE SONG

—COUNTERPUNCH, AUGUST 2002

At the opening show of Bruce Springsteen's new tour, the first thirty feet of floor space was separated from the rest by a bike rack barricade. Right behind the bike rack, a fellow in maybe his early forties, long hair, beard, motorcycle-style T-shirt and jeans, held a towheaded boy about ten years old. The kid had a crayoned sign: "Bruce Rocks." The father occasionally had exchanges with the security guards about the dad putting his son's feet on a ladder on the "wrong" side of the barricade. I thought, "What a drag if this is this kid's only chance to spend time with his dad, and he has to pretend he's interested in a middle-aged rock'n'roll star."

Late in the show, the band lit into "41 Shots," Bruce's song inspired by Amadou Diallo's shooting. They'd rearranged it, so when I heard a high, sweet "41 shots!" in my left ear, I looked toward Nils Lofgren. But Nils wasn't singing.

Then I realized that the sound came from behind me. I turned and there was the ten-year-old singing every word of the song in a voice to tear your heart up, especially on the verse where a mother reminds a kid his own age to be careful not to give the cops a chance to kill him. When the song was over, I thanked him.

I should have thanked his father, too. Kids learn songs like "41 Shots" only at home. That particular song got played a lot only by people who know that it could also be their kid lying on the cement. That was one hell of a father.

This comes to my mind a week later because I just learned my friend John Woods of Rock Out Censorship died this weekend. His huge heart gave out at age fifty-one.

Nobody but those of us in the censorship trenches ever paid much attention to Woods or ROC. They looked like they'd just gotten off work and were headed on their bikes for a beer. The kind of guys who are supposed to hate rock critics and not take anything seriously except sex and drugs. In truth, John's crew—which included Randy Payton and Kenny Moore—was tough, smart, fearless, and shameless. When it seemed like Tipper Gore had the keys to a steamroller in her purse, rather than backing up like the record labels, they put out a T-shirt. "Who made Tipper Gore God?" it said.

John Woods worked as a coal miner in his native northeastern Ohio. He deserted from the army and went to Sweden when that was the right thing to do. He organized welfare recipients when the mines closed. Later he became president of the Jewett, Ohio, Junior Chamber of Commerce. He always lived so close to the ground that you could never be sure his phone number was working. Yet he, Randy, and Kenny traveled on tours by Guns N' Roses, Metallica, Wu-Tang, and Rage Against the Machine. They turned up with their powerhouse tabloid newsletter, *R.O.C.*, pamphlets, shirts, buttons on a card table. They talked to—and accepted censorship "incident reports" from—kids who had to live with abuse from parents, "teachers," cops, and, for that matter, record store clerks for liking the wrong kind of music, wearing the wrong clothes, having the wrong hair—all the everyday crap that turns out Eminem and Axl Rose and Ol' Dirty Bastard and Zack de la Rocha, even Bruce Springsteen.

John loved the music and the people who made the music, as we all do. But he also loved the other people who loved the music and the musicians. To stand up for them, he slept in his car or on somebody's floor and sat in the heat and the rain and sometimes even the snow. He complained, a lot, but it wasn't about that. It was about the fact that nobody paid attention to music and kids getting fucked over, and about the government going on a rampage against the people who were least able to protect themselves.

Did I say he deserted from the army? In the Guitar Army, the greatest on earth, he belonged to the Joint Chiefs of Staff. I'm proud to have served with him.

ILLEGAL MUSIC

—*COUNTERPUNCH*, SEPTEMBER 2002

S eptember feels like harvest time for records. I've got here new ones by Peter Wolf, America's most underrated rock singer; Steve Earle, which is spiritually kin to *The Rising*, politically kin to the Coup; CeDell Davis, maybe the best Mississippi hill country blues album I've ever heard; stuff by Alvin Youngblood Hart, Buddy Miller, Bobby Bare Jr., David Baerwald, Gov't Mule, Todd Thibaud, and Jason & the Scorchers, whose surfaces I've barely scratched; and who knows what I didn't immediately recognize and slipped into the "It'll wait" pile.

Yet the new music I most want to listen to came anonymously in the mail, and you'll probably never be able to hear it at all.

The label on the CD said nothing at all. On the back of the jewel box, it just said: "nothing to fear. A rough mix by Steinski. Produced for Solid Steel / BBC London." A set of tracks with titles like "lolita (burning mix)" and "swan lake (beat poets)" and "the art of getting jumped." At the bottom the legend: "blame steinski for everything."

Steinski. It'd been years since I'd heard anything new by that master of early hip-hop mixology. The best record he and his partner, Double Dee, ever made, "The Payoff Mix," never even got released commercially, because clearing the samples would have been about as easy as rebuilding the Tower of Babel.

"nothing to fear" operates at the same level. Over fifty-nine minutes, it hits you with Ed Sullivan, Dion and the Belmonts, James Brown, fuzz guitar licks, Rocky and Bullwinkle, the Marx Brothers, synth riffs so elusive you can barely remember them, and an anonymous singer you know you'll never forget. Beneath all of it, the beat, the beat, the beat, stuttering, stomping, chattering, clattering, scratched and battered back and forth among turntables and samplers and who knows what other technological wonders. Gene Krupa beats. Clyde Stubblefield beats. Afrika Bambaataa beats.

Steinski didn't make "nothing to fear" to make money; he made it because he's impelled, every once in a while, to concoct a soundscape that tells you who he is and how he sees the world, and what that has to do with how we dance our dances. He made it to be played on the BBC's *Solid Steel* radio show, hosted by Coldcut and DJ Food. On the air, the mix was intertwined with interviews with Steinski and Double Dee.

How it got pressed in CD form remains somewhat mysterious. Apparently, the bootlegger initially took a master to a UK pressing plant, intending to create the Great White Wonder of hip-hop. But the machinery rejected it. Seems there now exists a technology called the "major label waveform CD database," which is capable of recognizing materials allegedly owned by the record label cartel. I thought this was a hoax, just something added to spice up the story, until I read a story in *J@pan Inc* magazine (June 26) about a company called Gracenote, which specializes in "music recognition service," the software that lets your CD player tell you which artist and track are currently playing. It's pretty easy to see how the RIAA and its international counterpart, the IFPI, could use the same technology to track "bootleggers"—or get pressing plants, which they have been known to raid, to do it for them.

Fortunately, not all pressing plants operate under RIAA scrutiny. Anyway, Steinski's work should be protected by fair use, because it is fair comment on the cultural artifacts deployed. But the major labels contend that there is no fair use, and get away with charging so much money per sampling that their greed has almost entirely devoured one of the most important aspects of hip-hop artistry.

It's pretty easy to see who was robbed here: not the artists who wouldn't get paid even if the labels did, not the labels, not even Steinski, so much as you and everybody else without access to the bootleg. Maybe we should make the destruction of artworks for commercial gain a felony.

THE POLITICS OF FILE SHARING

—*COUNTERPUNCH*, OCTOBER 2002

A bright young man spent a fair part of Saturday evening trying to convince me that file sharing and "piracy" were the reason that Eminem's new album has sold "only" 4 million copies, like his last one did, but only 4 million.

How many artists whose last records sold 8 million sell that many or more the next time out? He didn't know. The answer is damn few; it is probably more typical for sales of a follow-up to drop off 50 percent or more, and that was the case long before Bill Gates sold that evil gleam in his eye to IBM.

How long did it take Eminem's previous record to sell 8 million? About twice as long as the new one has been on the shelves. It reached those shelves early, by the way, because the record label convinced itself that downloading was killing its market. The most downloaded record of the year then had the largest first-week sales figure of the year. How did that happen? Could it be that the internet is more like radio than a back-alley music chop shop?

There are answers to all these questions, but we don't have them because the RIAA and the cartel for which it fronts are too busy trying to get us to pay attention to the smoke and mirrors of their propaganda.

The bright young man, who is twenty-three, bought it all, not that it affected his behavior. He said that he and almost all his friends never, ever bought records made by the RIAA cartel. They burn copies—mainly at work—or buy burned copies for $5 from stores that only sell pirates. I asked if he didn't think, given that the pirate copies have lousy sound quality and artwork, that what that mainly told us was that record prices are too high. He said that the industry couldn't survive or "support the artists" if kids sat at home downloading and burning copies of Britney Spears albums. I asked why the industry had to sell Britney and not a load of other stuff, but he said it just did.

Having been educated in a system that teaches the fashionable crackpot free-market theories and raised among people who until a few months ago thought those theories worked perfectly, the young man couldn't back down. It felt like I was herding him to the edge of a cliff. Since I don't think the drop is very steep or anything, but beneficial, I finally gave him a shove: I told him about the cartel's September settlement of the price-fixing case brought against it by forty-two states.

The settlement will cost the record labels $67,375,000 in cash, details of how fleeced record buyers collect to be announced later. In addition, the major labels will give the forty-two state attorneys general 7 million music CDs (valued at $75.5 million), to be distributed to "not-for-profit corporations, charitable groups and governmental entities such as schools and libraries."

Fred Wilhelms, who would be the industry's ethicist-in-chief if the industry had ethics (which it doesn't, because ethics violate free market principles), called a couple of the attorneys general to ask how the artists who made those 7 million giveaway CDs would be paid. The NY State Attorney General's Office said that the record companies were sure that the 7 million discs were covered under the "free goods" provision in standard artist contracts.

Fred asked if she'd like to buy a bridge. Free goods clauses state pretty clearly that the records are to be given away for promotional use, not sent to a lending library (and taken home and cloned). "I think the settlement does show how far the industry is willing to work with the artists on issues of mutual concern," Fred wrote me. "I think there will be more than poetic justice if Stevie Wonder or any of the other artists endorsing the MUSIC campaign [in favor of music industry status quo] are on that distribution list."

What this is really all about is getting the record labels off the hook for insisting that consumers be charged a minimum price for records.

That's right. The record labels don't want discount retailers to sell you records at the store's cost. There's actually a very good reason for this, which is that such retailers chase record-only stores out of business. But rather than address the problem in a legitimate way by lowering its ridiculous prices—which any retailer will tell you do more to kill sales than all the burners on earth—they chose a minimum-price scheme that years of legal precedent indicated would never survive scrutiny.

Who pays the price of being so stupid? The record companies, who will pay about $12 million each, or roughly half of what it cost EMI not to burden itself with another Mariah Carey album. And the artists, who will lose royalties on whatever part of their work the record companies chose to give away in violation of what is laughably called a "contract."

Do you benefit? If you want the blockbuster hits and live near Circuit City or Best Buy. You lose if you want something other than the big hits and can't find them—which you won't—at the appliance stores.

Would everybody gain if prices dropped across the board? Who could know. In the pyramid scheme called "the free market," it's against the rules to find out.

Addendum:

According to the new issue of *Billboard*, the settlement with the states in the price-fixing case now requires that the record labels pay royalties to the artists. Presumably, this is the result of Fred Wilhelms's phone calls, since there has been no publicity about the matter. This places the labels—presuming they honor an agreement for the first time in history—in the odd position of paying royalties on records they give away, while not paying them on records they sell, contract provisions notwithstanding. I think this is ironic, but could not reach Alanis Morissette.

In case you think I'm being cynical, the morning's email brought a flurry of reportage about HR5469, the House bill designed to create a royalty system for webcasters that doesn't put all but the biggest out of business. Once again, the RIAA arranged for Capitol Hill underlings to type up the bill in such a way that two crucial revisions were made against artists (and in its favor). The first provision eliminated direct payments to artists (meaning they would flow through standard label royalty channels, which is the accounting equivalent of being doused with acid and left to soak), and it also allowed the labels to recoup their expenses before making payments to artists (the accounting equivalent not of allowing the fox into the henhouse, but of handing him a napkin and a fork as he enters). Again, this language sneaked into the bill after the conference among the parties dependent on the bill ended, in the middle of the night, through staffers, not legislators, and entirely outside the democratic process.

AFTRA's Greg Hessinger sent out an email late this morning that "at this point, this information is outdated and completely contrary to the result ultimately achieved. The legislation actually REQUIRES direct payment to artists . . . ," which is true, but only because Rep. Sensenbrenner intervened (after a threat by Rep. Conyers not to vote for the bill if the language stayed) and revoked the changes; there is a somewhat amusing colloquy between Sensenbrenner and industry stooge Howard Berman from the Congressional Record nailing it down.

Unreported, meaning I don't know the answers yet and may never:

a) Since the "direct payment" is through SoundExchange, which is a part of the RIAA, how direct is it and how trustworthy?

b) What is happening to the staffers who inserted this language? What incentives were they offered to do this? Who at the RIAA—the only party to gain an advantage from the changes—got them to do it?

c) If the RIAA doesn't intend to steal (so to speak; I'm sure they've got another language inversion model) this money from the artists, why did they want these changes?

d) Why aren't the unions and RAC and other artist advocates demanding a public explanation of this behavior and the creation of procedures that will ensure it does not happen again, the next time the RIAA gets a hard-on for cash that belongs to music-makers?

e) If (d) isn't achieved, what evidence is there that "the system works"? Because the RIAA got caught? Last time they got caught, it took expensive congressional hearings and an expensive, full-pitch lobbying battle to get the cheating rectified. What will happen NEXT time?

At what point does somebody slap these bullies and tell them not to try to do it again? Or ban them from legislative conferences altogether? What protections are we being offered here? ("We" because even though all of us are not musicians, all of us are gonna pay part of this money, one way or another, and if anything is clear from the current copyright and other battles, it is that the American people DO NOT want to further feather the record company nests.)

AND THE BEAT(ING) GOES ON

—*COUNTERPUNCH*, NOVEMBER 2002

Cops in New York seized the opportunity provided by Jam Master Jay's senseless murder to declare the dawn of a new "hip-hop war" that allows them to put rappers under surveillance. There is no possibility of such a war, and if there were, the last people to be involved in it would be Run-D.M.C., consistent apostles of peace.

The minute it was discovered that one of the snipers came from Jamaica, MSNBC produced a shrink to compare the murder spree and the plot of the reggae film *The Harder They Come*. Yet no one at MSNBC has pointed out that Bush, Cheney, Rumsfeld, Powell, Ridge, Ashcroft, and Rice are crafting a lame remake of *The Magnificent Seven*.

The snipers' messages contained a common slang phrase (used by Ice-T in *New Jack City*, for instance), so *USA Today* rushed in a pundit who "revealed" a connection to the Five Percent Nation, a Nation of Islam offshoot that's influenced certain rappers. Media coverage portrays the 5%ers as villainous thugs. In fact, the 5%ers are best known for porch step philosophizing and their felonies probably amount to providing one another with smoke.

As Davey D (www.daveyd.com) points out, "police departments all over the country have been collecting and now have very detailed dossiers of rap artists and who they're affiliated with. From New York City which actually has a 'rap task force' to Oakland to Mountainview, California, where the police chief sits down and determines what RAP acts are allowed and not allowed to perform." New York cops declared the Zulu Nation, of Afrika Bambaataa fame, a "gang," then arrested thirty-four of its members for tutoring students in a Staten Island park, suddenly declaring it illegal for more than twenty people to gather in a public park. The "war on terror" features accusations that suicide bombers recite 2Pac lyrics, and FBI interrogation, and surveillance of hip-hop activists. Yet, as Davey D also points out, "Let's roll" came out of the mouths of DC rapper Doug Lazy California's Chill EB long before it came out of Flight 93, but nobody is giving hip-hop credit for that. This story stretches back to the 1989 arrests of five Harlem teenagers for raping and beating a jogger in New York's Central Park. According to the cops, these kids had been in the park "wilding," a supposed piece of rap jargon derived from Tone Loc's "Wild Thing," and meaning a vandalism spree. In reality, "wilding" came only out of the mouths of cops and the media.

In reality, someone else raped and battered the jogger; that person confessed and the DNA confirmed the confession six months ago. The forensic evidence used to convict the kids is unquestionably bogus. The cops coerced their confessions, as the kids and their families said all along. The state denied one of the police victims parole for thirteen years because he refused to deny he'd been framed.

The ongoing vilification of poor young people and especially minority youth began so far back that even *The Birth of a Nation*, another "wilding" fantasy, is but a midterm marker of its progress. As Jimmy Breslin wrote in *Newsday*, "The cops, news business and prosecutors—white to the last thought—decided to base their lives on a vocation that is essentially vicious: the framing of the not guilty."

Meanwhile, E. R. Shipp, a Black columnist with the *Daily News*, argues that the convictions represent an acceptable error because the kids must have been out there doing *something* bad. Shipp's words are important because they establish that this battle isn't purely White on Black. It's also privileged on poor, a category that cuts through racial lines.

That's why Eminem has two hit albums right now.

ACROSS THE BORDERLINE

—*RRC* #195, NOVEMBER–DECEMBER 2002

T he film that replayed itself in parallel while I watched Eminem's *8 Mile* wasn't an Elvis film or *Purple Rain*, but *Body and Soul*, Robert Rossen's 1947 boxing movie in which John Garfield struggles to survive in a world of fixed fights. It's not the plot that struck me as similar—the bouts in *8 Mile* are fixed only by the script—it's the way Eminem looks and acts.

Most of Eminem's acting—that is, all the emotional contradictions his character discovers in himself—comes out of his Pinocchio eyes and his small lithe body. In an early, defining scene, he takes a lonely late night city bus ride. He sprawls his lean body in baggy sweats across the backseat, and stares out at the barren streets of metropolitan Detroit with an intensity that suggests determination not to beat the bleakness but simply to fight it, without really caring who wins.

Director Curtis Hanson places Eminem in a world so cold and dirty you can practically smell its squalor. The Detroit streets seem as devoid of people as they are full of derelict buildings. Ninety percent of the people we see are Black, which must be a first for a film with a White star.

The subject here is cultural miscegenation—another reason it doesn't remind me much of previous vehicles for music stars. Elvis made forty films without ever getting to matters of race; *Purple Rain*'s message was that Prince transcended race (both true and impossible). *8 Mile* takes race as an inescapable social and musical constant.

The film's best musical moment comes when Eminem and his Black best friend, Future (Mekhi Phifer), are outside working on Eminem's junker. In his mother's trailer, her deadbeat boyfriend plays Lynyrd Skynyrd. In their bemusement at this cracker cliché, they begin freestyling to the tune of "Sweet Home Alabama," a hilarious commentary on how and why Eminem's impoverished trailer trash life sucks. Even more than the final scene, when Eminem wins over a Black club by fessing up to his honky roots, the scene drives home the idea that the only thing that might trump race solidarity is class solidarity.

Eminem says the movie's message is that "no matter whether you come from the north side or the south side [of 8 Mile Road], you can break outta that," if "your mentality is right and your drive is right." But he's wrong. The film actually shows that in a world where everyone is trapped, including prep school kids, the only way out involves using your individual drive and vision to tell the painful truth—it's not identity of any kind that can't be faked, but *emotional* authenticity.

So Eminem's victory comes not when he moons his White ass at a lesser opponent, but when he tells the whole truth about his trailer trash background. The decisive factor involves championing that experience as more authentic than his Black opponent's prep school roots.

So at the end of the film, when Eminem says he needs to work by himself for a while, he walks off not into a sunset but back to the bus stop, back to his factory job, which means to caring for his family, to accepting responsibility, to struggling as hard as he knows how to live in a more decent world. Is that what an artist would or should do?

Apparently.

NINA SIMONE

(February 21, 1933–April 21, 2003)

—COUNTERPUNCH, APRIL 2003

S onny Rollins once said that if Nina Simone was a jazz singer, then he didn't understand jazz. Nevertheless, a lot of her obituaries call her a jazz singer. They also refer to her as singing pop, cabaret, rhythm and blues, soul, blues, classical art song, and gospel. She had a different idea. "If I had to be called something, it should have been a folk singer because there was more folk and blues than jazz in my playing."

Maybe that's true of her piano playing. But her singing, not her playing, defined her. Mainly, it defined her as Nina Simone, sui generis. But if you need a label, try this one: freedom singer.

The term describes her militant presence in the Civil Rights Movement of the 1960s and the way that she sang, both within and without the limits of predictable cadence and melody. More than that, it describes what she sought. Like her good friends James Baldwin and Lorraine Hansberry, Nina Simone made art about wanting to live like a free person. This certainly didn't mean to live—or to sing—like a White person or, for that matter, an American. It meant living, and singing, like a person who not only counted on the promise, but lived in the actuality of the American Dream.

Personally, she could be haughty, with audiences as well as everyone else, but once the music started, her hauteur showed its real face: an unshakable, irrevocable commitment to her own self-worth, and by extension, ours, too. This is what Aretha Franklin and everyone else found in songs like "To Be Young, Gifted and Black" and it's what let Simone set "Mississippi Goddamn," otherwise a "protest" song, to a jaunty cabaret arrangement and fill it with jokes that turn out to be time bombs. The shadow that she casts across her blues, especially "Nobody's Fault but Mine" and "Work Song," represents not so much what it is to live without freedom as what it is to live with the fear of losing the sense of self that allows freedom to exist.

"I wish I knew how it would feel to be free," she sang, so delicately that it sounds like she feared the concept would shatter from merely being uttered out loud. But she ends that song on an entirely different note: "I sing 'cause I know how it feels to be free." In that moment, so does the listener. This tension animates virtually every one of the songs she sang and all of the songs she wrote, starting with "Four Women," which speaks like a condensed Toni Morrison novel twenty years early.

Her classical training made her wish that she could convey that spirit simply by singing her songs. If you hear her sing "I Put a Spell on You," "I Loves You Porgy," or "To Love Somebody," you know she could—she still stands as the greatest interpretive singer of the '60s, pouncing on songs by the likes of Dylan, Leonard Cohen, George Harrison, and Randy Newman with catlike grace and singularly personal insight. (This week, I find many of them too painful to listen to.) But once Hansberry convinced Simone that joining in the movement would not diminish but enhance her work, she took off in the opposite direction. No singer—no artist—committed herself or her work to the movement more fully than Simone, and she followed its twists and turns from the days of freedom marches to the less hopeful time of identity politics that lay just the other side. *I Put a Spell on You*, one of the great music autobiographies, spends at least as much time conveying her political attachments and adventures as talking about her music career or personal life.

Simone took the treacheries with which the movement ended so deeply to heart that she went into exile, first in Liberia, then in Barbados, finally in the South of France. She returned occasionally, always written up as a self-involved diva, but perceptive as always. She found her native country's racial and political malaise, she said in 1996, "worse than ever." In that respect, what a mercy that she will not, as planned, tour the U.S. this spring.

Nina Simone hadn't made an important record or written a well-known song since the early '70s, so in a sense her absence will not be widely felt. But she had a song about that, too. "I've forgotten you, just like I said I would / Of course I have / Well, maybe except when I hear your name." The words are Hoagy Carmichael's. The sentiment is hers. And ours.

I SHALL BE FREE:
THE BLACKLISTING
OF THE DIXIE CHICKS

—HARP, JUNE 2003

I n Chris Buhalis's "Talkin' Sounds Just Like Joe McCarthy Blues," John Ashcroft declares questioning him un-American, to which the singer replies, "It's called a democracy. You ever hear of give me liberty or give me death?"

"Don't tempt me," says the attorney general.

Six months ago, this struck me as hilarious. Right now, it just feels descriptive. Richard Johnson, a *New York Post* gossip columnist, declared a boycott against "Saddam Lovers." The only music artist he names to his blacklist is Limp Bizkit, adding that its fans are too stupid to "even know what Iraq is."

Wipe that smirk off your face. Hacks no more credible than Johnson drove the McCarthy blacklist. They ganged up, just like today's hacks. Go to celiberal.com and you can find a call to blacklist—that's the term they use—performers including Madonna and the Dixie Chicks. There aren't more music stars on this list because the blacklisters are too stupid to know System of a Down from the Coup. Gene Simmons, Kiss's lead cretin, leaped in to declare himself "ashamed to be surrounded by people calling themselves Liberal . . . spitting on the graves of brave American soldiers who gave their life to fight a war that wasn't theirs . . ." Simmons, like D.C.'s brave chicken hawks promoting the Iraqi invasion, dodged military service during Vietnam.

After Natalie Maines declared herself ashamed that she and Bush shared Texas, the Dixie Chicks found themselves banished from the great majority of radio stations. Stations put on orgiastic, DJ-hosted record smashings and burnings. One Chick had her home vandalized with pro-war slogans. Sales of *Home*, the group's current album, dropped 80 percent from 150,000 copies a week to 25,000. Yeah, the Chicks' *Home* still spent some time at #1, but that's more evidence that the country market is dead. Meantime, Clear Channel talk show bully Mike Gallagher put on an "alternative concert" for the opening date of the Chicks tour in Greenville, S.C., on May 1. The Dixie Chicks can expect pickets and hecklers at many other shows. (Delicious irony: It's an all–Clear Channel tour, CC's biggest of a very desolate summer.)

Major media portrayed the anti-Chicks movement as a groundswell from the grassroots. Nonsense. Doug Thompson of AmericanNewsreel.com found that the National Republican Party orchestrated it by spamming email lists as soon as the Maines remarks hit the news. The spam urged calls to radio stations demanding the Chicks be pulled off the air. Some of the early calls to country stations traced back to GOP national headquarters. Gallagher's "alternative" concert originated with the South Carolina Republican Party. Clear Channel, the most avid boycotter, has well-known ties to Bush, who will deliver for his pals by allowing the FCC to remove all restrictions on the number of radio stations a company can own.

The Chicks serve as an object lesson, but not the only one, by any means. The government overtly put activist/artist Michael Franti and his band Spearhead under surveillance. After Eddie Vedder delivered an anti-war rant—followed by a free speech rant when a fan told him to shut up—then impaled a Bush mask on a mic stand and slammed it to the stage in Denver on April 1, Mark Brown of the *Rocky Mountain News* led an April 3 story with "Incensed fans walked out of Pearl Jam's concert Tuesday . . ." Trouble was, Brown's review in the previous day's paper, headlined "Pearl Jam Show Will Make a Great CD," said nary a word about the walkouts and neither did any other review. Pearl Jam issued an April 4 statement denying that any such walkout happened. Who knows what pressures led Brown to his fable?

"Ed's talk from the stage centered on the importance of freedom of speech and the importance of supporting our soldiers, as well as an expression of sadness over the public being made to feel as though the two sentiments can't occur simultaneously," read the Pearl Jam statement. In reality, supporting American soldiers means opposing Bush and his fellow war-wagers (Republican and Democrat). The administration's current budget sharply reduces veterans' benefits. Already, soldiers subsist on such low wages that some of those in Iraq left behind families who qualify for what's left of welfare assistance.

If superstars face pressure and character assassination, what happens to performers on lower rungs of the ladder? The folk duo Sweet Polly (Akbar and Patricia Anwari) received a letter from Nico of the Lighthouse Cafe in Connecticut chastising them for singing "Travelin' Soldier," the Bruce Robison song that was the Dixie Chicks single before the Bush gang killed it. The nonprofit Lighthouse Cafe caters to an under-twenty-one crowd, exactly the group (with no memory of previous imperialist adventures) most susceptible to pro-war enlistment.

"I didn't hear the song but it had to do with peace (if that helps you know which song it was)," wrote Nico. "Also we have a policy at the cafe where we try to stay clear of politically charged topics. It is one reason I do not have poetry yet. I do not let people preach from the stage. Lighthouse is to be a safe place for people to come. A place of rest and freedom from the outside pressures." A place too peaceful for peace? This isn't McCarthy. It's Orwell.

Bruce Springsteen's statement supporting the Dixie Chicks took a welcome stride in the other direction, but it points out the absence of support from other artists. Let's see if his fans start tossing Springsteen CDs into the streets.

Buhalis concludes his talking blues by breaking into actual singing: "There ain't a man alive today / Gonna make me watch what I say / When I get them talkin' sounds like Joe McCarthy blues."

If so, best look for him down at the end of Lonely Street.

("Talkin' Just Like Joe McCarthy Blues" can be ordered from mp3.com as a download or as a CD from chrisbuhalis.com.)

THE ZEN OF REVOLUTION: MICHAEL RAMOS'S CHARANGA CAKEWALK

—*AUSTIN CHRONICLE*, APRIL 2006

Michael Ramos bears not a single distinguishing characteristic of the revolutionary. He's a quiet, unassuming, trim, and well-dressed man who has spent almost his entire career in subordinate roles in a variety of groups. He's been a member of the BoDeans and the Rembrandts and played accordion and keyboards for Patty Griffin, John Mellencamp, Paul Simon, and, currently, Los Lonely Boys.

Yet on the long bus journeys and overnight hotel stays that take up far too great a percentage of a road musician's life, Ramos uses Pro Tools to transform all the music he's played and has grown up with into a unique synthesis that blows apart preconceptions. Ramos has released two albums as Charanga Cakewalk, which is what he calls the result. It's a conceptual group, like Steely Dan, consisting of Ramos and whatever friends, acquaintances, and heroes he manages to corral.

The first LP, 2004's *Loteria de la Cumbia Lounge*, fused cumbia and electronica with a go-for-broke, rock & roll attitude in which whatever works is the right thing to do. The title referenced *lotería*—Mexican bingo—so Ramos festooned the package with the lushly provocative imagery of *lotería* cards: bride and groom skeletons, a sacrificial heart, brown beauty booty, ghostly couples in formal dance poses, and a heart plummeting downward like a comet.

As for the album itself, it might not sound revolutionary to ears attuned to rebellion in the form of tearing down the comfortable walls of the bourgeoisie and erecting monumentally simplistic two-chord slums in their wake. Charanga Cakewalk is revolutionary in an entirely different way: it's liberating.

Loteria de la Cumbia Lounge did what seemed previously impossible: bringing intelligent writing and diverse arrangements to compositions that were mostly cumbia in form and shaping out of techno's computerized stasis a much greater breadth of structure and emotion. Ramos inflected the music with Tejano, flamenco, meringue, salsa, ska, and reggae, plus a little cheesy garage rock tone, so whenever you felt comfortable knowing what would come next, it didn't. The result made both cumbia and electronica accessible to people who might not know charanga from cakewalk or techno from tango. It created a singular dynamic, a flow back and forth from the familiar to the exotic, from ease to disruption.

This spring's *Chicano Zen* goes much further, partly because the songs are stronger, partly because Ramos made it with a more-eager group of collaborators—many who heard what he pulled off on *Loteria* and wanted to participate in the new one. What Ramos created, a sound sensibility that transforms musical "play" from a synonym for work to something truly playful, doesn't come along very often.

On *Chicano Zen*'s "La Miga Hormiga," for example, Ramos builds up the story of a little ant who finds pleasure and honor in his simple work around a typical but particularly haunting synth figure that might be techno except that a drum comes crashing in, followed by a guitar, and then a truly thunderous bevy of Mexican percussion. In ten seconds he's taken the ear on a charanga cakewalk past a variety of expectations. And when the voices come in, Ramos and Lila Downs—his fellow charanga revolutionary—erupt from the midst of thunder and make the ant's ecstasy so palpable you just about have to dance.

That's what a revolution sounds like—not protest and rejection. Freedom. Liberation. Discovery. The zen of . . . bingo!

RING OF FIRE

Michael Ramos grew up mostly around San Antonio. He's a multi-instru-mentalist, specializing in keyboards and accordion, but also singing and playing trumpet, organ, and a little percussion.

"I'm Mexican," he told me last year. "My mom's family was Spanish. Growing up in Texas was a little tough because my dad would turn me on to the Beatles and the Stones, all the cool bands at the time, yet we'd go hang out at my grandmother's, and she's listening to really hard-core Latin music, cooking in the kitchen."

On *Loteria*, he wrote of his song "Romanticos Desesperados": *"My parents were a great dance team. I can close my eyes when I listen to this number and see them gliding gracefully."*

"So even at that point, it really moved me," he reiterates in person. "I secretly liked it. But it wasn't cool with all my friends, who were listening to the Stones and Jimi Hendrix and all that. So . . ."

So he recognized fusion when he found it.

"A perfect example: 'Ring of Fire,' Johnny Cash. Those horns! There were glimpses like that.

"The obvious bridges were like Carlos Santana and stuff. But then, whenever José Feliciano did 'Light My Fire,' I thought that was really cool. A defining moment for me was when we were in our big station wagon, and we were cruising down the road, and 'Me and Julio Down by the School-yard' came on the radio. Here it was: Top 40 radio and this guy is singing with this huge Latin group behind him.

"So then I thought, well, maybe liking Latin music is okay. And then, as I started getting older, instead of it becoming a source of embarrassment or whatever, I became really proud of it and really embraced it.

"Latin music has always been with me—and world music. When I was on tour with all these rock bands, the minute we'd get back on the bus, I'd have my headphones on, and I'm listening to the furthest thing from what I just got through playing. It was sort of my guilty pleasure."

CHISPAS

Just as Charanga Cakewalk is a revolutionary concept built on traditions, it's a studio endeavor born on the road.

"I did the bulk of it at home," says Ramos. "Whenever I'd go on the road, that was one of the things that used to kill me. I've been a sideman for so many years, it really is a struggle for me to be out touring most of the time.

"So I just figured, okay, what are the things that make it hard for me to be away from home? Number one, I basically have to stop working on my own stuff. So I took my laptop. Now they have it to where you can basically take a virtual studio with you out on the road. One of the tracks on [*Loteria*] I actually did in the back of a tour bus on a drive from Seattle to Austin that took us three days.

"We were out with Patty, and that's where her tour ended. They said, 'Okay, we'll give you the option of flying home, or you can ride the bus. Now, if you fly home, we only pay 'til this date, but if you ride the bus, we'll pay you a half week's salary.' I thought, 'Oh, that'll be easy.' But let me tell you, the only good thing that came outta that ride for me was that song.

"I was just going crazy, so I pulled out the old laptop, got the head-phones on, got a little keyboard, and wrote a tune. And it ended up on the album! Which I think is really funny. That's even more drastic than a hotel room."

"Chispas," the song that began on the bus, resembles a hypermodern Jimmy Smith tune, with synth and B-3 figures interlocking with heavily strummed guitar by David Pulkingham that invokes John Lee Hooker. The Ramos vocal, set so far back in the mix that the lyrics almost don't matter, has a West Coast hip-hop cadence (a sober "Wild Thing"), but the high-light is Becca Rodriguez's wordless sighs over the last verse that take the performance toward Gilberto territory. It's a world of music, even though, or maybe especially since, it grew out of a lone man's attempt to conquer nonstop-bus-ride boredom. A freedom ride.

MIL BESOS

When Michael Ramos first started putting together an album of his own music, he was already playing with Austin's Patty Griffin, a close friend. She was going to make an album, the one that became *1000 Kisses*.

"Before she started, she said, 'If you want to do some of it in Austin, we can.'"

When Ramos called her back two weeks later, she was already done.

"I was more hurt from a friend's standpoint than professionally," says Ramos. "So I let it go. I didn't stew for more than seven or eight days."

Culling through songs for his album, Ramos remembered the Spanish ballad "Mil Besos" ("1000 Kisses"). "I remember it from when I was growing up. It was just so beautiful. I said, 'You know what? I gotta record this. I don't know what I'm gonna do with it, but I've gotta record it.' So I called Patty up. I was going down the road, I was on my cell phone, and I said, 'Patty, you gotta record this song. It's great, it's great, it's great.' She said, 'What's it about?' I said, 'It's about this guy who kisses a woman and loses his heart on her lips.' She said, 'Oh that's great, it'll be the title track.'

"Here she thinks I'm still trying to muscle my way onto her record, and I was talking about it for *my* record! But when she said, 'Oh, great,' I said, 'Okay.' I snuck it in through the back door."

"Mil Besos," cut at Ramos's house, sounds like it was made fifty years ago in a studio floating somewhere between Manhattan, Madrid, and Mexico City. It has a simple, elegant arrangement, led by a basic clave, joined by strings, and finally that husky, breathy vocal. The song swells and swells, yet always complements the singing, never competing with it, while still incorporating three marvelous solos: Brian Standefer's on cello, and Ramos's on both accordion and piano. The latter can't last eight bars. It's fifty times smarter and more gorgeous than any of the myriad efforts at recording standards in the post–Tin Pan Alley era. Ramos's father had the best review: "I didn't know Patty Griffin was Mexican."

After his first album got such strong reception, Griffin, who sang on its unreleased precursor but not *Loteria*, began taunting Ramos: "You wouldn't let me sing on your record." Ramos taunted back: "You better be careful, or

I'll make you be on my second record." He was seeking a song to do with Austin's Ruben Ramos, perhaps the greatest living exponent of northern Mexican (or South Texas) singing, when he fell upon a track from an old José Feliciano album, "No Soy Feliz." It dawned on Ramos that the song would work beautifully as a duet between Ruben Ramos and Griffin, "two [singers] who would never be in the same room together."

It's at the other end of the spectrum from "Mil Besos," a strongly rhythmic tune, with the singers trading lines at the start and ending in harmony. By the time Ruben Ramos gets to "No, no, no!" just before the bridge, it's already a triumph. Michael Ramos expresses his pride in it with typical modesty.

"José Feliciano is one of my heroes. I'd love him to hear that track."

In a better world, Feliciano might be sick of hearing it on the radio by now.

GAUCHO

Chicano Zen isn't so much a star-studded affair, although if you're a fan of great singers, having Ruben Ramos, Downs, Griffin, and Martha Gonzalez on the same LP is awe-inspiring, as it's a reflection of Michael Ramos building a community around his concept. It's not a stretch to compare it to a group of musicians who gathered around that ultimate studio band, Steely Dan, in its heyday. Charanga Cakewalk is in its own way just as singular, the music it plays equally intricate and engrossing, not to mention inviting.

On the first album, although he used several other players, Ramos seemed to be working in isolation, following his own instincts. "If I felt a song getting a little too traditional, then I started throwing electronica in," he explains. "If I felt it getting too electronic, then I tried more traditional. I tried to make it a thing, as opposed to two things put together. I really wanted to do something that was modern yet pointing people in the direction of what cumbia music and what great Latin music is at its core, which is melody and rhythm."

At the same time, "I wanted to show people that you can actually use technology, and it doesn't have to sound canned or cheesy or whatever. It can sound beautiful and warm. An instrument is an instrument, that's the way I see it."

On *Chicano Zen*, the edges of his isolated vision blur a bit, which opens the sound further. He was surprised to find, often through comparisons in reviews, that quite a few other artists were working on a similar approach: Downs, Quetzal, harpist Celso Duarte. And he incorporated more ideas from others in the creation process. At one point, Quetzal's Martha Gonzalez and her husband, Quetzal Flores, came to stay with him and basically barred him from the studio for a day or so. When they emerged, Gonzalez had written lyrics and recorded vocals for "Vida Magica" and "La Corriente," tracks Ramos had thought instrumentals. The result is an audible and exciting progression.

"I could take what I already started, but I didn't want to wander the same roads," he says. "I wanted to push it just a little bit farther."

There's less synthesizer on *Zen*, because there's a much larger palette, yet the result is, if anything, a greater synthesis. In fact, the success of *Loteria* let him do several things. Most important, it let him make *Chicano Zen* and to make it on his own terms. It also let him take a band on the road for the tour with Downs, and led him to manager Gil Gastelum, who also handles his friends in Quetzal and David Garza, among others.

"At this point, I can do whatever I want to do," says Ramos.

What he wants to do is make sounds that reflect himself and his concerns. To me, the two most moving tracks on *Chicano Zen* are instrumentals: "Gloria," the boisterous, modernist ranchera he created in honor of his mother, and "El Ballad de Jose Campos Torres," a haunted piece of synth and piano written in tribute to the Mexican youth beaten and drowned by Houston cops, who were fined $1 each—something that happened in 1976 and is still honored in Houston today.

"So many people think of what happened to Jose Campos Torres," Ramos told me recently. "But I got thinking about him as a person, who he was, what he felt, how he lived."

As for "Gloria," its composer addresses the song in *Zen*'s liner notes: *"When you listen to this imagine the smell of warm homemade tortillas and Spanish rice simmering on the stove."*

Both of these thoughts, in this time and place, are revolutionary.

"I was born in the wrong era," said Michael Ramos. "But there's nothing to keep me from going back there."

Or from bringing that past into our future. If you don't understand these things, the best suggestion would be to begin your exploration of *Chicano Zen*, the sooner the better.

GREETINGS FROM NEW ORLEANS, LA

—RRC #216, MAY 2006

In a time of warfare against a phantom enemy abroad and a war against the poor creating phantom citizens at home, up pops Bruce Springsteen with an album titled *We Shall Overcome*. He didn't have New Orleans in mind when he started making it in 1997, but both the music and the ways he's using it speak directly to the situation there today.

Deciding to start his current tour with the Seeger Sessions Band at the New Orleans Jazz & Heritage Festival on April 30 reflect Springsteen's sensitivity to the issues of poverty and racism and his ability to pick up on a catalytic event. What Vietnam veterans were twenty years ago—a powerful symbol of the people the system tries to erase from view—New Orleans is today.

Discussion of Bruce's new album has focused on its subtitle, *The Seeger Sessions*, probably because people are puzzled by what it means. The song selections don't seem nearly as political as their source, Pete Seeger. Yet four of the thirteen—"O Mary Don't You Weep," "Jacob's Ladder," "Eyes on the Prize," and "We Shall Overcome"—have at one time or another been used as "freedom songs." "Pay Me My Money Down" is that rare thing, a song that truly protests the situation it describes. "John Henry," "My Oklahoma Home," and "Mrs. McGrath" are explicitly about oppressed folk. That's almost two-thirds of the thirteen-song album.

One reason the album seems to avoid politics is "We Shall Overcome" itself. Springsteen's version downplays its spirit-rousing aspect; instead he sings it as one of his desperate love songs, even changing the chorus from "Deep in my heart" to "Darling, here in my heart." The result is a lovely ballad of two people against a hard world, and a violation of the collective spirit that the song stands for. He sings "Eyes on the Prize" in the same emotional mode, but it works a lot better.

The difference between the two is that on "Eyes on the Prize," Springsteen uses his band to build an arrangement that brings in voices and instruments to illustrate a community spirit taking shape out of the dark shadows inhabited by lonely isolated souls.

The music Springsteen makes with his biggest-ever band (thirteen members on the record, seventeen to twenty on stage) abandons much of what has defined his sound. In particular, the stiff rock beat has given way to syncopation. The instrumental focus is on the drums, with the melodic contributions emerging from fiddles and horns, rather than guitars and keyboards. The vocals, both his own and the multipart harmonies, are freer than anything he's recorded. After three albums of tragedy, the mood here swings toward joy. The album's tone is sometimes silly and once in a while fearful, but it's never doomed.

Bruce wrote none of the songs, yet *We Shall Overcome* is as personal as any of his records. For once on a studio recording, you can feel the unaffected pleasure he takes from making music, from working with other players and singers.

New Orleans right now is an eerie place, but not just because of the devastation. Abandoned cars and strewn rubble, even the scent of rot, are all over the place in Detroit and, for that matter, Asbury Park. What makes New Orleans different is that despite all the hype about reconstruction, nothing is being done. The housing projects are empty, looking more than ever like prisons. The upper Ninth Ward's population is decimated; the lower Ninth Ward's population is gone. But it's not just people that are missing. So are cranes, building equipment, and construction site supplies, even as the courageous volunteers of Common Ground are hard at work in the Ninth, with a blue-roofed house in each part of the ward serving as a center for returning residents, for cleanup, and for visitors.

Musicians in particular are struggling right now, and one reason is that tourism—40 percent of the pre-hurricane economy—has dwindled so badly. New Orleans does have a great Indigenous music community, but the gigs that pay have long been played by outsiders.

The Jazz & Heritage Festival offers a lot of jobs for musicians, but the most prominent and best-paying main stages, even the themed tents for jazz and gospel, mainly feature stars from far away. The splendid group of New Orleans icon Allen Toussaint appeared on the main stage right before Springsteen, but with Elvis Costello stepping in to sing several numbers.

Tourists will come to see, hear, and eat the music and culture of New Orleans and the Louisiana swamplands. But to get enough of them to fill the huge fairgrounds racetrack and gain national attention, not to mention lucrative corporate sponsorship, the promoters of Jazzfest need artists like Bob Dylan, Dave Matthews, and Springsteen. (The festival is run by a non-profit corporation, which doesn't mean a lot of money isn't being made.) This aspect of New Orleans may thrive—but it's hard to see how it will do much to change conditions there. It's equally hard to see how presenting a festival with a more local focus would help rebuild the city, either.

Music can do a lot of things, though. Above all, it can provide inspiration and foster connection. Springsteen's always been a man on a mission when it comes to those jobs, and changing bands and singing traditional songs didn't affect that. If anything, this is the strongest outreach he's made in years, stronger than *The Rising*, because he's playing a species of dance music, designed to activate the ass and the mind. And in New Orleans, as backstreets.com noted, "Bruce wasn't preaching to the choir for the first time in a long time."

Springsteen was not only starting a new tour with a new band and new material, but he's Bruce Springsteen, the rock star who is supposed to rise to the occasion. He needed a set that lived up to the drama of closing the first big event in New Orleans since the flood.

His big brass section added Crescent City flavor, and drummer Larry Eagle's fat, syncopated beats kept the cadence right. And Springsteen kept things focused. "O Mary Don't You Weep," the opening song, ends with "God gave Noah the rainbow sign / No more water but fire next time." "Eyes on the Prize," with its recurrent "Hold on," also invoked an embattled spirit: "The only thing that we did right was the day we started to fight." But the show found its legs and definition with a sequence that began with the refugee anthem "My Oklahoma Home Blowed Away," and ran through the Irish antiwar ballad "Mrs. McGrath" before peaking with the Depression-era anthem "How Can a Poor Man Stand Such Times and Live."

Springsteen introduced it with a statement about how shocked, furious, and ashamed he felt about what he'd seen since hitting the town, then dedicated his rewritten version—"Them that's got, got out of town / And them that's not got left to drown"—to "President Bystander." After that, he had the crowd.

With his somber "We Shall Overcome," he gripped them tighter. By the end of it, even violinist Soozie Tyrell turned to wipe back a tear. That wasn't the climax, though. For the encore Springsteen came out and began to sing "My City of Ruins." As he described that "blood red circle," then pleaded for us to "rise up," tens of thousands of fists raised in the air. Thousands of tears formed a new salty flood.

The concluding "When the Saints Go Marching In," also slowed down considerably, should have been anticlimactic. But Springsteen unearthed verses rarely sung, beginning the song with "We are traveling in the footsteps of those who've gone before." In the ruins of America's oldest big city, those words resonated like a midnight echo in an abandoned housing project.

But I left contemplating the last verse, sung by this tour's Bruce sidekick, Marc Anthony Thompson of Chocolate Genius. "Some say this world of trouble is the only one we need / But I'm waiting for that moment when the new world is revealed."

Those lines took my understanding of one of Springsteen's best lines—"Don't waste your time waiting" from "Badlands"—and turned it around. And that made me consider what it would mean to reveal a new world in this life.

We need patience to wait for the new world to reveal itself, that's true. But we mustn't waste that time merely waiting, because only struggle and refusal to surrender can bring that new world forth.

Music can't change the world. But sometimes, it delivers some pretty great marching orders.

YOU'VE GOTTA GET
INTO THIS PLACE

—RRC #218, OCTOBER 2006

I've got to be the only person in the world who watched Harry Carson's induction into the NFL Hall of Fame this past summer and thought of Al Kooper and Wayne Kramer.

Don't get me wrong. I thought plenty about Carson, my favorite player on the smashmouth New York Giants of the 1980s. But Carson's induction brought Kooper and Kramer to mind because, like them, he was asked to wait an unconscionably long time before being inducted. And like them, until he was selected, Carson maintained that he found the whole procedure so ludicrous that he didn't want any part of it.

Like Carson, Kooper and Kramer have impeccable credentials for induction, yet Al's never been on a ballot and Wayne's band, the MC5, has only made it that far a couple of times.

Al Kooper led Blood Sweat & Tears for its only listenable album, played in a seminal New York City blues-rock group, the Blues Project, and created the Super Session project with Michael Bloomfield and Stephen Stills that helped inspire the jam band concept. He also discovered Lynyrd Skynyrd, produced the band's most important records, and served as a sideman on three of the greatest records ever made: the Rolling Stones' "You Can't Always Get What You Want," Jimi Hendrix's *Electric Ladyland*, and, oh yeah,

Bob Dylan's "Like a Rolling Stone," to which he contributed the greatest B3 organ riff ever heard.

Wayne Kramer's guitar playing with the Five cut a narrower furrow just as deep. Echoes of his style—Chuck Berry meets Pete Townshend at more than maximum volume—resound in contemporary bands like the White Stripes and Mooney Suzuki, not to mention such Hall of Famers as the Clash and Sex Pistols. If Kramer didn't invent punk, he and his band perfected it long before Malcolm McLaren ever laid eyes on Johnny Rotten. In recent years, Kramer has made a fabulous series of solo discs, with his slash-and-burn guitar chops tamed only for his occasional forays into post-beatnik storytelling in the vein of a Motor City Bukowski.

My guess is that, like Harry Carson, were they to be inducted into the Rock and Roll Hall of Fame, both Kooper and Kramer would greet it as the honor it is. But one of the things that makes the Rock Hall unique is that you can never be sure of that. There have been some significant snubs: David Bowie didn't show up for the induction ceremony the year he made it and Rod Stewart found it necessary to wash his hair on his big night. Last year, the Sex Pistols, being the Sex Pistols, got more mileage out of Rotten's nasty letter spurning their inclusion in the Hall than they would have received if Sid Vicious's ghost had turned up to accept in person. I didn't take Roger Clemens very seriously when he said that he wouldn't show up at Cooperstown if his plaque showed him as a member of the Red Sox rather than the Yankees, but perhaps Kooper and Kramer are made of sterner stuff. And who knows what would happen if the Rock and Roll Hall of Fame had the smarts to select Motörhead?

As Arlo Guthrie remarked when he stepped onto the stage in the Waldorf Astoria's ballroom to accept an Early Influence Award for his father, Woody, "If my dad was alive, I don't know where he'd be tonight, but it wouldn't be here."

The family of another Early Influence inductee, Mahalia Jackson, demanded that her commitment to singing gospel not be defiled by placing her among so many devotees of lust and mammon. To its credit, the Hall ignored them.

But then, what choice does it have? Rock'n'roll has spent its first half century acting out the implications of Walt Whitman's life lesson: "Do I contradict myself? Very well, then I contradict myself." Rock'n'roll is the home of rejection, refusal, rebellion and, from time to time, riot itself. At the same time, rock'n'roll as conceived by the Hall of Fame voters may start with Elvis and Little Richard, but soon enough fans out to incorporate James Brown, George Clinton, and the giants of punk, girl groups, and (this better happen sooner than later or there really will be a riot goin' on) hip-hop. It's a term that represents not one thing but a set of them, and that set actually did conquer the world of music. There's not a place left on the planet where you can be safe from it.

It's wise to remember Whitman's sanguine response to self-contradiction: "I am large, I contain multitudes." Words that might, better than any song lyrics that come to mind, be carved above the entrance to the Hall of Fame building in Cleveland.

For my part, I promise as a writer and broadcaster to continue to agitate for my friends Al and Wayne to be in the Hall. Whether they like it or not. After all, part of the fun of writing about rock'n'roll is that you get to contradict yourself, too. For instance, even though I play the role of nemesis among Deadheads, I think the Grateful Dead very much belong in the Rock and Roll Hall of Fame. After all, dopey though their music mostly is, they are very famous. [This originally appeared in the August issue of *Hall of Fame Magazine*.]

BONO'S BULLSHIT

-COUNTERPUNCH, MARCH 2007

I read with growing dismay each successive paragraph of David Carr's fawning *New York Times* business section piece on Bono, the (RED) campaign, and *Vanity Fair* yesterday morning. Later, I read the more interesting piece from *Advertising Age* that shows that all the Sturm und Drang from (RED) has generated $18 million for African relief—I wonder if that'll even be enough to replace the condoms Bono's "effective" friend the Shrub refuses to allow U.S. government–supported agencies to deliver. You can be dead certain that it is hardly a match for the combined profits that the corporations for which (RED) fronts expect to pull out of all those products.

What maddens me most is that articles like this are built upon a cascading series of false premises, so I thought I'd catalogue the ones in the *Times* column.

- Bono is a "rare" rock star. Almost every rock star has some kind of charitable endeavor.
- Only the opinions of celebrities (the pope, Bill Gates) are of any consequence in getting the job done.
- Wealth and charity are somehow a "contradiction." Unless there is wealth, there can be no charity in the sense that Bono and Carr use the term (which is quite a bit different than, say, St. Paul's definition).
- Bono is not part of the "Sally Struthers" thing. But of course, his entire project depends on sustaining the image of Africans as unable

to fight for themselves, which is one reason one encounters no Africans—certainly no poor ones—writing for these Bono guest edits. It also depends quite a good bit on their continuing to be humiliated by their poverty (presuming they are, other than in the minds Bono loves most).

- "The crucial role that commerce will play" as a new thing. That has been the barking sales pitch of imperialism and its missionaries from the first day that Europeans landed in Africa. (If Bono didn't think that history began when Jeffrey Sachs conned his first Russian, he'd know this.) Bono doesn't really contend that corporations have a "crucial role," anyway. He premises this statement on his insistent, addled idea that they are the only vehicle by which the problems of African poverty and disease can be solved, despite the fact that everywhere on earth that these corporations exist, there is a great deal of poverty and disease.

- The bizarre assertion that, in this case (but there is always something equivalent to this), China wants to invest in Africa as somehow a boon to the poor. It is either the opposite (the Chinese invest in Africa because they can exploit African workers even more than Chinese ones) or irrelevant (since the profits will go to China, not whatever part of Africa the Chinese are invested in). By the way, Bono knows that there are a couple dozen nations that comprise Africa and that Chinese and other corporations invest in one or more of those, not the continent as a whole, right? I read the whole *Independent* issue and never heard a peep about this reality.

- "Africa is sexy." How many hundred years of racism does that tightly packed cliché contain?

- "People need to know it." If, after all these years of grandstanding, even the kind of person who reads *Vanity Fair* doesn't know it, what does that say about the (RED) approach?

- Changing the subject as soon as the topic of extreme wealth comes up—changing it to AIDS, the only time (it would appear) that AIDS comes up in the interview. Talking from both sides of his mouth as usual: if 5,000 people a day are dying, as they are, for what, exactly, do Bush and Blair and Bono's other powerful cronies earn their high marks?

- Refusing to discuss his ownership of *Forbes*, ostensibly because it's off the topic. It couldn't be more on topic given that Capitalist Tool Bono is about to edit a slick magazine, claims he lives in the world of media, claims that such commerce-friendly publications have a "crucial" role to play.

- Bono sees the world through rose-tinted glasses. The (RED) campaign is based on an entirely cynical view of what motivates humans.

- Bono would have been a journalist. In fact, he did freelance a few pieces, universally undistinguished ones; his more obvious career choices would have been either a priest or a pimp.

- "Striking fear in the hearts of writers." As if this piece weren't an example of how he carefully selects easily intimidated stenographers to do his bidding. (Would a real journalist have stopped at "I don't want to talk about" *Forbes* or let him get away with changing the subject to AIDS when the topic of his own arrogance comes up? Or that if he did quote Bono in those cases that he shouldn't have written a little detail about the contradictions Bono is avoiding, as I have managed to do in about a sentence each here?)

How long before people will call a con a con? How many more people have to die in Africa before we acknowledge that this process is a fraud and a failure and that the evidentiary trail is not short but quite long (it's been twenty-two years since Live Aid)?

DIFFERENT STAGES: THE DIVERGENT PATHS CARVED BY ONE DISEASE, IN LIFE AND ON FILM

—AUSTIN CHRONICLE, MARCH 2007

*C*razy Sexy Cancer is almost a comedy, which is pretty good for a documentary about a thirtysomething woman with a rare cancer. The fact that it exists at all is a little mind-boggling: young adults with cancer are so widely ignored that being swept under the rug would make them more prominent. The icing is that it's about an irrepressible woman named Kristin Carr—a young actress turned "health junkie"—who refuses to accept that she's sick and gets away with it.

I know Kris Carr because she and her colleagues at Red House Pictures sought out my family in 2004. They did this because we run a foundation with two missions: research and treatment of sarcomas, which are the kind of rare cancer Kris has, and the well-being of young adult and adolescent cancer patients. They also did it because our foundation is called the Kristen Ann Carr Sarcoma Fund.

Kristen Carr, my daughter, died of retroperitoneal liposarcoma in January 1993. In February 2003, Kris Carr was diagnosed with epithelioid hemangioendothelioma. The tumors are cousins among the fifty-odd sarcomas, which are about half of all types of cancers, but add up to only 1 percent of all cases of cancer. Kristen and Kris are unrelated except in spirit and cultural background: two beautiful New York City women who imagine themselves fearless and invincible until the roof comes down.

Cancer is not an ennobling disease. A lot of cancer patients—like a lot of people with gingivitis and the common cold—are selfish or angry or just plain jerks. What can you expect from humans who are poked, prodded, poisoned, cut open, denuded of all body hair, and brought within a few heartbeats of death—if they survive at all? There is no adequate description of people who confront the terror, despair, and sheer pain of cancer and still manage to think past their own problems.

Kris Carr doesn't just portray one of those in *Crazy Sexy Cancer*. She shows how it's done. That means we get to see her in painful moments of tearful self-pity, scared out of her mind. It means listening to some of the loopiest practitioners of "complementary" medicine I've ever seen, including the Hippocrates Health Institute in Florida, where we are allowed to witness how to use blades of wheatgrass as an anal suppository. This is not as menacing as Dr. Robert Young's explanation that all disease is caused by excess acidity in our bodies. (See www.quackwatch.org for an explanation of why it not only isn't, but couldn't be.)

Kris believes intensely in this stuff, but she eventually figures out that what she eats isn't who she is any more than what's hanging around in her liver and lungs is. One of the last scenes in the film shows her at the sink with wheatgrass, no blender in sight, but she's laughing. At the Hippocrates Institute, she piles a plate with raw food and says straight into the camera, "This is a plate full of chi. It is also a plate full of gas."

From the beginning, she acknowledges how scared she is—and turns that fear into a kind of protective irony. She is outwardly perfectly healthy—extremely energetic and radiantly beautiful, in fact—which is both confusing and infuriating. Her medical oncologist, Dr. George Demetri (an eminent sarcoma researcher/clinician), assigns her the toughest of all cancer regimens: watchful waiting, which means doing nothing until the disease makes the first move. If you want a cancer treatment that will really piss you off, this is it.

Kris shares the stages with three other patients. They also survive, but the real point is their shared wit, I think, the skewed perspective that being a young person with a life-threatening disease gave each of them. I haven't laughed like this since the last time I sat down with one of the young patients and survivors I know.

Near the end, Dr. Demetri tells Kris that, for the time being, she's free to think of her indolent cancer as nothing but a wart. Kris, who hates the idea that she's incurable, doesn't know what to think or feel, let alone say.

"Are you happy?" asks her father. "Because he's pretty happy. And I want you to be happy, if you can be, just for a minute."

It's a funny place to feel envious, but having stood in the same kind of room and received other news, there I was. I'm pretty sure I'll feel the same way at the festival screening, but that's okay. I'll see one of the Kris Carrs move off to live with all the hope and love the world has to offer. It makes me want to laugh with joy. And cry for the same damned reason. When you find a film that can give you both of those in an hour and a half, your watching it twice probably isn't half enough.

THE FBI AND THE GODFATHER (OF SOUL)

—COUNTERPUNCH, JUNE 2007

I don't know what anti-censorship activist (and longtime *CounterPunch* contributor) Phyllis Pollack expected when she filed a request for James Brown's FBI file under the Freedom of Information Act. I figured she might find some information about his international connections, his work in the civil rights movement, and his meetings with President Nixon and Vice President Humphrey.

There is nothing in the file she received about any of that, which doesn't mean that the Bureau doesn't have it. FOIA requests are routinely given the back of the government's hand, especially by the FBI.

What the feds have released about James Brown is dynamite, though. All of it relates to an accusation made in January 1989 by his then-wife, Adrienne. Mrs. Brown accused local police and judges in South Carolina and Georgia of violating her husband's civil rights. The FBI pursued the case for about ten days and then so listlessly that to call the investigation superficial would give it way too much credit.

Both James and Adrienne Brown tell a very different story than what the public heard. Only an article by Jesse Jackson in *Jet* got it anywhere near straight. The charge that sent James Brown to prison was a so-called "blue light violation." It's all but unprecedented to be given six years in prison for such a crime (refusing to pull over for the cops), let alone receive that punishment from two states. (A young White man sentenced for the same violation the same day received a suspended sentence.)

James Brown wasn't sent to prison because he was a PCP-crazed soul man with a gun. He went to prison because he fled the cops, all right, but he fled them with good reason. For eighteen months Brown had been targeted for harassment by cops in Aiken, South Carolina, and Richmond County, Georgia, which sits right alongside Beech Island, South Carolina, where the Browns resided. It began when Brown got into a fender bender on the Georgia highway he had to use to get home. That one resulted in Brown being jailed after some very dubious proceedings, and allegedly being punched in the mouth.

The FBI report also reveals that Brown did not lead cops on a high speed chase through two states. The police admitted that they followed Brown, but they never "chased" him—they never even turned on their lights or sirens. Nevertheless, there were seventeen bullet holes in the cab of Brown's truck when it was over. Brown did have a shotgun, of course. It was unloaded and "inoperative." Allegedly, the police shot into his car while it was parked in South Carolina, where Brown came to a stop and began talking to local officers. (One Georgia officer took the trouble to knock out the glass in the passenger window with the butt of his gun.)

The allegation that Brown was high on PCP came from a local police analysis of an improperly administered blood test. The cops first said that it showed Brown high on cocaine, then changed their story. The next day, when Brown was again arrested, he was not out careening around the countryside high on anything. He was at the Georgia War Veterans Home in Augusta, visiting his father.

There had been a couple of police visits to the Brown home. Adrienne offered credible explanations for each of them. One wound up with Brown agreeing to put on a benefit concert for local disabled children, but it was "a failure due to the fear of the local Black population of the police, who boycotted the concert."

Brown's version of the incident that sent him to prison conforms in its essentials to his wife's. Brown adds that, while handcuffed, he was punched in the jaw by a cop.

Adrienne Brown also claimed that the trial was unfair, the judge strongly involved in jury selection, a change of venue denied even though ninety local news reports had carried only the police version of the events. Brown had left the country for a European tour, but returned, ill-prepared, for the trial. Nevertheless, the judge forced him to spend the entire trial in the local jail.

You may think that this is just James and Adrienne Brown's attempt to rationalize his misbehavior. That's what you're supposed to think. You're also supposed to think that James and Adrienne Brown had a terrible relationship, that he abused her and may have fired his gun at her. If that's true, then why would Adrienne step up to try to get James out of prison? Why do James, interviewed in prison, and Adrienne Brown, interviewed in an FBI office, tell essentially the same story? Why is there no record in the FBI report of a contrary version of the story from the police? Because the Feebs held it back to protect the guilty officers? Or because they didn't bother to talk with the Georgia and South Carolina police on the record?

Most important, why did no one except Jesse Jackson manage to put even a semblance of the Browns' side of the story into print when America's greatest living musician was sent to prison?

Most mysteriously, where is the FBI's account of the rest of the political and social activism that occupied James Brown's attention during the late 1960s and much of the 1970s?

BONO (HIMSELF) CHALLENGES ME TO A DEBATE

—COUNTERPUNCH, OCTOBER 2007

On a perfectly pleasant evening at the end of May, my colleague Gavin Martin and I were sitting with most of the E Street Band and a few dozen others in the bar of the Merrion Hotel in Dublin after a Springsteen show. It was getting on toward midnight. The room was conversationally loud. I was drinking red wine because I can't stand Guinness, never mind my last name.

The noise level rose noticeably as another troupe entered. It was U2, in full, and their manager, Paul McGuinness. Gavin and I looked at one another in trepidation. We knew what probably came next and sure enough, 'round the corner of the couch came a man dressed in a ginger suit with ginger hair, possibly the recent victim of some surgery, but nonetheless recognizable as Bono Himself.

Himself did not plop down on the couch—there wasn't room and both Gavin and I have trained ourselves against obeisance even to godlike celebrities. So Bono leaned over and began to engage us in conversation. He spewed out theories, analyses, opinions, and attitudes. All he got back were monosyllables and mumbles. We weren't talked out, exactly. Maybe kind of dumbfounded, that He was living out such a perfect caricature of himself.

That's a little unfair because He did eventually ask what we were working on. I don't remember what Gavin said, because I was busy inventorying what I didn't want to talk about: not my book about why *American Idol* is evil (because I feared the response) and not the one about the civil rights movement (because I didn't want to lose my temper about that moronic song that says Martin Luther King did not lose his "pride" when he was assassinated, as if MLK were a preening, pretentious pop star). So I said, "Actually, I've been thinking a lot lately about celebrity politics and how ineffective they are."

I have been. I started at No Nukes (the MUSE concerts), which did succeed, with help from Three Mile Island, in shutting down the U.S. nuclear power industry for twenty-five years. But after that, I couldn't think of a problem that actually gained a solution from celebrity involvement: AIDS is a bigger crisis than ever, hunger is rampant precisely where hunger was rampant at the time of Live Aid, nuclear power is making a comeback in the States, and celebrity endorsements failed to elect the last several presidents. (Which is one reason the McCain-Palin complaint that Obama is nothing but a celebrity is preposterous—they wish.)

Then again, my thinking wasn't so sharp that night. Bono seized my statement and, with a look of determination, declared: "I think I know something about that. And you're dead wrong." I said, well, not as far as I could see. He said, "No. It does work . . . I think we should have a debate about this, Dave. A public debate."

I responded that I had a satellite radio show called *Kick Out the Jams*, two hours every Sunday, and we could do that debate any week he'd like. He said that sounded good to Him, I said I'd put the folks at Sirius to work on it that very night. We parted soon after. A weird story, I thought, but put in a call to Sirius just in case.

He had plenty of wiggle room, Gavin being my only witness. But the next night, Bono told my wife, "Tell Dave not to forget about our debate." Paul McGuinness was standing right next to them, too.

U2's New York office took a couple weeks to get back and then said that the debate would happen, after the band completed recording its new album. (The release date has now been pushed back to January.)

I figure, if it does happen, I can't exactly win—celebrity counts for something, after all—even with the facts on my side. I also think it'll be fun, and some additional listeners (and readers—*RRC* will of course provide a transcript) will get the point. Which is empowerment of those who are not celebrated, who are in fact the wretched of this earth. Those people have voices, too, and the solution to many of these problems is to hear them, speaking for themselves, not through a bullhorn controlled by Bono and Bob Geldof into the ears of politicians who are deaf as a matter of principle.

And if it doesn't happen, believe you me, I'll have even more fun. I'm thinking that, now that the record is due in January, the time to begin the count for "*Kick Out the Jams* Held Hostage" is probably March 1—it's not only a Sunday next year, it's also my birthday.

Of course, I'd rather present the debate . . .

BIG SCAR ON
THE HORIZON

—*RRC* #225, SPRING 2008

A s *RRC* disclosed in September, last May U2's Bono confronted Irish journalist Gavin Martin and myself in the lobby of Dublin's Merrion Hotel. He asked what I'd been working on. I said, "The premise that celebrity politics has been a pretty much complete failure." Bono replied that he wanted to debate the topic in public. He reiterated the challenge the next evening. The witnesses included U2's manager, Paul McGuinness, and my wife, Barbara Carr, among others.

I made sure that Sirius Satellite Radio, which was to broadcast the debate, knew about Bono's invitation. By mid-June, U2's New York office confirmed the plan, asking only that it be delayed until U2 finished recording its next album. I kept it public via *RRC* and my Sirius show, *Kick Out the Jams*.

In November, U2 manager Paul McGuinness rang me. After some brief personal palaver—I like Paul, even though I know he's alluded to me as a "Trotskyist" behind my back—McGuinness sheepishly said, "Bono has asked me to ask you if he can withdraw" from the debate.

I said, "Sure." McGuinness expressed gratitude that I was taking it so well.

"Of course," I added, "this was a public challenge. Backing out's not gonna be private." I did not ask why Bono ducked the debate. Maybe he'd come to his senses, as his apologetics for world capitalism disintegrated with the stock, housing, and employment markets. Maybe he was too busy preparing the banalities he'd blare on the new album.

In the wake of the New Depression generated by Bono's tutors in world finance, it's hardly necessary to issue a point by point refutation of his statements about how the world works. Based on Bono's response to criticism of U2's tax avoidance, he plans to carry to the grave the ardently stupid globalization orthodoxy of *Forbes*, the Wall Street cheerleading rag he co-owns. Can there be anyone else who's ventured a deep thought in the last several months who still believes that the only path to change involves bending the knee to the powerful?

As for the lyrics, don't jump to the wrong conclusion. It can't be denied that Larry Mullen, Adam Clayton, and the Edge can still make fascinating music. Bono's yelped vocals are another matter, his hollow lyrics—where every platitude yields to an obscurantist pretension and back again—yet another. Unfortunately, even if he'd come up with a lyric as great as "One," Bono also carries into each project his offstage political pronouncements, and his fawning affiliations with war criminals such as Tony Blair and George W. Bush.

I don't know why Bono spit the bit on debating these issues in a public forum with a well-informed antagonist. Maybe he decided that he'd fucked up and was about to lower himself by going head-to-head with a journalist. Maybe he doesn't want to deal on the spot with descriptions of his repeated appearances at the conferences of the leading capitalist nations where he's yet to ask his first hard question about anything but Africa; about his settling for promises from world leaders that patently weren't going to be kept, and never doing more than mewing when they weren't; about why it is that Zambian economist Dambisa Moyo, by no means an anti-capitalist, observes that she met him "at a party to raise money for Africans, and there were no Africans in the room, except for me"; or why so many other Africans have complained that he claims to speak for them but has never so much as asked their permission. In regard to the last, I did receive more courtesy than Andrew Mwenda, the Ugandan journalist Bono cursed for raising such questions at an economics conference. (But then, I'm White and Celtic-American.)

It certainly isn't my fault that I have to say "maybe" about all of this.

Bono never got back to me, or had any of his handlers get back to me, about the ground rules for our projected "debate"—his term, not mine. I'd have settled for an honest interview, although "debate" would have been more fun, even though the result was inevitable. No matter how many people sided with my being able to see through the kind of thing William Burroughs once poetically dubbed "a thin tissue of horseshit" it wouldn't be enough to outweigh Big Time Pop Star status.

I don't know. More to the point, you can't know, either.

U2 could be in a fair amount of trouble. The band is old by rock standards, and on the cover of *Rolling Stone* Bono looked much older than the rest because of a physical makeover that tries to deny it. *No Line*'s first single flopped on the radio. The band's decision to have its song publishing company flee Ireland for a tax haven in the Netherlands has been subject to protests in the streets of Dublin and has no obvious justification, despite Bono's fatuous counterclaim that it is his critics who are the hypocrites because free-market values were what created the "Celtic Tiger" of Dublin's capitalist boom economy. The Tiger's death throes look to be particularly messy, in part because of capital flight of just U2's kind. The band's attempt to alter the Dublin skyline with its Clarence Hotel expansion is another example of its ruinous distance from everyday Irish reality.

Bono's self-promotion fares much better on this side of the Atlantic than at home. For instance, he got away scot-free in the American press after declaring during the inauguration concert, "What a thrill for four Irish boys from the north side of Dublin to honor you, sir, Barack Obama, to be the next president of the United States." But Shane Hegarty wrote in the *Irish Times* that only one of the band now lives on Dublin's working class Northside, while Bono has lived more of his life on the Southside.

"During the band's performance of 'In the Name of Love,' " wrote Hegarty, "he described Martin Luther King's dream as 'Not just an American dream—also an Irish dream, a European dream, an African dream, an Israeli dream . . .' And then, following a long pause reminiscent of a man who'd just realized he'd left the gas on, he added, '. . . and also a Palestinian dream.' This was his big shout out to the Palestinians . . . You can't help but marvel at this latest expression of Bono's *Sesame Street* view of the world. Hey Middle East, we just have to have a dream to get along.

"Just ignore the sound of those loud explosions and concentrate on Bono's voice."

So listen, Bono, if you decide to suck it up and face me, I'm still available. I can't win a debate, we both know that, and why you'd want to continue to look feeble and cowardly when you have virtually nothing to lose . . . Well, that's another question I suppose you'll never be asked.

It doesn't mean that those questions are going to go away. Maybe for the tamed tigers of the American pop press, but not for me, or for those people in the streets of Dublin calling you a tax cheat, or for the Africans who feel insulted by your ignorance of their lives, or for that matter, the fans who wonder why you insist on siding continually, if slyly, with the powerful against the powerless.

FANTASTIC JOURNEY: ALEJANDRO ESCOVEDO RETRACES HIS STEPS

—*AUSTIN CHRONICLE*, JUNE 2008

For the last sixteen years, Alejandro Escovedo has been one of America's two or three greatest popular music artists, but if you just moved to Austin, you probably don't know it. If you live somewhere else and know the longtime local, perhaps it's because you saw the YouTube video of him performing "Always a Friend" with Bruce Springsteen & the E Street Band April 14 in Houston. Maybe you were a subscriber to the late, great *No Depression*, the roots-music bible that in 1998 named him Artist of the Decade. They got it right.

It's almost funny Escovedo became more prominent singing one song at the Toyota Center arena than he did in fifteen years of playing some of the most thrilling shows anywhere. I've seen him solo in a room with twenty people, as a duo with another guitar or a violin, with the scabrous glam rock band Buick MacKane, and with the Alejandro Escovedo Orchestra. I've dragged people by the ear to see him at midnight simply by saying, "Other than Bruce, he's the best live artist I know." I got it right, too.

Real Animal, his ninth release, is his *Born to Run*, the album that justifies every superlative ever thrown at him, and it does so by retracing his journey from Orange County, California, where he grew up, to Los Angeles, San

Francisco, and New York. The focus centers on the music he loved and the life he lived before arriving in Austin in the early 1980s. It's not a throwback to other bands he's played with or led, Rank and File, the True Believers, and Ronnie Lane's last, Slim Chance. Rather, it's a throwback to the music of the Stones, Bowie, T. Rex, the Stooges, and all the other rock bands that inspired him. It was even produced by Tony Visconti, who made all those great Bowie and T. Rex records.

(Starting with this album, my wife, Barbara Carr, began managing Escovedo, which has nothing to do with me, other than it's my pleasure to report it. She and her partner, Jon Landau, also manage Bruce Springsteen, as they have since 1980. If I weren't married to Barbara, what I'd do is toss in a few superlatives about how great it is that Escovedo has such prominent, empathetic, and professional management.)

The new disc is the second Escovedo effort to appear on Back Porch, a division of major label EMI, not a milestone most great performers have to wait until they're in their fifties to achieve. Like the man says in "Chelsea Hotel '78," his new song about living in the legendary New York City bohemian hotel at the same time that Sid and Nancy were getting themselves dead there: "It makes perfect sense (*it makes no sense*). It makes no sense (*it makes perfect sense*)."

One reason *Real Animal* is so much better is that Escovedo's superb instinct for finding the right collaborators kicked into overdrive for this project. Even before EMI's Ian Ralfini hooked him up with Visconti, he had begun songwriting with fellow roots-rockist Chuck Prophet. Eventually, they'd write every song on the album together.

"Chuck was a perfect foil, because he had grown up in Orange County," explains Escovedo. "He knew the culture. He was also a surfer. He understood all of that stuff."

The payoff comes in a song like "Swallows of San Juan," a latter-day "Surf's Up." The surfers "crawl up on the shore, roll in the mud and the clay," and behind them the surf is "breaking bigger and harder than anyone's ever seen." It's a song about going back, except you can't. You can't stop trying, either.

"For us, it was wanting to roll around in the music. The source, right?" said Escovedo in early May, when we talked at the Sirius Satellite Radio studios in New York. "The metaphor being the swallows would always build these beautiful mud nests. They would also always come home to this beautiful mission. It was gorgeous. We always went there as kids, in elementary school, on field trips to the San Juan Capistrano Mission.

"My parents would also take all our relatives that would come to visit there because it was so beautiful. I remember it came to represent everything that was beautiful about Southern California at the time. So now, of course, there aren't as many swallows coming back . . .

"[The song] was just about really wanting to get back and roll around in it again. Just roll around in the mud. It's kind of Darwinian, I guess, very much about that primitive, that primal scene."

"Swallows" is a slow song—not a ballad in any other sense—but there are plenty of hard-rocking parallels on *Real Animal*, notably the title cut, an anthemic tribute to Iggy Pop and his Stooges (but mostly Iggy). One smart decision was using Escovedo's road band. It's an odd assortment for a guy who declares at the beginning of one new song, "All I ever wanted was a four-piece band." If you don't expect that to mean guitar, bass, drums, and *strings*, you don't know Alejandro Escovedo's music. These are essential collaborators.

He's worked with drummer Hector Muñoz, who plays like a mighty beat beast throughout *Real Animal*, for twenty-five years; violinist Susan Voelz for about twenty; Brian Standefer, the cellist, for thirteen; guitarist David Pulkingham, with whom he does live gigs when he's playing acoustic, for six. Bassist Josh Gravelin, formerly of Cotton Mather, is the newcomer. Prophet was until lately the other guitarist. He departed to fulfill commitments to his well-trenched solo career.

Real Animal is "the first record in which the band has been involved in the creation of the whole project," affirms Escovedo. "And I mean from the very first. The first song we wrote together was a song called 'Slow Down,' which closes the album. I think it was two days later, maybe that very night, that I took it to the band. We were playing Antone's, and we ran through it at sound check, and we played it that night. We had a lot of gigs going on at that time, so all these songs, as they were coming, we were playing them the very same night that they were written. It was a year in writing the record. By the time we prepared to make it, we had been playing these songs for over a year."

This is where Tony Visconti's skills really came into play. The album's virtually live. Moreover, Visconti's also a terrific arranger and can do charts on the spot, thanks to his handy song flute.

"To work with Tony Visconti was a dream come true, really," says Escovedo. "Not only because of the Bowie and T. Rex records, but the way he used strings on those records. I hope I'm not giving away any of his secrets, but he carries a recorder with him all the time, the kind you have in elementary school. So as he's listening to these tracks being played, he's suddenly coming up with a melody figure. Like 'Hollywood Hills,' let's say.

"He's playing it on his recorder, and then he writes out these perfect charts for a string quartet. And they're very well-written. He hands them out to the strings, and they go over it a couple of times, and it's done, and there you have it. It's an all-in-one thing with Tony."

He pauses. Escovedo often speaks most softly when making his most passionate statements. He does that this time.

"Not only is Tony qualified with all these talents, he's a wonderful human being, too. So it was a pleasure, a real pleasure."

Except for a few tracks on the 1998 live compilation, *More Miles Than Money*, no other Escovedo album comes as close to the full spectrum of music he generates on stage as does *Real Animal*. The basic mode is classic rock, but only if your version of classic rock includes the Stooges and strings. What it most reminds me of is the Stones' *Sticky Fingers*, with lyrics by Pete Townshend, although it's been a very long time since even Townshend wrote these kinds of confessional narratives. The opening bars of "Sister Lost Soul," which is blatant Phil Spector, find Hector Muñoz getting closer to the heart of the opening beats of "Be My Baby" than anyone I've ever heard.

We're not talking concept album, exactly, much less rock opera. Not all the songs relate to the theme. "Sister Lost Soul," arguably the musical heart of the album—its "Sway"—doesn't. There's a trio of songs, for instance, addressing the world to which his parents moved him from San Antonio in 1957, when he was six.

"My parents told me we were going on a vacation. We never went back to Texas. We left everything behind. I mean we left our horse, we left the dog, the cats, everything. We were literally going on vacation. It was my grandmother, my mom, my dad, and all the kids in this little sedan, stuffed into this complete *Grapes of Wrath* thing. And we went west, you know."

In Orange and Huntington Beach, California, Escovedo's father found work as a plumber. "He said that we left because of discrimination in Texas and that the unions in California, which they didn't have in Texas, made it a right-to-work state."

The Escovedo patriarch, Pedro, who died in 2004 at age ninety-seven, also worked as a musician sometimes. Eight of his twelve children grew up to be musicians, notably Coke and Pete, adept Latin-jazz drummers, and Javier, with whom Alejandro formed the True Believers. It wasn't only the music, either. By the time Alejandro was entering his teens, he was completely submerged in Southern California culture.

"Surfing, surf music, all the great ballrooms that were having bands," he relays. "And this one record store where this guy would order me all the import records from England and all the magazines. I'm reading about Bowie and those guys in *Sounds* and *NME* and *Melody Maker*, and stuff like that."

Neither the surfing culture nor the rock culture provided absolute insulation from the culture of his own home. In his 2002 play and accompanying album, *By the Hand of the Father*, Escovedo described the plight of immigrants from Mexico like his father, who came to the U.S. early in the twentieth century. He'd written about it once earlier, in the True Believers' "The Rain Won't Help You When It's Over," his first great song, and the first song he ever wrote. What he couldn't get at was his own generation's dilemma: a loss of connection with Chicano roots that went hand in hand with being refused full acceptance within the modern Anglo world.

"I really wanted to address the fact that the children of these men who crossed the border and started new families in the Southwest—courageously and recklessly—were now immersed in this new sixties culture. Influenced by English bands, I used to wear green velvet suits and snakeskin boots, wanting to have Keith Richards's haircut and be a surfer at the same time.

"Surfing was an Anglo kind of thing. Very racist in a way. And in the Chicano culture, you were abandoning your culture by wanting to be a surfer.

"So I was stuck in this kind of no-man's-land. They used to think I was Hawaiian as a surfer, right? I would go for it so I wouldn't get my ass kicked.

So I was Hawaiian for the day or whatever it took to get out of some hairy situation. It's an interesting thing; I've always wanted to write a whole thing about that."

I'm not sure he's done it here, either, but it's an important point, because the distanced eye of a troubled outsider can be felt in several of the lyrics, like "Smoke," which is set in Rodney Bingenheimer's English Disco, the Sunset Strip nightclub frequented by very young Anglophile teenagers; "Swallows"; and the forlorn barfly lover in "Hollywood Hills."

The music's about inclusion, the way rock & roll always is, even when the words complain about being excluded. Escovedo describes the Nuns, his first band (he was twenty-four, a late bloomer in every way), as the product of crashing film courses in San Francisco.

"We just wanted to make this film, based on the Stooges in a loose way, like Iggy's song 'Dum Dum Boys.' It's about these misfits who can't really play. Since we couldn't play, we thought we'd play ourselves because we kind of looked cool. So we became the band, and the movie was never finished. We became the Nuns. That was the beginning of my musical career, really. We rented a guitar from a music store.

"We were horrible people," he adds. "We were despicable."

He's kidding (*he's not kidding*).

"It's one of those things where we never should have been a band. The singer had never been in a band, didn't even really listen to records other than Stones records. His girlfriend loved Mick Jagger, so he had to emulate Mick Jagger. We did everything wrong. We had two lead singers, and then a keyboard player who was also a singer. Her thing was so different from the rest of the band. She was our Nico. She did this very Germanic, all-dolled-up kinda thing.

"We were just complete misfits."

Yet from the time they first played Mabuhay Gardens, with a band led by Chip and Tony Kinman of Rank and File as the other act on the bill, the Nuns helped define the San Francisco version of punk. The city's eclecticism was what made that scene different from New York's or London's or the one in L.A.

"San Francisco had such a bohemian atmosphere. We'd go around North Beach and hand out free tickets to the Cockettes—what was left of them—the Angels of Light, and you know, Bruce Conner and all the people who hung out at City Lights Bookstore. So it was a slightly older crowd, a totally different trip. We brought in all kinds of things. It was a multimedia circus in San Francisco."

That's an insider speaking. Directly afterward, the outsider shows up.

"The Nuns could never find a gig, because San Francisco was pretty much run by Bill Graham. So for bands like us to play, you had to find your own gig . . . or find somebody who was crazy enough to let you play in a bar.

"We got a gig on Fisherman's Wharf. It was one of those things where they had the speakers out on the street to lure the tourists in. As soon as we plugged in and cranked it up, within half a song they threw us out of the bar. We had lost our gig right away. So we went back to our rehearsal studio on Folsom Street and put up a sign: 'If you came to see the Nuns, we're at so-and-so address on Folsom.' The only two people that showed up were Chip and Tony, who had come to see us. So they came to our rehearsal, and we performed for them. We did our full set for our girlfriends and Chip and Tony."

Back to the insider again. Except that he then says the Nuns are still a band, only "now they're supposed to be vampires."

On *Real Animal*, "Nuns Song" and "Chip 'n' Tony" have very little to do with each other, except that both are among the album's more belligerent songs. (The title track, by far the most antagonistic, wouldn't have been out of place in Buick MacKane's set list.) Why "Chip 'n' Tony" is set this way is interesting, since that pounding beat is exactly what Rank and File reacted to. They stepped outside of punk, keeping the attitude but not the beat. From this outsider move came alt-country, which is, let's face it, one long insider story.

Even here the stories tumble together, much the way Escovedo's musical interests haven't so much blended as converged. "Chelsea Hotel '78" describes living in the New York landmark, where he moved just after the Nuns had opened for the Sex Pistols' final show at Winterland in San Francisco, 1978. It was punk time.

"We came to New York, we lived in the Chelsea, and we toured the East Coast by Amtrak. We were on $5 per diem back then. I remember the day that I came down to the lobby and Sid was checking in, him and Nancy, with Jerry Nolan and Johnny Thunders [of the New York Dolls] in tow."

The change came when Chip Kinman moved to New York, too, and he and Escovedo decided to do a country-punk band. Rank and File belonged in New York about as much as an orange grove.

"It was the worst. We used to put ads in the paper looking for a country western drummer, and we'd get guys who'd say, 'Yeah, I love the Riders of the Purple Sage.'"

They landed a tour: seven gigs in seven weeks. On the night Ronald Reagan was elected president in 1980, they left for Dayton, Ohio, with $25, a bag of pot, and a roast chicken. All of it was gone when they reached the first show. Eventually, they made Austin, which was filled with people they didn't know, except for Lester Bangs, who had moved there because he had friends, or *a* friend, in writer Ed Ward.

"We played at Raul's; it was still open. The Armadillo had just closed. And I just fell in love," smiles Escovedo. "I remember calling New York and saying, 'I wanna move here.'"

"Everyone was just so friendly, and the food was so great, and the musicians . . . I mean, suddenly I see Townes [Van Zandt] in person for the first time. Blaze Foley is there, Pat Mears, Jubal Clark—all these great songwriters, man."

He hadn't written a song yet, but songwriters were already a passion.

Leaving Austin, Rank and File finally made it to its last few dates, which were in the Pacific Northwest. Along the way, they picked up Tony Kinman. Chip on his own was one thing. Chip and Tony together were another. On the drive back, the rhythm section quit. Escovedo and the Kinmans reconstituted the band back in New York and stayed just long enough to be able to afford the move to Austin, where they lasted a year or so, just long enough to permanently embed Escovedo as part of the city's music culture.

This account untangles the story in a way that does no justice at all to the flow of *Real Animal*, which is a narrative of something else: of perseverance, commitment, faith, perhaps even aging wisely.

"The first solo album, [1992's] *Gravity*, is really the Austin experience. That and *Thirteen Years*," he says. "With this record, I really wanted to get away from those things. I didn't want to address the things that I had on *The Boxing Mirror*. I'm done as far as that's concerned."

2006's *The Boxing Mirror*, produced by another one of his heroes, John

Cale, is a journal from a dark night, the period when Escovedo's father died and when he faced death himself as a result of hepatitis C. During this period, benefits were held and *Por Vida*, a tribute album, appeared, all the kinds of things that usually happen when a beloved musician is dying.

Then Escovedo found a hepatitis treatment that worked. Today, he looks great, with that shining, high-cheekboned face, the brilliant child's smile, and the pomaded hair slicked back, clothes always chosen to fit perfectly, and sometimes, amazing shoes. (The current pair is very red and very pointed.) To see him, you wouldn't guess he has seven children, the oldest almost forty, the youngest under ten, let alone that he was sick unto death not long ago.

At the Continental Club, on the Sunday night of South by Southwest 2008, where he performed the whole show without ever touching his usual quartet of guitars, he was in command of his material in a new way. The energy level remained as ever in the red, but the attitude behind it demonstrated a different confidence. He introduced "Slow Down," the first song he and Prophet wrote, which wound up as the last track on *Real Animal*, by talking about what it means to get older. To get old, even. Losing one's father does that.

"That was huge. You know how you think you're prepared for all these things? I was not prepared," he says. "[*The Boxing Mirror*] is a really beautiful album, a dark album, somewhat dark. Not in a downer way, but it addresses some serious things, you know. With this album, I just wanted to tell a story. I wanted it to be like a movie."

Real Animal tells the story he has to tell: his own. A story so old it always seems new, because it is, as James Baldwin wrote, "the only light we have in all this darkness." Looking back, the pain of it never outweighs the pleasure. The Nuns may have been crazy enough to turn into vampires, but Alejandro Escovedo not only survived the experience, he got a great song out of it. The Chelsea may have been the place punk rock went to die, but it was also where you could meet up with Neon Leon, who was busy prefiguring Prince. Ronnie Lane may have had his life wrecked by a horrible illness, but Alejandro Escovedo, who once faced a similar horror, has just made his finest album and looks fit enough for many more.

"If you asked me what my music is like, I really couldn't answer that in one sentence. I couldn't give you a sound bite," he insists. "Because it's about so many things. It's about my brother's bands, the larger bands, and the arrangements of Duke Ellington, which somehow seeped into all the stuff that I was doing. Then you take 'Sleepwalk' by Santo & Johnny, and Brian Eno, Mott the Hoople, and Ian Hunter's songwriting. You take all those things and throw them into one thing, and somehow you come up with what we've tried to create over the years."

"Slow Down," the first which is last, begins with an incredible scene. The singer walks the beach holding hands with his new love, out on the strand. On the pier, a band plays. "Close your eyes, and you can hear the music in the wind," he tells her. "Out on the pier, that's the Ike and Tina Turner Soul Revue. I don't know what this means to you, but it was everything to me."

I know this is his story. It's also mine, though somehow, in my version, it might easily be the Alejandro Escovedo Orchestra up there. The image is indelible. It does slow you down, the way anything does when it takes your breath away. It's a gift, and like most gifts, it both makes no sense and makes perfect sense. And the person who gives it is always a friend.

INTRODUCTION
TO SECTION 4

The 2010s

In the end, we all have our limits. And that means we all have our own ideas of what's right and what's wrong. I'm not so much of a hypocrite to think I know how to weigh those scales. I don't. And it bothers me. But you can't let things that bother you always keep you out of them.

It's because I'm a journalist. At the end of the night, there I am with a pen in my left hand and a pen in my right hand. And I'm an American: people fought and died for the right to do what I'm doing. Absenting yourself does not make you absent. It does make you gutless. The thing I hate about these "serious" journalists is that they don't want to pull their socks out of their shoes to make sure justice is attained. Me, I'd piss on those shoes.

I talk a lot about this thing: trying to be fair. That's a simple way of saying it. Trying to be fair. If my old man had been more fair, he probably would have beaten me up only half as much as he wound up doing. And I'd be a much better person. No doubt in my mind about it.

At one point, I asked myself—for some months—how was I going to balance what I did and wanted to do, how do I deal with that in the light of having children and grandchildren? I wanted a fairly normal life. This is insane but true: I just thought I was being normal the whole time. That's one of the reasons I irked so many people. I've thought to myself—on the death penalty or some other issues—this goes so far over the line, I can't do what I should do. But it hasn't happened. I don't think it has.

At a certain age, you're cocksure about a lot of things that are wrong and wrong and wrong and not very right. And that's okay. There's the Springsteen line (from "Tunnel of Love"): "You've got to learn to live with what you can't rise above." (People think I'm always quoting Springsteen; I don't want to disappoint them.)

What do I think of having my writing collected like this? I like enough of it that I'm proud; and I dislike enough of it that I'm anxious. And I'm very flattered. And I'm very cognizant that I have a lot of friends who are important to me in a lot of different ways. And I hope I can live up to them.

—*D.M.*

AMERICAN IDIOT: FINALLY, A MUSICAL THAT ROCKS

—COUNTERPUNCH, OCTOBER 2010

Producer Vivek Tiwary invited me to *American Idiot* on Sunday night, composer Billie Joe Armstrong's last performance as St. Jimmy. I'd seen the show opening night, when Green Day attended but did not perform, unless you count the last curtain call. I've been thinking ever since about the next time I'll see the show, and that's something that Sunday didn't change at all.

Some of my friends may find this remarkable, because I'm a notorious loather of Broadway musicals.* Hated *Rent*, thought the music in *A Chorus Line* was worthless, liked the first act of *Dreamgirls* pretty much, despite myself. With *Tommy*, I liked what Des McAnuff did to straighten out the narrative and the way the production used video elements more than

---

* Love straight plays, have since I saw a collegiate *King Lear* in junior high school. When I first moved to New York, a friend worked at Circle Rep and I got to see a batch of plays, including the original production of Lanford Wilson's *The Hot L Baltimore*, that rank with my greatest cultural experiences. I even liked *A Raisin in the Sun* in its Puff Daddy incarnation, though not because of Puffy. My friend Vivek was a producer on *Raisin* and he's got a more prominent role in producing *Idiot*, but I'm not sure I'd risk *The Addams Family* even for him.

that version of the music. (I'd forgotten 'til now that it also played at the St. James.)

But *American Idiot*, as rewritten and directed by Michael Mayer, is such a breakthrough that it no more needs Billie Joe's charisma than it does an orchestra. (Billie Joe did a fantastic job, creating a very different Tony Vincent, sly and crazy rather than sinister and slithering.)

When Billie Joe as St. Jimmy appeared at the top of the stairs, high up at the back of the stage, the audience went off like a rock concert. But it didn't stop the show for more than a few beats, any more than similar mania stops rock shows. *American Idiot* is way too close to a rock concert for that. A great rock concert, one that renders you alert to everything from the ways you've changed or haven't since you went to your last one to how this one is going to change you, too.

Idiot has very little to do with any of the shows mentioned above, although like McAnuff's *Tommy*, it uses video screens and a few other elements on its simple, efficient, but high-tech set. The performances (particularly from the Idiot himself, John Gallagher) are way better than anything mentioned above, *Dreamgirls* included, yet they are Broadway not rock'n'roll performances—that is, you always know you're seeing an interpretation, and you're meant to know it.

What makes *Idiot* different and important is very simple: it trusts the music. The show is high volume, rock'n'roll show loud—they've had to turn it down in order to avoid bothering the play across the street—and the musicians, a very fine eight-piece band handpicked by Green Day, rock to the bone.

The singing challenges, even if it never changes, the Broadway paradigm. Walking out of *Sweeney Todd* years ago, I asked Brian De Palma why I hated such shows. He said, "Well, you love stories and you love music. In musicals, story is compromised by having to stop for the songs, and the music is compromised because it has to tell the story."

That's part of what I mean by trusting the music. This music can tell the story by itself, we know that from the album. And by music I mean music: the sound of each song, not just its lyrics.

In rock, slurring notes (thus, inevitably blurring verbal phrases) is a requirement, part of the link to the South and to blues. By that measure,

Broadway singing is marred by excessive enunciation. Part of what letting the lyrics slur and be buried in sound means is that in *Idiot* the actors make music with facial expressions much more similar to the way that they speak than in conventional musicals. One of my favorite memories from Sunday is thinking, "Gee, I'm sitting in the fourth row and in no danger of seeing anybody's tonsils."

Trusting the music in this way also means trusting the listeners. Between the volume and the slurring, there's absolutely no danger that the audience can fully grasp in one sitting any plot points established by the lyrics, especially in a show that probably doesn't have ninety lines of spoken dialogue in ninety minutes. The trick is not caring—or rather, giving the performers the permission to act as if all is perfectly understood.

Which is back to trusting the sounds. Or as Pete Townshend elaborated in an interview last year, "In a pop song the function was different to the songs from music theatre. There was already a story being experienced, by the listener—the context was already established." That is, you know things about the story because of the sounds and the fragments of lyrics you do acquire, not from the lyrics as a whole.

The *American Idiot* plot isn't all that hard to grasp anyhow, being a story many times as old as rock'n'roll's evolution into rock, which is when it hardened into almost a formula: drugs, sex, war, music, and a whole lot of pain on the way to some specks of dawning maturity. It's not a story to be trivialized (though many have tried), but like every kind of aural epic, the quality comes down to how passionately it's rendered. On the album, Green Day treated it like autobiography without ever denying the inherent clichés. Gallagher and his on stage mates, Stark Sands and Mike Esper, greet the challenge of relaying it with only partial help from the lyrics, as if it were a brand new thing in the Broadway world—which I think it is. So *American Idiot* seems excited about itself, which is what makes me want to go there some more.

A lot of this has to do with Michael Mayer's courage in letting it happen like this, but I think it's also about who the show brings into the St. James. You can see Sunday's post-curtain number on YouTube and it's worth seeing. As every night, the entire cast appears with acoustic guitars to sing Green Day's "Good Riddance (Time of Your Life)." It's a beautiful moment because it is a rock song in the Townshend mold and because it speaks to what someone—like me—might take from the show: "It's something unpredictable / But in the end it's right."

Sunday, before everybody else started strumming, Billie Joe brought a folded piece of lined paper out of his pocket and laid it before him on the stage. He crouched over it and sang a farewell to the show. When "Good Riddance" ended (this part isn't on YouTube), he accepted a bunch of roses from a fan in the front row. He paused, then handed her his guitar. The entire house roared its approval.

Security personnel confronted the girl with the guitar when she got to the aisle. She clutched it tightly as her girlfriend chastised the women from security: "He gave it to her." "It's not his," the woman from security replied.

For about two minutes it was a standoff, with the crowd hooting its outrage. ("You're going to like what's in the papers tomorrow a lot more if she keeps it than what'll be in 'em if she doesn't," I muttered to Vivek, who already knew that.) Then somebody sent word from backstage—probably that Billie Joe's wages could be docked for the price of the guitar—and the fan left with the guitar. The crowd went nuts again. Not so much because this was justice. But because it was looking for another excuse to go nuts again.

You wonder why I want to go back? That's so rock'n'roll, I'm pretty sure it doesn't happen at rock shows anymore.

THE GREAT GENERAL JOHNSON

—*COUNTERPUNCH*, OCTOBER 2010

G eneral Johnson died last week. He wrote the first great rock'n'roll song not about rock'n'roll itself exactly, but about why the music would prevail. And he wrote a ton of other stuff, though that one and "Patches," his deeply affectionate reminiscence of hard times in the rural South, got the attention.

"It Will Stand" was a prophetic voice in its way, as much as James Baldwin's was. "It swept this whole wide land / Sinkin' deep in the hearts of man." Grown-ups must have thought he was nuts. It was 1961. Rock'n'roll was out of fashion since . . . oh, maybe the plane crash. Two years might as well have been forever. Who else believed that music would have a comeback?

Every kid who heard it. I was ten, it never left my mind all through the crap about the Beatles, long hair, too simplistic . . . Ten years of blah blah blah.

And that whole period at Invictus Records . . . man! At that point, he was the most powerful ally Holland-Dozier-Holland (who owned the joint) possessed.

In that time, the early '70s, General Johnson wrote some of the greatest anti-war songs: "Men Are Getting Scarce," "Bring the Boys Home." He wrote the greatest anthem of the down-low, "Band of Gold." He wrote Laura Lee's

"Wedlock Is a Padlock," which Loretta Lynn ought to have covered. Not to forget Honey Cone's rendition of his version of "One Monkey Don't Stop No Show," which I actually like better than Joe Tex or Oscar Brown Jr., and I don't hardly ever like anything better than Joe Tex. Beyond that, "Westbound #9" was just classic, like an updated "Expressway to Your Heart" from the Motor City.

For his Invictus group, Chairmen of the Board, Johnson wrote about fifteen great songs including "Patches" (I think that they did it before Clarence Carter defined it). The Chairmen also had a stage act that is totally underrated, with wild-ass Harrison Kennedy adding a P-Funk thing. I remember him racing through the streets of some theater, in New York or Detroit, I can't remember, à la Shider, only wearing lime-green jockey shorts instead of the diaper.

I interviewed them for *Creem*, but can't remember what I wrote. Maybe nothing. I was taking it in, but maybe not ready to spit it back out. It was one thing to see Funkadelic, a Black rock band, but it was another thing for that kind of outrageousness to pop up with vocal groups. It made me ready for Labelle and Sylvester, probably.

Then all those beach music records, a steady stream of them it seemed like, as they worked the Carolina beaches. Just dance grooves—I never found a great song in any of those various albums they did for little labels down there. Never found any bad songs, either. Which is tougher than it might seem.

To me, General Johnson was a giant. A ton more interesting than a sometimes-inspired hustler like Solomon Burke.

Probably that's just my problem, but . . . what if it isn't?

TO SET OUR SOULS FREE

—*RRC #229, SUMMER 2012; DAVE MARSH AND DANNY ALEXANDER*

Y ou might wonder, for good reason, why we are writing about Springsteen's Wrecking Ball *five months after its release. Some of the reasons have been personal. But there are better reasons why we're speaking up now, and speaking in the way that we are. Part of it is that we both like to listen slow, and listen frequently. Too much music writing now seems hasty and undigested, and that takes a toll. (Deadline perceptions are fine if there's nothing important in the details, vastly inadequate if there is.) More important was our desire to hold off until we'd heard a larger dialogue: Just what would the world make of this record and what would we have to add to that conversation? But that dialogue has been slow in coming. Most of what was written and said about the album missed the overriding sense we have that this record speaks directly to the Arundhati Roy/Grace Lee Boggs maxim: "A new world is possible. A new world is coming. A new world is already here."*

Because we listen both as long-term Springsteen fans and as activists, that's what we heard here from early on. It's a big part of what makes Wrecking Ball *something different, especially in the way these songs interact with the dialogue about the movements for social change currently taking shape in our society. This album doesn't sound like anything else he has done, and its call stands apart, both musically and lyrically. It calls for us not only to react, emotionally, psychologically, even spiritually, but also to act, to not just stand but fight "shoulder to shoulder and heart to heart," the last words sung on the record.*

Such a call requires—demands—a response in kind: detailed, direct, and the result of lots of interplay between our own ideas and those of others. So we've taken our time and as much space as we needed to use. We hope this is part of a beginning.

Bruce Springsteen's *Wrecking Ball* opens with an alarm, with air-raid sirens blaring and tribal drums kicking. The singer, recognizing the enormity of what he's dealing with, begins in quiet caution. He knocks on the palace door; he desperately seeks a map to bring him home; he stumbles over once-kind neighbors turned callous to his suffering and their own. Like the man in "Rank Stranger," the Stanley Brothers song that influences so many rock dystopias, the singer can't believe the devastation he's seeing, not in the streets but in the faces, the gestures, the way people are standing and moving: "Where's the eyes, the eyes with the will to see . . . Where's the work that will set my hands, my soul free . . . Where's the promise from sea to shining sea?" There's one thing he needs to make sure of: he chants it obsessively, as if himself amazed that he still fully believes it, even against all this evidence that it can't be true: "We take care of our own, we take care of our own / Wherever this flag's flown, we take care of our own."

Trying to figure out how to realize that promise occupies the bulk of this album, the most complete narrative work Bruce Springsteen has created since the trilogy that runs from *Born to Run* to *Darkness on the Edge of Town* to *The River* (1975–1980). At the end of the first two albums in that series, we found his central character left wounded and stranded, on a hilltop above those who'd given up, with no choice but to come back down into the valley of mundane reality, where he has remained ever since. But now that mundane world itself has become tinged with fantasy, swept up in a phantasmagoria of all-against-all: marauders, carrion eaters, and blank-faced rank strangers who, though some have intentions every bit as noble as those of "The Promised Land" and "Born to Run," find the game impossibly rigged. Those "different people" who came down here to "see things in different ways" have indeed swept all away before them. It's a haunted place now, beset by vultures and wrecking balls. Even with their bones picked over, it seems the dead may have better advice to offer than the living.

Determined to pull out of this world without options, Springsteen begins by deploying some of his old tools: layer upon layer of guitar against swelling keyboard, driving percussion, exuberant backing vocals, and lush strings. We've known this guy for decades, and part of what we know is that, at his core, he's just as desperate as *Wrecking Ball*'s first track makes him appear. But he's not nearly so bereft of new ideas as our first reaction to desperation implies. He has, as he so often does, the other possible reaction to desperation, the one that generates alternatives rather than merely succumbing to realities—the ace in the hole called hope. He also has new collaborators, who helped him find loops, samples, an array of new instruments—many of them antique—and, most startling, new beats as well. The surprise is the dawning realization, as he moves remorselessly through a dozen songs describing this grotesque landscape and its denizens, that Bruce still believes that if we look hard enough we'll discover that we, too, have just as much reason for hope as for despair—and at least as many devices for realizing that hope. Particularly the hope that, if not America, at least Americans can remember what life is supposed to be all about, and then . . . well, then, act like they believe it, mainly. And beyond that, can get to the hard work of change, not as rank strangers but "shoulder to shoulder and heart to heart."

In the world Springsteen invented for himself (and us) forty years ago, hope was an abundant commodity—hope came cheap. Today, hope's so much harder to discover that most of the time it seems practically beyond price. Nevertheless it's the indispensable key to solving the fundamental question posed by *Wrecking Ball*: Can a society that's torn apart "from the shotgun shack to the Superdome" function on its most basic levels? Should it? Will it? It's all too obvious (to everyone but the willfully blind) that we no longer take care of more than a few. But how do we admit it to ourselves and begin again?

Springsteen literally prayed for some force—human or supernatural, maybe both—to provide him with this answer a decade ago, in "My City of Ruins." Now he's telling us what *he* thinks. He's singing not just about changing the dialogue, but altering the way we behave. That is, he wants to begin—he wants all of us to begin—confronting our own weaknesses and illusions. Springsteen presses a point he's made since he first called out, and it's fundamental to dismantling those lies we tell ourselves: "Nobody wins unless everybody wins"—taking care of me and taking care of you can't be separate options. They have to become part of one process.

Like any great musician—and this album marks him as one, not just a great songwriter or supposed poet—Springsteen's process begins with listening, hearing what's around him and what's within him. James Baldwin said it: "[T]he man who creates music . . . is dealing with the roar rising from the void and imposing order on it as it hits the air." On *Wrecking Ball*, Bruce creates from what he hears a catalogue of what he calls his own: a cross section of American voices and sounds that connect to various pieces of himself. And that first song's emergent voice, proclaiming the necessity of our commonality in order to retain our ability to rave on as individuals, is an almost predictable piece of what makes Bruce Springsteen who he is.

But with his very next step, the tone turns darker. "Easy Money" bursts forth with bombastic percussion accompanied by handclaps. Springsteen sings with an all-but-indecent braggadocio and a twinkle in his eye—veteran fans may recognize the kid who tossed the bus driver a quarter and told him to keep the change. Seemingly mundane preliminaries (getting dressed, taking care of the pets) give way to busting the town wide open. It sounds like this guy's out for nothing more or better than kicks. And then he states the grim facts as he knows them, and he knows them well: "There's nothing to it, mister, it won't make a sound /when your whole world comes tumbling down." He notices that "all the fat cats . . . just think it's funny," and he's made a choice. If he has to be a fool, he's not going to be their fool. The music evokes gangster charisma, a recklessness as infectious as it is cynical. The soaring shout and hoot and holler of his vocal, the steel guitar, fiddle, and exuberant backing voices travel alongside it, taking hold before the point emerges clearly: "Easy Money" tramples the line between an ordinary fool headed for destruction and a rock and roller bound for glory. It's anything but a plan to confront Springsteen's own illusions, much less the illusions of the larger audience. Such a way out isn't even on offer. Yet the song does possess a seemingly unsinkable spirit. Such swagger can make holding tight to one's illusions seem like enough, but the way it works out, generally only the fat cats are still smiling at the end. This might well be the character in "Ramrod," except the guy in "Ramrod" wasn't looking to kill anybody. That's how much or how little the world has changed.

"Shackled and Drawn," a work song through and through (like "Night," "Factory," and "Youngstown," among numerous others before it), begins with a spry guitar figure over pounding percussion. This one's about awakening to a realization that if wages aren't quite exactly slavery, they certainly leave the worker "trudging through the dark in a world gone wrong." It rejects the 9mm nihilism of "Easy Money," but the only replacement offered is a primitive "Badlands" slugged out on an anvil. When the lyric asks, "What's a poor boy to do but keep singing his song?" he's obviously asking a personal question—but also an ethical question and, in a collapsing economy, a practical one. It's certainly the only way this artist knows to move closer to taking care of his (and ostensibly our) artistic concerns while "up on Banker's Hill, the party's going strong." He hangs on to that last word so that it all but evokes the rhyme "wrong" before returning to the chain gang: "down here below, we're shackled and drawn." But the moment of ignition comes when a female preacher's voice calls out, "I want everyone to stand up and be counted tonight," and Springsteen shouts back, relieved to find that somebody *is* alive out there.

The narrator of "Jack of All Trades" could be any of the guys we've met so far. But he could also be any of a hundred other characters Springsteen has created, from the little kid with his feet rooted in the earth and his head in the stars in "Growin' Up" to the father who drives with his son on his lap in "My Hometown" and returns to walk through the town square, wondering when it all *really* went to hell in "Long Walk Home," or the man in "Countin' on a Miracle," hearing a new heartbeat as he lays against his wife in their sleeping bag and tries to figure out how he's going to take care of yet another life. "Jack" is sung in the voice of a man whose best moments have been left behind, down by the river or in the aisles of a supermarket or in the dust of Iraq . . . or maybe there are pieces of him scattered in all those places, and many more. (Any Springsteen fan could give you a list three times this long and twice as specific.) But there's a reason he can speak so frankly as he sits with his hands around a cold coffee cup, leaning across the kitchen table, looking straight into the eyes of the person he loves most and telling the biggest lie of them all: "Honey, we'll be all right."

The music uses the chords of "When the Saints Go Marching In" (in Curt Hamm's trumpet solo, it simply is "Saints"), and they bear what that song always carries, a vision of the certain finality of death so unquestion-able that all arguing must cease. Which doesn't mean the details don't matter—the way he sings "the banker man goes fat," so that it threatens to resonate as "fair," is the best example. He sounds weary on that line, like he's almost sighing, and the fairness is understood to be that of yet another rigged game. It just means the truth is what it is, a pitiless pathway to the grave. If you take it seriously enough, you're likely to want to take someone else with you—and if you go one step beyond that, you wind up in the coda, a Tom Morello guitar solo so remorseful it beggars any language but its own sounds. And the violin that follows that hums the same tune, albeit maybe another verse. Maybe the one that talks about "when the moon grows red with blood."

The tragedy of Springsteen's career may be summarized in the reaction of many of his veteran American fans to the appearance of this epic song in concert: they get up and head for the toilets and the concession stalls. It's not that they don't get it. They *won't* get it. (In the European shows, the song is accompanied by a stillness and silence so deep it carries a jolt.) And so, as Springsteen says for the first but not the last time on this album, "it's happened before and it'll happen again." Now's the time for your tears.

The shimmering starlight emanating from the final note of "Jack of All Trades" opens the door to the full-blown fight song that follows. "Death to My Hometown" begins in Celtic delirium, pounding drums offset by hand-claps, a penny whistle, a touch of banjo. Vocals enter, but they're chanting transcendental Pentecostal incoherencies. There's a hint of cannon fire. But the clearest noise of all, perhaps unintentionally not buried in the mix (or maybe situated there with perfect calculation, like a Motown tambourine), comes almost three minutes into the song. It's a gun being cocked—and like the good student of Chekhovian drama he is, having now mentioned the option of the gun in three out of five songs, Springsteen makes sure this one goes off, though you'll have to listen up to hear it. (That this is buried in the mix cannot be accidental.)

Do we know the character Springsteen portrays here? He's not the guy standing by the roadside, kicking a dead dog—although they might be related. He's not the maniacal nihilist who calls himself Johnny 99. He's maybe more like the guy in "The Big Muddy," who believes "You start on higher ground but end up somehow crawlin'." Except *this* guy refuses to crawl—that's what that shotgun's for, a way of keeping him on his own two feet. It's how he takes care of his own.

This infuriated Irish-American damns his enemies, gives them names ("marauders," "vultures," "greedy thieves"), declares in sputtering rage that the greatest of the injustices is that they "walk the streets as free men now." But what sort of justice would he have them face? The gun goes off, but without repercussion . . . And when he has the bastards most clearly in his sights (and this guy's vision is a lot clearer than Jack's), he suggests that something else is what might work: "Now get yourself a song to sing / And sing it till you're done / Sing it hard and sing it well / Send the robber barons straight to hell."

It's a rock'n'roll answer. But it's also something else: it's straight out of the beloved community that produced the most effective American social change of Springsteen's lifetime, the Civil Rights Movement. For this ever-moral (and moralizing) artist, the song is always mightier than the shotgun. Hold that thought.

Hold it tight against what comes next.

"This Depression" sounds not nearly so much depressed as desperate, and not the desperation of the outlaw who's crossed some invisible line, more that of a man who's being slowly tangled by the lines of hip-hop beats, ethereal keyboard washes, floating wordless backing vocals, and more Tom Morello guitar, which tools through this soundscape of isolated misery as if it's on a lonely Jersey Girl's journey between stars . . . although this certainly isn't the lights of the sun, let alone where the fun is. More likely, it's a roughly spackled ceiling dropping paint chips onto her Sistine Chapel dreams.

The nakedness of the song's self-disclosure marks it as utterly contemporary. The voice stripped of bravado, or even energy, to face the struggles ahead, suggests the dead ends and bad dreams of "The Promise" and (more so) "State Trooper," where the singer declares "the only thing that I got's been botherin' me my whole life." But whether "This Depression" refers to the character's personal clinical depression or an international economic depression, or more likely both, it's absolutely not a way out. In fact, it's not even a coherent response to the threat we've just been hearing about. He keeps declaring, to some unspecified "baby," "I need your heart," although the musical heart of the song, its pulsation, stumbles around like it might give out (or give up). And you have to wonder if he might be staring into a mirror. Until you see that, if that's so, it's because we all are.

In the midst of a vinyl revival, one thing you'd imagine would be mentioned more often is that Bruce Springsteen is approximately the last artist whose records almost always divide as if side one and side two were pertinent digital terms. On *Wrecking Ball* the turn from "This Depression" to the title track clearly marks the story's emergence as a struggle toward light, after six songs cursing the darkness.

That light doesn't exactly pour in. These lyrics are the ultimate mixture of the personal and the political on an album where that particular combo is the daily special. Although the song's metaphor depends on the planned demolition of Giants Stadium in the Jersey Meadowlands after the Springsteen run of shows there in 2009, even back then it wasn't "about" the disappearance of a major concert venue or even a quasi-historical site. Bruce first sang it on September 30, 2009—one week to the day after his sixtieth birthday, annus horribilis for any rock star. It was also a year since Springsteen traveled the campaign trail with Barack Obama, and ten months since Obama's administration had begun squandering whatever chance there may have been that the vultures of Wall Street would no longer walk the streets as free men.

It's a funny song, but the humor's anything but light. For every "mosquitoes grow big as aero-planes" and jangly guitar lick, there's "when all our victories and glories have turned into parking lots," a mordant summation of both the man and the building's career highlights. We are urged to raise up our glasses to those who have fallen ("because tonight all the dead are here"), but we are much more surprisingly and unsentimentally instructed that the way out of the mess is to "hold tight to your anger and don't fall to your fears." That's not the advice of a nice guy from the backstreets. It sounds more like the admonition of a seasoned barroom brawler.

More than that, we're told that even after the game is decided and the wrecking ball is heading straight for a sock in our eye, we have to hold tight and not fall because "hard times come and hard times go / and hard times come and hard times go / and hard times come and hard times go / and hard times come and hard times go / and hard times go" and then, his voice coming down on the words like his strings on a power chord, "Yeah, just to come again." This is a man who's sick of laughing in the face of defeat after defeat. This is a guy who won and then watched the victory turn particularly sour. This is a guy who's not sure anybody within earshot (give or take the band) is on his side and isn't letting that stop him.

This is the tragic hero, finally learning the fundamental lesson that repeating the same mistakes over and over again is worse than insanity. Springsteen here is like Bo Diddley, condemned to endless repetition and delighting in it, too. Condemned to learn the lesson and to spit in the lesson's eye. Condemned to act crazy and finding in that the greatest delight of all.

It's not that the endless cycle of hard times doesn't matter. It's that it matters so much—and so does what so many have learned about the unsettling ways in which what matters presents itself, opportunities as well as obstacles. At the end of the song, with the whole band in full swing and a wordless chorus pressing relentlessly forward, what you're hearing is precisely a group admitting its own (very mortal) limits in order to risk whatever it takes for hard times to come again no more.

The record's musical turning point hinges on not only tearing down walls, but reaching through the rubble for helping hands to rebuild. "Wrecking Ball" itself shifts the focus of the horn arrangement from Clarence Clemons's tenor sax to Curt Ramm's trumpet, but that's a product of inevitability. Producer Ron Aniello is new, as are almost all the engineers and mixers. And though this is a rock album, there's hardly a track where the E Street Band appears intact. Instead, dozens of different musicians and singers appear, from so many different genres that many songs defy classification. The lyrics suggest that junking the whole works might be worth the risk, but he's not just saying it—the idea is made more plausible because it emerges from greater *musical* risks than Bruce usually allows himself.

Suitably then, the first song after this cataclysmic anthem is a reach of the hand. "You've Got It" begins as a wooing, with only voice over acoustic guitar. Electric guitar, piano, and steel guitar turn the second verse into a country-flavored seduction, celebrating that thing the loved one has that makes her like no one else. Once the singer observes, "You can't read it in a book / You can't even dream it," the full weight of the album's sound kicks in with bluesy guitar and soulful horns. By the end, it's apparent this song's about the creative heart of the album—that individual human spark that makes us fall in love, yes, and that same spark that binds us together and lends us surprising strength in numbers—like the massive band second-lining onward into the unknown beyond the fade-out. A thing so elusive and so fundamental that it's hardly any wonder that the first time Bruce played it live, he explained it in terms of the Higgs boson.

Springsteen's writing has edged toward outright gospel since the turn of the century. "Rocky Ground" is the payoff—one of his most musically dramatic and emotionally lavish productions ever. The opening samples a Pentecostal preacher proclaiming, in a voice that sounds remarkably like Bruce's own, "I'm a soldier!" over and again. The gospel choir that follows— the Victorious Gospel Choir of Asbury Park, New Jersey, with which Springsteen's worked before—caresses what will become the song's chorus: "We've been travelin' over rocky ground, rocky ground." The bed is a synth echoing "Streets of Philadelphia," before a particularly liquid guitar riff sets the stage for Springsteen's hoarse recitation of the verse. He begins where he left off in his other gospel choir song, "My City of Ruins" from *The Rising*, exhorting, albeit with quiet sadness, his flock to "rise up," a term never more saturated in political and religious conflict. He shows which side he's on immediately, invoking the expulsion of the money changers from the Temple, as well as the prospect of (perhaps divine?) retribution, in death and in life. But the second time through, "Sun's in the heavens and a new day is rising."

When Springsteen finishes, Michelle Moore steps out of the choir and delivers a rap. It's written for an impoverished woman, a mother, but she could be that "Wrecking Ball" character ("You pray that hard times, hard times come no more"). Her prayer is simple: "That your best is good enough, the Lord will do the rest." Still, in a sleepless night, faith curdles to doubt and "only silence meets your prayers / The morning breaks, you awake, there's no one there."

"There's a new day comin,'" the song declares, but the voice sounds like Bruce Springsteen, not God. And as Michelle Moore's voice fades out, repeating the title phrase, what's left is more than a moment of doubt. The song is an answer to the challenge posed in "We Take Care of Our Own": If the cavalry stayed at home, what now? The stark answer is that all that's left is us.

And as the choir opens the next to last song, "Land of Hope and Dreams," recasting a staple of Springsteen's live shows since the E Street Band reunion in 1999, that's right where the answer stays. This rendition is that much more intense, edgier, louder—even Little Steven's mandolin has some added urgency—because that choir is present to connect Springsteen's Woody Guthrie elements to those he took from Curtis Mayfield and the Impressions, a secular cross between "This Train Is Bound for Glory" and "People Get Ready." What this means is that the weary traveler finds love even as the material losses multiply. But it's not God she meets in that field where sunlight streams. It's just that ordinary guy, the same one we've known since "Born to Run" and "Thunder Road," "a good companion for this part of the ride." Surrounded this time by (and seemingly at one with) whores, gamblers, thieves, lost souls, and just plain sinners alongside the saints and winners, the journey remains just as important as its destination.

The pledges of religions and governments are one thing. The bond between individual humans is what always seems truly sacred in Springsteen music, and it has to be carried out, step by painful step. Forgiveness is possible—hell, forgiveness abounds—but the price is as high as it's meant to be. Those bells that ring might be the bells from the courthouse in "Long Walk Home," because their promise is defined exactly the same way. They are "bells of freedom ringin'." And if, as Springsteen has long contended, the real issue in his songs is whether love is real, then the only qualification might be "in this life." It's heartbreakingly real here, heartbreaking because that is one long, long ride. But it can't start unless we get on board.

However religious he may be, Bruce Springsteen for sure believes that, each and every night, all the dead should be with us. It's one of the joys of this record that Clarence Clemons makes his final appearance on "Land of Hope and Dreams," in the heart of one of the band's greatest songs, in a performance that actually tops the live one.

But the Big Man, like Phantom Dan before him, is gone and he's not coming back any more than your good manufacturing job is. The question isn't whether that's true—only a politician would pretend we don't know that answer—the question is what we are going to do about it. To really set off on the trip to the Lands of Hope and Dreams, we need to find ways to accept who we really are, to fight off the vultures and the marauders, to rise up so we can hear those bells of freedom ring.

To Springsteen, the dead still have a role to play—just as they do in "Wrecking Ball," they reappear in the finale, "We Are Alive," a mocking, dead-serious merger of Johnny Cash, mariachi, Morricone soundtrack music, and a little of that old devil dust.

A bass note from what sounds like scratchy vinyl opens "We Are Alive," then folky guitar and some truly outré whistling. (The whistling could also be termed "ghostly" and given that the E Street Band's on stage whistler was Clarence, maybe that's a better way to put it.) But then the mariachi horns arrive, and a bass and drum figure out of "Ring of Fire." The singer starts looking up at calvary hill, but he's immediately distracted by "a grave-yard kid" lurking among the dead, listening to corpses tell their stories. The singer kneels and places his ear to the headstones, so he can hear them, too. The first three are a dead railroad striker, a little girl killed in a civil rights–era bombing, and a border crosser who expired in the Southwestern desert as he attempted to reach the U.S. It's not much of a reach to connect the gamblers, workers, jacks-of-all-trades, fighters, and athletes—each, like all of us, systematically isolated.

But not only are these dead not content to be silent, they're not even content to watch us forever screw up. They are about to issue marching orders, not in order to evoke the old days, but to ensure that we have the best possible new ones. "We are alive!" they exult. "And though our bodies lie alone here in the dark / Our spirits rise / To stand shoulder to shoulder and heart to heart."

The singer dreams himself dead—carried under to confront the worms and the dark and the loneliness. Then the voices appear again to remind him: "We are alive . . . our souls and spirits rise / To carry the fire and light the spark / To fight shoulder to shoulder and heart to heart."

Call it a rock'n'roll version of magic realism, if you wish, but you still won't have nailed the biggest, most significant change Bruce Springsteen has wrought in his work—and perhaps therefore himself—with *Wrecking Ball*. The man with the amazing ability to remain a mere moralist while traveling on presidential campaigns has finally discovered his politics. And so he's willing to strongly suggest what we might do if we would like to rid ourselves of the vultures and thieves who pillage our lives. Even if he does put his ideas in the mouths of the dead.

Maybe that's as it should be, the musician listening to the voices he's gathered and relaying what they say. Those ideas he hears are living things, never more vital than at these moments when we all feel out of options. What matters most is not that the speakers are the dead (or even that the dead aren't in the most important sense gone), but that we are alive—right here, right now. All of us: the Jack of All Trades, the punk in search of Easy Money, the ones who've got it and the victims of the death of their hometowns, the ones starving on rocky ground or discovering that the lack of a job shackles them as much as the drudgery of a job ever did. Not to mention those sure that the train holds no place for them. *Wrecking Ball* leaves no one untouched, unmarred, or at the very least unchanged. But the people out there in the dark, listening, aren't buried. They're still moving and the future lies in the ways in which they move—together and apart, bonded and isolated, terrified and overjoyed, in hope and in despair—as they always have moved when hard times come and come again. *Wrecking Ball* dares to put all of them together on that train to the certain nowhere that is our only blessed future, and then it does the unimaginable: it tries to start a conversation. In its own way, armed with not much more than a song to sing and a belief that if we travel over this rocky ground together there is a promised land at the other end, it aims to change the world.

Whether it succeeds in changing it, of course, isn't up to Bruce Springsteen. It's up to those who hear his call. It's up to the ones who are alive out there. It's up to us.

[Many thanks to Daniel Wolff and Craig Werner.]

CRY, CRY, CRY

(Bobby "Blue" Bland, January 27, 1930–June 23, 2013)

—COUNTERPUNCH, JUNE 2013

Bobby Bland was, in his prime, the most powerful blues shouter of all time, though capable as well of a caressing tenderness. "Turn On Your Lovelight" is what the rock world knows, I guess, but the man's legacy is also in "Ain't Nothing You Can Do," "Farther Up the Road," "I'll Take Care of You," "I Pity the Fool," "Cry Cry Cry," "If You Could Read My Mind," to my ear the finest "St. James Infirmary" of them all, the entire *Two Steps from the Blues* album (which is, without any doubt in my mind, the best Southern soul album, even including Otis's; it has the impeccable and beautiful and scary "Lead Me On," for many, including me, the greatest performance of his career). The list goes all the way up to his Malaco sides, particularly "Ain't No Love in the Heart of the City." It is not true that Bobby Bland never made a bad record; it *is* true that his ratio of great to mediocre is as high as any other singer you can name, in any genre you care to cull.

To call him Bobby "Blue" Bland always seems so redundant to me— like, as if he could be heard for so much as eight bars and you wouldn't know that this was his core, his essence and, one way or another, a heap of your own. But you can make too much of this essentialism—finally, you know Bobby Bland's name and music less well because he was like his audience: he was a key voice of the Black Southern working class from the '50s onward. His role was to play the shouter from the anonymous ranks, the totally heartbroken man among an all-but-totally heartbroken folk. (And of course, once in a while, shouting with exuberance all the greater because of that everyday heartbreak.)

He was completely nonintellectual about the whole enterprise, as far as I can tell. Told Peter Guralnick that his ambition was to be able to sing each song the exact same way, every time he sang it. A strange kind of perfectionism, I guess. But his command of tone and phrasing was so great that, for me, he held the place that Frank Sinatra held for a lot of other people. "Lead Me On" in particular has never not brought me to tears, not once, though I sometimes listened to it many, many, many times in a row—when I was by myself, the way that particular act of allegiance is best performed. And you know what? He sings it the same way every time.

Perfection is what he knew a *lot* about. And I, especially the I who found him on the radio and held him very close to the center of my being for the better part of half a century, will never be able to thank him enough. Or often enough. Or even express what I'm thanking him for altogether adequately.

I will tell you the real truth: he was, for me, probably the greatest blues singer of *any* kind, and the reason I can say this now instead of at the beginning is quite simple: I started listening to *Two Steps from the Blues*: *"No matter what you do, I'm gonna keep on loving you and I'm not ashamed, oh no, I'm not ashamed."*

WHAT IT MEANS TO LOSE PETE SEEGER

—*COUNTERPUNCH*, JANUARY 2014

I met Pete Seeger about forty years ago on the *Clearwater*, a refurbished nineteenth-century sloop that had begun its then seemingly hopeless task of cleaning up the shores and waters of the Hudson River. Like a lot of the things that Pete got involved in, it was a hopeless task until it turned out to be common sense.

That day, we cruised Long Island Sound, if I remember right, from Port Jefferson to Oyster Bay, which is not very far, and back, which is still not very far. It was worth every minute, and would have been if only for the chance to spend time aboard the 106-foot, single-masted *Clearwater*, a gorgeous vessel, stable even in Long Island Sound's considerable chop and carrying as cargo volumes of lore and lessons about the costs of environmental neglect.

You could say that those early *Clearwater* voyages were the precursors of the present-day celebrity cruise, but with fewer celebrities. No more were needed. Pete Seeger was not only the enduring star of American folk music, he was its leading evangelist and one of the greatest singer/musicians this part of the planet has produced. I remember Pete singing, though not what songs, and some lectures about the important work of the ship and the ecology of the Sound and the Hudson River region, though not their specific content. The presentation did its best to be as folkie as a much-darned pair of wool socks, and unmistakably also an event with a star and a crew and an audience, never exactly commingled. It was also a strong, healthy political event, by which I mean that each of us left with a sense of mission and some ideas about how to execute it.

I wasn't there to clean up the Sound, though I was glad to be part of the movement, or to hear Pete perform, though I knew the importance of his music. I was there to write a story for *Newsday*, the Long Island daily. I did what you do in those situations, where you don't know anybody and nobody knows you, which mostly means I watched and listened and took mostly the kind of sensory notes that you don't write down on the spot.

When we docked, everyone headed for the parking lot. Pete and his wife, Toshi, had several bags. I introduced myself, not only because we were meant to talk for a few minutes, but as a prelude to asking if I could help carry their stuff.

I got no further than "Hi, I'm Dave Marsh from *Newsday*," before Pete turned to me and snapped—and I mean snapped, like he was already booking me for malingering—"Grab a couple of those bags. It's good for white-collar workers to do physical labor." Thus spoke the Harvard gentleman to the brakeman's son who'd never owned a necktie. And no, I didn't come up with my usual smart-ass retort. He was Pete Seeger, who had changed not only my life but the world, and the alternative to silence was insulting him as much as he'd just insulted me, and . . . well, for once it was not in me.

That incident was one of the best lessons I ever had several times over. I learned lessons I'd chew on for, apparently, the rest of my life: the relation between stardom and shyness, between changing the world and retaining your self, and between trusting your perceptions and remembering not to suppose anything until you've made sure the person about whom you've just supposed it is not a cartoon. And I mean it, I've always been grateful because that dressing-down has saved me all manner of grief, and not only in things about celebrity. The most important lesson, you see, was about recognizing a difference between loving something and liking something, even when that something is someone. A great teacher may or may not inspire great affection, and he or she may not even teach the best lessons deliberately. So it turned out that Pete and I were in many social and professional situations over the next forty years without ever getting to know one another much and that isn't surprising. Mainly because I didn't learn my lesson all at once. Though I think I did learn, finally. I'll tell you about it later.

I respected Pete Seeger so much that my teenage self forgave him for writing "Kisses Sweeter Than Wine," which to my ears was sheer bathos, and for deriding Bob Dylan's beautiful electric music, which to my ears was the absolute poetry of a world in chaos.

One side of what he did was somewhat foreign to me. Years later, my friend Jon Landau and I were talking about folk music one day, which inevitably came around to talking about Pete. Jon told me a story about Pete appearing at his left-wing summer camp, or maybe it was Earl Robinson's music school. I said something I thought was appreciative and Jon stopped me cold. "You don't understand," he said. "He was Elvis."

To me, he was more like a father figure or anyhow that's the way I made sense of him after I understood that he had many metaphoric children and was glad of it, though not always of the way that they behaved, musically or socially. (Hmmm, that is like Elvis, isn't it?) He could be amazingly contradictory—a sign of humanity not deity. In his 1972 anthology, *The Incompleat Folksinger*, which collects among other things many of his columns for *Sing Out!*, Pete wrote about a tour of Czechoslovakia he made in 1964. He was especially thrilled to go to a particular club and hear the groups playing guitars, which happened to be electric.

Back home, Pete was not only immune to Beatlemania but hostile to folk-rock. Maybe it was because, as Pete said, he couldn't hear the words due to the high volume, but he should have known more about music than to use that to justify attacks on the songs themselves. I'm more inclined to think that he didn't like "Maggie's Farm" with the Butterfield Blues Band because of the loud absence of explicit social commentary and Pete's acknowledged absence of feeling for postwar blues.

I am trying to reckon with the complexity of Pete Seeger as man and artist. It is not an easy road to travel, especially not today. But it never has been.

Ten years ago, more or less, there was a panel discussion at a Folk Alliance conference that wound up in a tangle when Nora Guthrie said that Pete had refused to allow Madonna to issue a recording of "If I Had a Hammer" because she'd changed the lyric to "If I had a hammer / I'd smash your fucking head in." (I don't know if that's funny. Depends on how she sang it, doesn't it?)

Another complex folk music elder, Chris Strachwitz of Arhoolie Records, also on the panel, thought that Nora was responsible for the rejection and scolded her for not asking Pete to make the decision, since he would surely have supported free speech. I was the moderator and tried to help out by asking Nora if what she meant was that she had communicated a decision made by Pete himself. She said yes. Chris began to sputter, well past the point of coherence for a few seconds, and finally a single sentence burst out: "WELL . . . well . . . well . . . then Pete's not God anymore!"

He never was. He never needed to be. Like everybody else, Pete Seeger set examples good and bad. We might pause here to take notice that, though his feet were of clay, he had a remarkable ability to keep them shod. By which I mean, his transgressions may have been personal, but they were very rarely public and he knew how to back down. In 1967 or so, he made a record using electric guitar—not played by him—and somewhat heavier beats. And then returned to doing what he did, as he should have.

Pete Seeger was such a prodigious talent, so young, that the godlike was expected of him. Born in 1919, the son of the ethnomusicologist Charles Seeger, he grew up in a left-wing household. It was the mandarin left wing: like his father before him, Pete went to Harvard. He began his prominent performing career in 1940 on CBS Radio, alongside Lead Belly, Woody Guthrie, Burl Ives, and Josh White (the show was heard only in New York because the cast was integrated) and a year later was a founder of the first important left-wing folk group, the Almanac Singers, which defined protest singing. Pete Bowers, he called himself then—he had to, as his father was currently a government employee who had been blacklisted during World War I for espousing pacifism.

After the war, Pete formed the Weavers with Lee Hays, Fred Hellerman, and Ronnie Gilbert. Their songs were not always topical, because McCarthyism had begun, but the political songs were always there and they had big hits. Thus "Kisses Sweeter Than Wine," though the Weavers also rearranged Lead Belly's "Good Night Irene" into one of the most important hits of 1950. Seeger and Hayes were a formidable songwriting team. Because of them, the Weavers also produced some of the most enduring postwar protest songs, notably "If I Had a Hammer." By 1953, they were blacklisted by broadcasters. "If you had seen us coming down the street," Toshi Seeger, Pete's wife, told me once, "you'd have crossed over to the other side of the block." I looked dubious. "That's exactly what people did," she said.

Toshi, at least as formidable and complicated as her husband, allowed herself the bitterness Pete never expressed. They had a lot to be bitter about. After being smeared as a Red, Pete became an unusually uncooperative witness before the House Un-American Activities Committee in 1955. HUAC had caused the Hollywood Ten to be imprisoned for contempt of Congress in 1950. The Ten lost for standing on the First Amendment as the basis for their refusal to testify. Since then, it had become the practice to stand on the Fifth—the nonincrimination clause—rather than freedom of speech and association. Pete returned to the fundamental issue: "I am not going to answer any questions as to my association, my philosophical or religious beliefs or my political beliefs, or how I voted in any election, or any of these private affairs. I think these are very improper questions for any American to be asked, especially under such compulsion as this."

This was not godlike. It was human—stubborn, flouting all sound advice, courageous. It was also not quite as futile as it immediately seemed. In 1957, he was charged with contempt of Congress. In 1961, Pete was tried, convicted, and sentenced to a year in prison. In 1962, he won his appeal, a landmark case in ending the blacklist. But the consequences rolled on: the Weavers reformed in 1955, but mainly as a live act. They recorded for small labels, but their music could not be broadcast. Nevertheless, they played the major role in popularizing "Wimoweh (The Lion Sleeps Tonight)," "Sixteen Tons," and "Kumbaya."

Pete was never idle. In the fifties, he wrote *How to Play the 5-String Banjo*, invented the longneck banjo (three additional frets made it longer than a bass guitar), popularized the twelve-string guitar (he'd learned from Lead Belly), and created the brilliant "Goofing-Off Suite," using classical themes by Bach, Beethoven, Stockhausen, and Grieg alongside Berlin's "Blue Skies" and a batch of folk tunes. When John Hammond at Columbia finally got him a major label record deal, one of the first results was "Where Have All the Flowers Gone," probably the most beautiful anti-war melody ever composed. Pete championed the burgeoning topical song movement in the best possible way: he crammed the songs into his albums and concerts. He also took up world music, not as a stylistic synthesis, but as a collection of pieces that, taken on their own terms, resonated with one another, from Africa ("Wimoweh") to Cuba ("Guantanamera"), even Europe. It was Pete who suggested that SNCC needed a singing group, and it was Toshi and Pete who befriended and cared for Bernice Johnson Reagon when the SNCC Freedom Singers broke up. He made children's albums and live albums and thematic albums and mere collections of songs. He was instrumental in starting the Newport Folk Festival. He was on the editorial committee of *Sing Out!*, the *Rolling Stone* of the folk revival. And he played a major role (if not the central one—that credit he always gave to Guy Carawan, and rightly so) in adapting and popularizing the most important song of the twentieth century, "We Shall Overcome."

Pete made a live album called *We Shall Overcome*, recorded at Carnegie Hall in 1963. It was extremely well-edited, I don't know by whom. The running order of the album—thirteen songs of the forty performed—has absolutely nothing to do with the order of the concert, but it's more focused, gets to the point more directly and clearly than the show did. Alas, the digital version is the whole thing. (It's easy to make a playlist of the original running order—the original track listing is at the Wikipedia entry for the album.)

I heard the *We Shall Overcome* album at age fourteen, when I was the son of budding George Wallace supporters, living in an Up South town full of Ku Klux Klansmen and packs of freelance racists, and going to quietly but adamantly all-White schools. The headlines had been filled every day for the past year with Freedom Riders, preteens slaughtered by bombs placed in churches, nonviolent demonstrators attacked by dogs and high-pressure hoses. And that was just in the South. Racial turmoil was a constant presence in southeastern Michigan, not just Detroit. The one true thing I was being told about this was that it meant the world, or a world, was coming to an end. The one set of contrary facts I held in my head was almost entirely musical, not the early songs of Bob Dylan, but Motown and early soul music that insisted, obliquely but powerfully, that freedom meant everybody or it didn't mean anything.

Buying *We Shall Overcome* was more the product of exploration than rebellion. What it inspired was rebellion's necessary partner, conviction. Most important, the conviction that there really must be a better world, somewhere, and that it was open to the likes of myself. Pete Seeger's version of a protest album offered a vision, and the core of that vision was not so much any particular songs but the gentle persuasiveness with which he introduced them, the passion with which he laid out their origin or history or contemporary relevance and the power with which he encouraged all present to sing them. What transformed *We Shall Overcome* from a powerful collection to something with deep historical significance was the presence of the SNCC Freedom Singers. They lent not so much authenticity as boldness and authority to "Oh Freedom," "If You Miss Me at the Back of the Bus," and particularly "Keep Your Eyes on the Prize." They made struggling for equal rights seem like something even a blossoming but isolated teenager could do.

As Daniel Wolff pointed out to me the afternoon that we learned of Pete's passing, he did this kind of teaching all the time. Seeger believed in singing, he believed it was good for you in all sorts of ways. He was, I recall, fond of reciting his father's dictum that a country's cultural health could best be ascertained by how many of its citizens sang and made music. I was just one among who knows how many—a number surely in the hundreds of thousands, maybe the tens of millions, over the sixty years or so that Pete performed—who had their lives turned if not upside down at least askew by the power of his conviction, by the contagion of his vision.

If nothing else, Pete Seeger made me understand how far behind enemy lines I was living—he showed me the road that had to be traveled, if I really wanted to live. He did this the same way that James Baldwin and Elvis Presley and John Coltrane did it: by example, and with the same generosity and the same sense that the world was packed with a load of insurmountable cruelty and that, nevertheless, the truth was that something better had managed to survive within it. Which meant, for each of us, a choice and a chance.

It may even be that Seeger, whose rectitude often communicated, at least to me, a whiff of the Puritanism he inherited, offered a more direct route to this not-at-all specious salvation of spirit and society than anybody else, and for the oddest reason: he thought smaller. He genuinely believed that one more singer, one more nonviolent resister, one more example of gumption and love, one more song, one more guitar, was an important thing. And, this I am sure about, he genuinely believed that that was mainly what he, himself, was: one more.

That, and nothing more meek, was why Pete Seeger eschewed the celebrity path. (Ask yourself this: If Burl Ives could become a big star looking like that, what could the young Pete Seeger have become if he'd just given over a few names?) Pete could seem innocent, but you'd be a fool to believe it. He paid the price and he had seen the bill coming, too.

If all you know about Pete Seeger is a protest singer, a ragtag Red, a spinner of false hope, a doddering old man walking that hopeless line (but never by himself, you may have noticed), then you missed it. If all you know is the famous songs—most of which I haven't even mentioned—you might even then not see it whole. Pete Seeger lived his life every day in the possession of what he envisioned.

There is one song that to me expresses this vision almost perfectly, maybe the greatest of all the lyrics he wrote and in the performance on his mini box set, *A Link in the Chain*, possibly his greatest recorded vocal performance. It is called "Oh, Had I a Golden Thread." It's sweet in a way the hard boys, left and right, fear, as they ought to. "Far over the waters I'd reach my magic band / To every human being so they would understand." He makes it true. He makes those who hear him want to make it truer.

Without such a vision, the folk process that we talk about (or used to, before the scene shifted to singer-songwriters meditating on their inner lives—alas, almost never about the banality of them—and the preening cultists they attracted) isn't worth much. But there is another question, which is whether Pete's vision of freedom carries forward, whether it stands, whether it can be nurtured and sustained.

I am sure it will be and my conviction came, perhaps predictably, on the last night of the Rock and Roll Hall of Fame's magnificent Woody Guthrie tribute in 1996. Pete already wasn't singing very much—Arlo led the night's final song, which you knew was going to be "This Land Is Your Land" before you ever saw a ticket. But you didn't know that the whole cast, including many of the conference's speakers, would be on stage leading the singing.

It had been a night of triumphs: for Ani DiFranco and the Indigo Girls, for Dave Pirner and Jimmy LaFave, Billy Bragg and Jack Elliott, Bruce Springsteen and Pete, too. But the most powerful triumph was that group sing—above all for the spirit still embedded in a potential national anthem yearning for a country to become worthy of it. It floored me and, really, it seemed like the moment caught everyone. John Wesley Harding and I, old friends, walked into the communal dressing room afterward, arms around each other's shoulders, tears in our eyes. And there was Pete, with tears in his eyes.

I think it was the first time I'd ever truly seen him. He was pleased, I understood, not so much that the night had carried Woody and what he represented forth in such grand fashion. What I remember seeing in Pete Seeger's eyes was a sense of relief. He knew something that night—if I'm right—something important about not just Woody's work, but his own. Which meant also the work of all the people he'd learned from, and all those who'd taught them, from the slaves who came up with "O Freedom" to Mother Bloor writing the labor history Woody made into music. He knew that folks would try to carry it on, in both spirit and substance.

That linkage is the golden thread and its purpose now is weaving the garment of human survival, which was the explicit theme of Pete Seeger's last few decades on the planet. A rainbow design without which we cannot live. A design that shows us why and how to keep the most important thing that Pete Seeger represents alive.

We cannot experience the full measure of what it means to lose Pete Seeger until we realize that this burden is not his to carry anymore. Now it's on you. And me.

Got any bags you need carried?

[Thanks to Craig Werner, Danny Alexander, Daniel Wolff, and Lee Ballinger, without whom grief might have overwhelmed coherence.]

THE ANTI–PETE SEEGER

—*COUNTERPUNCH*, FEBRUARY 2014

A s a life member of the Folk Alliance International and until recently a member of its board, I'd like to be able to congratulate the organization on its move from Memphis to a much better situation in Kansas City.

But the first annual FAI conference in KC will feature Al Gore in a special presentation, for conference attendees only, of his quasi-prophetic fantasy, *The Future: Six Drivers of Global Change*. It makes me feel like FAI is dancing on Pete Seeger's grave. Does it really matter much whether they're doing it out of ignorance or making a deliberate effort to steer folk music far to the right of where its political and social allegiances have traditionally belonged?

Am I overreacting, refusing to come to grips with contemporary political reality and with Al Gore, the wronged should-have-been president, moral beacon, intellectual paragon, and his role as a leader of the ecological movement?

Gore's approach to solving the world's problems centers on venture capital firms, such as his own Generation Investment Management and the firm Kleiner Perkins Caufield & Byers, in which he is a partner. Exactly how he rationalizes such projects of these firms as AOL, Amazon, Electronic Arts, and Google as good for the environment and harbingers of a better future isn't all that interesting. It's just the usual neoliberal blather, the liberal version of the conservative lie that a rising tide lifts all boats. Neither ever asks whether everybody has a boat, or whether the boats we do have will carry all the people now living, let alone coming generations, or how there can be life-sustaining air, water, soil, and minerals if the depredations of high-tech capitalism, which are at least as devastating as those of earlier versions, are allowed to continue.

Folk music is supposed to side with the people whose lives are ruined, from West Virginia to Japan, not the exploiters who mask and attempt to explain away the all-but-irreversible damage that has already been done in the name of "growth." The question that no Gore speech or PowerPoint has ever answered is "Sustainable for whom?"

It's a question to which previous generations of folk musicians and activists associated with it have never failed to demand answers.

Gore's six drivers include nothing remotely related to the kind of human-scale empowerment projects (for instance, the civil rights and anti-war movements, Operation Wall Street, and labor rights) that folk music has traditionally been involved with.

From this point of view, Al Gore is the anti–Pete Seeger: deceitful where Pete was honest, cowardly where Pete was brave, an apologist for continuing to destroy the environment where Seeger was an ecological champion, a censor where Pete stood on the rock of the First Amendment even when Congress and his own lawyers told him it was a loser. (Pete won his case.)

Above all, Pete Seeger was a champion of music, all kinds of music, in America and the world, whereas Al Gore spent much of the '80s berating and belittling popular music, even helping convene a Senate hearing on the "threat" of lyrics to the nation's children. Ten years later, in typical fashion, he denied he'd even attended most of the conference, although he was the only senator who was present for all of that travesty (take a look at www.youtube.com if you must, but I was there and my own eyes swear to it). He and his wife, Tipper, wanted to raise my kids while at least one of theirs turned out to be a drunk (or was that a druggie?) with a penchant for driving while intoxicated. (Is this unfair to Al Gore's kids? Much less unfair than the Gores were to the kids—current and former—who loved and found emotional refuge in heavy metal and hip-hop.) Finally, the moral exemplars' marriage dissolved as Al was found creeping out of a massage brothel in the middle of the Oregon night.

One wonders if Al Gore ever met Pete Seeger. It's hard to imagine where it might have been.

It couldn't have been at a peace rally—as congressman, senator, and vice president, Gore voted yes on every war question from Grenada to Iraq to Yugoslavia. He pretended to agonize over whether to support the first Bush invasion of Iraq but, it turns out, this was simply because he was guaranteed to get network TV time with his speech.

It couldn't have been at a rally for women's rights. Gore never supported abortion rights more than half-heartedly, and while in the House, played a meaningful role in ending federal financing of abortion—which had the effect of denying any practical right for the poorest American women to exercise their freedom to choose.

It couldn't have been at a rally for the environment, because Al Gore's so-called "environmentalism" ends just about where the deep commitment of Pete Seeger began. Gore is the kind of ecological advocate who damns, say, timber mining in Brazil while either supporting or never uttering a peep about coal companies strip-mining the Appalachians. Gore grandstands as Barack Obama's moral scourge on the Keystone pipeline, but he treads much more carefully around actual energy executives. His inherited wealth stems from favors done for his father, Senator Albert Gore Sr., by Armand Hammer, the owner of Occidental Petroleum. Al Gore's environmental forte is failed adventures in public relations, such as his mild support for the Kyoto Climate Accords, a cost-free move since there was never any realistic chance of ratification by the U.S. Senate.

It's not possible that it would have been at a labor rally. Gore blabbers about "growth" and "jobs" just like every other neoliberal bullshit artist. He also was a prime champion of NAFTA, which has been devastating to workers' rights and livelihoods in both the United States and Mexico. (He "won the debate" against Ross Perot during the '92 election, but Perot, reactionary as he is, was right to sneer at the baloney Gore was spouting.) In the 2000 election Gore claimed he agreed with unions "90 percent, but not on free trade." This is about like the claim that humans share 98 percent of their DNA with chimpanzees.

God knows, Al Gore wouldn't have met Pete Seeger at an Occupy Wall

Street event. Gore's politics have never been remotely inclusive—he is another neoliberal devising programs "for the poor" without consulting anyone who is actually poor. (The first Senator Gore used to boast about his country roots and being sent to a one-room schoolhouse. He never did mention that the vast majority of the children around him—White as well as Black—had no schools to attend at all. They were already too busy working for a living as sharecroppers and miners.)

Gore and Seeger definitely would not have bumped into one another at one of the annual rallies held at Fort Benning, Georgia, to protest the continued existence of that dictator/torturer training camp, the School of the Americas. Pete never missed one. Gore was never there because he backs U.S. foreign policy, which essentially attempts to treat the nations of South and Central America as a string of colonial outposts led by children who must be instructed by the self-proclaimed grown-ups in Washington.

And for God's sake, it wouldn't have been at any kind of music conference because, for two decades, Al Gore has been scorned as wannabe censor and father of the PMRC. He was the eager assistant for his now ex-wife Tipper in her falsehood and fantasy-ridden campaign against rap, heavy metal, and rock that didn't abide by the Gore family's supposed Baptist principles.

Pete Seeger was one of the half dozen greatest figures in American folk culture.

Al Gore was a congressman and senator who opposed gun control and declared that homosexuality was not another "normal optional life style." (It also might be said that while Pete Seeger was a remarkably coherent, focused, and cogent writer and speaker, Al Gore has the verbal felicity of a wooden carving.)

This is the man behind the "frank and clear-eyed assessment" of the present that Folk Alliance International will present as an exemplar of "The Future." It's hard to know what Gore's going to talk about, but it's most likely to be an extension of his self-promoting film, *An Inconvenient Truth*.

There is also the significant question of whether Gore is being paid to do his "presentation." In early February, Gore was paid 100,000 English pounds (more than $160,000) for a speech to the Forbes Forum. In the history of the Folk Alliance, singers and musicians making appearances have never been paid. In most cases, they must pay for their own travel and lodging. It is hard to believe that Gore's PR machine would not be braying loudly if he were giving away his precious time and PowerPoint to struggling folk singers and banjo players. It's even harder to believe that the FAI, whose board isn't even interested enough to have a fundraising committee, is spending the big bucks. It will be a wonder to see how the FAI membership reacts if Gore's fee is revealed . . . or if the FAI refuses to reveal it, for that matter.

Is it absolutely morally "wrong" for the FAI to invite Al Gore despite all that he has done and represents? Of course not. Is it entirely reasonable to draw the conclusions drawn here about what that tells us about the FAI? Of course it is. It would be one thing, for instance, to invite Gore to speak on a conference panel with divergent views about the future. (That might even be refreshing, since so much folk discussion centers on the past.) But what the FAI has actually done is given a green Bernie Madoff a platform for his sales pitch.

Coda: One might wonder what Pete Seeger would think of a right of center (the center being the American people, not the denizens of the Beltway) politician at a folk music festival. I don't know. But I do know this:

In October 2000 with the presidential election between Al Gore and Shrub Bush running neck and neck and a third candidate, Ralph Nader, running on the Green ticket while receiving substantial support and also receiving vicious jibes and threats from loyalist Gore supporters, I attended a dinner party of about a dozen at Harold and Natalie Leventhal's Riverside Drive apartment. Early in the evening, we were each asked to state our preference in the upcoming presidential campaign. It got to Pete about halfway through. He talked about how he had been doing this a long time, and about his thoughts on splinter political parties. To him three choices was not enough. He said, if I remember the number right, that what was really needed was about eighteen different parties: a party for the vegans and a party for the pacifists and a party for . . . I don't know, he might even have said a party for the fascists. (I don't think so.) What he meant was, I know myself well enough that nobody can bully me.

And then he said: I'm voting for Ralph Nader.

INTRODUCTION AND REQUIRED POST:
DA DOO RON RON

[Da Doo Ron Ron was an annual online forum of friends, critics, and fanatics of pop music, curated by Alexander Shashko, lecturer in the Department of Afro-American Studies, University of Wisconsin.]

—JANUARY 2016

I'm Dave Marsh, I've been writing about music for a very long time (1969–present seems long to me, anyhow). Most of what I've written about is, I guess, driven by an urgent sense of needing mileposts to live my life by. And I have to say that, for me, if not you or her or the guy hiding in the other corner, trying to narrow it down to one is a nice parlor game. But the fact is, at least for me, that the whole reason I write about, and listen to, so much popular music is that if you dive deep enough, often enough, you really do find concepts to live by.

It seems to me that the danger of our mutual assignment is that we all take it as a chance to talk about lyrics.

But if you really want to find those songs that make you understand why it ain't no sin to be glad you're alive, I don't think it's the words. Or if it is, it's what the words sound like, the noises that surround them, their cadence, the textures of the voice or voices, the slash of a hand against strings that can and sometimes do cut to the bone, the sheer exhilaration the combination of these elements and more can produce in so many different ways. These things remain amazing across decades, and new ones take us all by surprise (often leading to dismissal, disdain, outright loathing). A new approach, a new voice, a new instrument, a new way of juggling the parts so that the focal point changes (think James Brown, Afrika Bambaataa, Dr. Dre, who's next?). Out of that emerges, at the best of times, a voice or several voices and what they are seeking by singing is a way forward to find something that seems much more elusive to me now than ever it did when I was younger and the world still simple. Each new wrinkle offers an array of things: a perch from which to observe, a stillness on which to reflect, a sonic chaos to match the inner one, a way to look at something important in a different fashion, or something that seemed trivial blown up to monumental proportions. (Kisses! Glances! Stumbles!)

And all of that is about living your life, and all of it is a kind of guidance, or at least a map made by someone. Might be a short journey (but how would you live without those one-hit wonders; I'm thinking Afroman at the moment), might be a long one (I am about to shoot the rapids of a river with some old friends). Might be just around the corner to the light of day.

I don't think I can really answer the question without feeling like a traitor in the morning, but I can give you a couple of examples. One is "Closer to Free" by the BoDeans. Forget about Sammy's singing—it's really about that opening "yee-hah," so hick it has to be true, and the way Kurt and Sam sing "free" at the end of the verses, as flat truth, no exaggeration, the noise is all the action, but less than half the truth. It's just what it feels like—people who've known each other long enough to get past the bullshit and look each other in the eye and say it. It's my favorite love song and it's not about love at all. Maybe. It is literally true that I have never listened to it once without repeating it another two or three (or five or ten) times.

And then, "Everyday People." No getting around those lyrics, whether you're listening to the rawness of Joan Jett or the thrilling desperation of Sly and his family. Listen to Larry Graham's bassline, changing the game for everybody. Sly built it as (or from) a child's song, and it's just about that basic, right down to a "scooby dooby dooby" so perfectly rendered that, to this day, nearly fifty years after I first heard it (and I can tell you exactly where I was and who I was with), I don't know if it's sarcasm or the real call to arms. It's going nowhere—it's already where you or I or they or all of us need to be. "Everyday People" is generally regarded as merely homiletic—the preacher proclaiming that we can live together. But that's not what it's about, and if it were, then it would be just hot air: that version of "Everyday People" is nothing anyone's lived yet, and there's precious little reason to think that we ever will. But Sly is not a preacher so much as a prophet, here to warn not what will happen (that is bogus prophecy) but what may befall those who are inattentive.

So I have gradually come to the conclusion that what matters, what really matters, is "We got to live together." It's not a dream, it's not optional, it's the essential thing for survival. And that is why most of the lyric is a litany not of how many different ways people accept and love one another, but a list of the many ways in which we hate, disparage, abuse one another. And then, when you've absorbed that, faced up to our, which means your (not to mention my) own capacity to ruin everything in the service of nothing, then you get to know what a horror it is to declare "I am everyday people."

Because we are the same whatever we do. So . . . why don't we do better? The song doesn't know and doesn't try to pretend it knows. Other than that one piece of what might be news: we're all the same. The music is unquestionably joyous, at least most of it, but if that's all you take away . . . it justifies Sly's every sardonic smile.

It took me a long time to accept that this truth was in this beautiful song. But I guess that's the part I want to live by. Or rather, I don't want to live without. We could probably live together if all that was wrong with our lives was just you lying to you and me lying to me. But lying to ourselves . . .

(I love false endings.)

JIMMY LAFAVE IN THE PRESENT TENSE

—AUSTIN CHRONICLE, MAY 2017

on't want to get out of this car," sings Jimmy LaFave at the beginning of "Blue Nightfall." Then he pauses. One . . . two . . . three . . . four seconds. Not a long interval, but you could take up residency in the cavern of possibility this particular silence builds.

The band rolls on, tearing it apart in fully synchronized agony, but your ear wants more of that voice, the very instrument of pain. A great many things beg revelation in this ticking down, least of all an ending. The voice cracks a little, bumps over a phrase, lingering briefly on a key syllable and then, expressing quite patiently, the obvious truth—the one you can't bear to be without:

"It's a blue nightfall. Now I weep."

The band continues, but LaFave stops. You can almost hear shards of a broken heart hitting the floor. You'll be forgiven for wondering if you're the only one that's shed anything-but-metaphoric tears. Or for wondering if there's really someone, somewhere who weeps no more, or whether it's just . . . everybody. Impossible to grasp fully why in such moments a listener feels so much more alive.

Listening to a genuinely great singer—Smokey Robinson or Joe Strummer, Patty Griffin or Mary J. Blige—is to accept a unique sacrament. It may raise you high or smash you flat, but you'll visit places you've barely imagined as well as those you know so intimately as to call home. Stopovers that confront you with your deepest fears, destinations driving your highest hopes.

Jimmy LaFave is one of those singers. And not only on "Blue Nightfall." All of the veteran Austinite's recordings and even more, his live performances, are extraordinarily rich in these moments.

Once, on my SiriusXM radio show broadcasting live Sunday mornings, I asked him to sing "On a Bus to St. Cloud" as a duet with its writer, Gretchen Peters. They both balked. Then the former sort of shrugged and they did that most beautiful of songs justice. It wasn't perfect. It was extraordinarily human.

"I don't think I really understood that song until I heard him sing it," Peters told me after LaFave covered it on 2001's *Texoma*.

AUSTIN SKYLINE

Jimmy LaFave doesn't simply possess a great voice. He taught himself how to use it. How to make it better.

Wise, tough, tender, elegant, gritty, he sings Bob Dylan songs like he owns the copyright. His national debut, 1992's *Austin Skyline*, included four Dylan covers. Besting the author of "Girl from the North Country" on the *Freewheelin' Bob Dylan* track isn't a stretch, since it's been done before, but usurping him on "Leopard-Skin Pill-Box Hat"?

LaFave captures all the honky-tonk the latter calls for. He keeps the rock rolling and when he starts to sing, you realize that the damn lyric is a really smooth hipster running a verbose come-on with uncommon panache. Originally, I'd heard it as crazy. LaFave made it crazy like a fox.

One night at the Cactus Cafe—I'm not sure what year, but the club was packed out in a way that hollers "South by Southwest"—LaFave explained that someone close to him had just lost her sister. The UT listening room remains possibly the finest space I've ever heard music in, as perfectly attuned to the kind of music played in it, as it is tiny. You can have your emotions turned upside down in there, and you can also have a ball, like the time a bunch of us played kazoos behind Molly Ivins. On the most memorable evenings, people in chairs and with their backs to the bar or the wall or standing in the doorway are exalted by music.

That night, when Jimmy LaFave sang Dylan's "Not Dark Yet," every heart was not shattered (that wasn't his purpose), but opened. It felt a little like a baby being born. New magic filled the air, something you'd imagined but never taken this far even in fantasy.

It proved one of the few truly perfect performances I've ever experienced. Tears on my cheeks and joy in my heart spring from simple recall of that performance. On that night, at that hour, Jimmy LaFave achieved undeniable greatness.

There are two recorded versions of him singing "Not Dark Yet." He brings so much of himself to the version on 2007's *Cimarron Manifesto*. The longer he sings it, the deeper it goes. His accompanists, particularly guitarists Andrew Hardin and John Inmon, plus keyboardist Radoslav Lorkovic, crank up that tune. They don't just support, they toss him into the air and catch him clean on the way back down. They love him because he has the courage to step up to this. They get the cost—to Dylan, to LaFave, to whom- or whatever the song's about originally—so they synchronize themselves more completely to live up to it.

The best "Not Dark Yet" is the live take from 2014's *Trail Two*. In my soul, it's from that night at the Cactus Cafe. This one's gentler, more intimate. He sings it a little more like Dylan, rushing the words here and there, and elsewhere pausing for a breath, as if surprised by what's coming next. It's a man counting off heartbeats of his unforgiving yet also absolutely honest interpretation of what it's like to succumb—to hear and see and feel your humanity laid waste.

"My sense of humanity has gone down the drain," wrote Dylan, which is honest because it isn't true—a paradox worth pondering. A couple of lines later, if you listen real, real close, you can hear the voice that's made it through so much tremble. Just a little, just enough. The fragility lays bare palpable courage.

You can't understand it from anybody's mere verbal account, but it's there to be found—in the breathing, in the timing, in the wonder expressed at what the song has to say, and the horror that it's yet incomplete. You get there eventually; that's what Dylan says in the last line, "It's not dark yet, but it's getting there."

Or you don't.

It's that simple. It's that painful. It's a lot like knowing that Jimmy LaFave is dying.

BUFFALO RETURN TO THE PLAINS

The first time I met or heard Jimmy LaFave was at the Woody Guthrie tribute conference put on in Cleveland in 1996 to benefit the Woody Guthrie Foundation & Archives and Rock and Roll Hall of Fame. I saw a lot of old friends and made several new ones at that event. I met him with Greg Johnson from the Blue Door, a folk/rock/singer-songwriter/Jimmy Webb club in LaFave's home state of Oklahoma.

At various Folk Alliance and SXSW events, we regathered, our ranks expanding as more musicians became old friends. It's a great social circle but requires some heavy dues: you either have to know how to perform or have to have something to say about it that has not yet been totally refuted by concrete evidence.

LaFave's singing struck me immediately. So did his songwriting. AllMusic's Thom Jurek, one of the most astute music critics and historians in the country, thinks his third album, *Buffalo Return to the Plains*, is a virtually perfect folk album, the best of its time. The title song, "Burden to Bear," "Going Home," "Rock & Roll Land"—the more you look into it, the harder that judgment becomes to refute.

In a city crowned by world-class singer-songwriters, Jimmy LaFave nestled near the top from the time he arrived in 1985. The company he keeps on that list is impressive, but more remarkable is that he goes about all of it—composing, recording, performing—with an awareness that he's an Oklahoma-Texas folk musician. Hints of Lynyrd Skynyrd appear on the first couple of albums, including "Rock & Roll Music to the World," but his allegiance is to Woody Guthrie and those who followed him. LaFave played an instrumental role in keeping the focus of the Cleveland Guthrie show, while also proving pivotal in development of the Woody Guthrie Center in Tulsa. He became leader of the troupe that toured the Guthrie show, "Ribbon of Highway, Endless Skyway" (see "Two LaFaves," below).

He's written insightfully about his native soil, the red dirt region that spawned him and his conception of self. More quietly, he's kept up the

Guthrie tradition of writing about the common man, in praise of justice and equality, against the rape of the land, always siding with the fate of the poor and underprivileged. In hindsight, he seems more political than Guthrie, especially in the live arena, where most of his audience encounters him.

At the Folk Alliance conference in Kansas City this past February, when I saw him for the first time in over a year, I mentioned he had written the first song about Donald Trump.

"I did?"

"Yeah, it's on *Buffalo Return to the Plains*. Pretty much every line of it."

We laughed for a moment. His showcase the next night turned out to be one of the most passionate shows I've ever seen, partly because half the audience had heard how sick he was, but mostly because he was playing like it was his last time on stage. At the end, he said wryly, "I wrote a song about Donald Trump twenty years ago and didn't even know it."

Then he sang "Worn Out American Dream."

I see no refuge for the weary
I see no handouts for the poor
I see no sense of satisfaction
On all the ones who just endure
All the slings and arrows slandered
Against the face of the poor man's dream
Where the rich circle in like vultures
Picking all their pockets clean.

Devastating, especially when he came to "Come on, face your situation. It's just as desperate as it seems."

BURDEN TO BEAR

A year earlier, I'd gotten a call from our mutual friend, Val Denn, who's been Jimmy LaFave's agent and de facto manager/agent for most of the time I've known him. She gave me a recap of the conference, which I'd not attended, and then, a little shakily, said, "Jimmy found some kind of growth in his chest."

"How big?" I asked, and was told the size of a pea. It was protruding, not soft and squishy. I told her it was urgent to get a biopsy because the chances were 1,000 to 1 it might be a sarcoma.

I know a lot about sarcomas. In the autumn of 1992, my twenty-year-old younger daughter, Kristen Carr, had a routine gynecological checkup. A growth was found in her abdomen and when it was biopsied, it was identified as malignant. Sarcoma is the rarest of rare cancers.

There are approximately 1 million cases of cancer discovered in the U.S. annually. Only 1 percent of these, 13–15,000, are sarcomas. They're so rare that most surgeons have very incorrect—lethally incorrect—ideas about how to remove them. Biopsy and identification are crucial, because sarcoma pathology is regarded as the most difficult in all of medicine. On top of that, while sarcoma accounts for a small fraction of all cancers, it nevertheless yields about two-thirds of all types of cancer. One distinguished researcher told me there will eventually be about five hundred types identified.

Sarcoma is cancer of the connective tissues—fat cells, bones, cartilage, fibrous tissue, the lining of organs, blood vessels, lymph nodes, muscle, and many more—meaning they can appear anywhere in the body. There are no symptoms until the tumor becomes large enough to interfere with an organ or system. When someone has a tumor the size of a watermelon, that's often a sarcoma. When you wonder why it wasn't discovered earlier, remember that no symptoms does not mean "a few."

Half of all sarcomas are treated by surgical resection. The other half result in amputations, debilitating additional surgeries, eventually death. If more initial surgeries were done by surgeons with specific sarcoma expertise, the survival rate would likely be notably higher.

Jimmy LaFave had some advantages. His sarcoma was small (sort of), it was identified at an early stage, and it was visible. The surgery appeared successful, but the margins weren't as clear as they needed to be and the tumor recurred almost immediately. Additionally, sarcoma in the trunk of the body is much more lethal than sarcoma elsewhere. You can amputate your arm or leg, but you can't do the same to your bladder or heart.

Jimmy faced major issues immediately and not all of them physical. Even if a medical solution could be found, even if all the family and psychological issues could be surmounted, how would this affect his career or, for that matter, given the chest involvement, his ability to sing? Repeated recurrences and then proliferating growth resulted, even with the most promising chemotherapy. No new sarcoma drug has been developed in about forty years.

I advocated coming to New York, where my family works closely, as the Kristen Ann Carr Fund, with a sarcoma team, one of the world's best. After analyzing the options with amazing calm and decisiveness, he told me that if he had to die, then he didn't want to do it in New York. He wanted to be in Austin with the people he loved, on the land that inspired him. He didn't want to be laid waste by chemo if it was only a stopgap. He wanted to write songs, maybe record, do his shows until he couldn't gig anymore.

I had to get off the phone and sit for a while as the truth sank in: Jimmy LaFave was the bravest of all the cancer patients I've known. He wasn't refusing treatment. He wasn't "giving up without a fight." He'd chosen to live, really live.

DEPENDING ON THE DISTANCE

Sarcoma will eventually cause Jimmy LaFave to die. I wrote this story as much in the present tense as I could, even though I know he is now very, very ill. It's the last chance I have to honor his commitment to life.

He's faced the situation and all the sadness it brings, but his American Dream is no wasteland. It's a hero's tale and I hope it inspires generations. He, and his music, deserve that much.

Postscript

When one reaches a certain age, and is famous, and relatively healthy, one is often called upon to write eulogies for one's aging friends who are also in their dotage. I remember once meeting Lord Goodman, the great Labour peer, and being asked to accompany the old chap to the toilet, where he announced that he had one piece of advice for me. "Pete," he said gravely, standing at the urinal. "Don't grow old." I advised him that I'd already made a few bob (a few bucks, too) out of that notion and asked him why he thought I should throw myself off a bridge before I reached his age.

"Because old men can't piss properly."

I know all these posh pronouns make me sound like Prince Charles, but—as he is often required to do—I have been called upon to do my duty to a very, very old man who played a big part in my life and career, Dave Marsh. I can't award him a Knighthood, but I can pretend I think I really know him.

Dave was a biographer of the Who, and interviewed me on many occasions. Among others, he conspired to wring some juice out of the wrinkled dry lemon that the Who (and myself as a part of it) has often appeared to be. But by the miracles of lies, money, frippery, fiction, absurdity, and managerial brutality, the Who have survived to produce more acidic liquid, however insipid, and it seems so have I. It's nice to be regarded as useful.

So, to Dave Marsh.

I think I probably met Dave in Detroit. He was then a founder of *Creem* magazine, that survived (so it seemed then) by featuring Kiss on the cover every week for about twenty years. It's no wonder Dave ended up disliking them so much. Occasionally there might be glimpses of bands that were less appealing to the young Kiss fans who mainly enjoyed, it seemed, looking at older men's tongues. The Who might then feature. Dave was not always kind to us. He wasn't always kind—period. It was about fifty-fifty, I think. His truth, his opinions, and his critique were always sharply penned, and he expected great things from us, from me especially. He was literate and smart, and regarded rock music as a new form of sociopolitical force that had massive potential for change for the better. Culturally, artistically, and politically. I believed this, too. It was hard for both of us to live up to. Compared to jazz, blues, and folk music, so much rock was just self-serving *blah*.

In later life, however, he has proved to be the most forgiving loyal friend and advocate. We became especially close in 1993 when I was almost resident full-time in New York while *Tommy* was on Broadway. In the early part of that year I attended a party to benefit the Kristen Ann Carr Fund (Kristen was Dave's stepdaughter who had died of cancer). Somehow, after eleven years of white-knuckle sobriety, that night I accepted a glass of Rémy Martin cognac from a wily female fan, and the evening took flight, and so did I. That year was one of the happiest of my life for a number of reasons, and it began with Dave and I sitting at a table talking about what really matters in life. Journalism, duty, truth, acquaintance, friendship, and finally family. I'm not sure we even mentioned music.

Who was I talking about? Ah yes, Dave Marsh. It's sad I can't be at his side to remind me of my worst behavior, laugh, and perhaps weep a little. Because in the end, when you get to your late seventies, you realize that your best friends aren't always those you have seen often, but those who have cared about what you do and who you really are. I'm talking about me, of course, Dave caring about who I am, and what I do. *How many friends have I really got? I can count them on the one hand.* And so, in memory of fine critique—good and bad—over the years, I hereby give Dave a finger.

—*Pete Townshend*

Index